Peter Hamel, who was born in 194
psychology and sociology in Muni
subsequently spent three extensive perio
studyed Eastern traditions of music. He
composer and musician.

Peter Michael Hamel

THROUGH MUSIC
TO THE SELF

How to appreciate and experience music anew

TRANSLATED FROM THE GERMAN BY
PETER LEMESURIER

ELEMENT
Shaftesbury, Dorset ● Rockport, Massachusetts
Brisbane, Queensland

First published in 1976 by Scherz Verlag
Berne, Munich and Vienna
English translation © Peter Lemesurier 1978

First published in Great Britain in 1978 by
Element Books Limited
Shaftesbury, Dorset SP7 8BP

Published in the USA in 1991 by
Element Books, Inc.
PO Box 830, Rockport, MA 01966

Published in Australia in 1991 by
Element Books Limited for
Jacaranda Wiley Limited
33 Park Road, Milton, Brisbane 4064

Reprinted 1991
Reprinted 1995

Printed and bound in Great Britain by
J W Arrowsmith Limited, Bristol, Avon

British Library Cataloguing in Publication
data available

Library of Congress Cataloging in Publication
data available

ISBN 1–85230–136–8

To My Parents

Contents

Introduction

Music – for the ancient Greeks 'the art of the Muses', a noble activity promoting the growth of mind and soul – has fulfilled a variety of functions in the Western world during the course of its long history. It has accompanied sacred rituals, has been used in support of the ruling-classes while simultaneously serving as a popular art-form, has often degenerated into the cheap self-indulgence of vulgar songs, and finally, through the efforts of many highly-gifted composers, has developed into the art of music with which we in the West are nowadays familiar. Today it displays an almost limitless variety of forms, a veritable labyrinth of the most heterogeneous styles. Moreover the music of the Far East and of other non-European countries is nowadays impinging more and more on our consciousness. These often very ancient musical traditions, most of which are today being adulterated in their native countries by Euro-American influences, hold for Westerners a primitive fascination, and are now bringing a strong influence to bear on our own music-making. In our own time a new 'spiritual' music is being developed, one which goes beyond the usual ideas of the experimental avant-garde. It is the result and consequence of the great revolution of consciousness that began at the turn of the century, associated with such names as Einstein, Planck, Freud and Jung, and whose musical side has been influenced by composers such as Schön-berg, Bartók, Orff, Messiaen and Cage. Today it is possible to approach music on the one hand with the apparatus of modern atomic science and on the other through the perceptions of depth-psychology.

It is the responsibility of spiritual music to learn from all musical traditions, to track down long-forgotten sources and to bring back into the limelight the original function of music – its links with the deepest in human experience – without, in the process, falling into a naïve eclecticism. There is abroad at present a strong urge to open up once again those stopped up wells of music which alone can reveal the way to a new type of musical experience encompassing man's being in its entirety.

It is my purpose in the following pages to reveal and to re-search the elements of a new musical integration. In the course of the various chapters, whatever the starting-points of their respective researches, an attempt will be made to stretch a great arc : from, on the one hand, contemporary theories and new approaches to composition in the realm of group-improvisation, via the no-longer ignorable encounter with non-European music, magic mantra and ritual, to the astonishing and nowadays demonstrable parallels between the laws of acoustics and the human psyche – taking in musical meditation, self-experience through breathing, singing and playing, and a variety of tried and tested exercises for individual and group-work on the way.

Ever since the journey to the Third World has become *de rigueur*, the encounter with the magical and mythical cultures of Asia, Africa and South America has provided us with a road of re-discovery leading us back to long-buried elements of our own consciousness. The suggestive powers of musical resonance are once more being felt and are re-awakening in us dormant aspects, hidden depths of experience.

Whether in avant-garde music, in Jazz or in Pop music, we have been witnessing a trend towards a more soul-oriented, in-troverted musical language. The increasing public interest in spiritual music, both recent and non-European, as well as in the ever-more-widely practised methods of deep relaxation which use oriental music as a basis, and in the psychologically-inspired use of breathing, sensitivity-training and collective vocal improvisation as an aid to meditation – all this suggests that, here too, the future rôle of music will not be confined merely to one particular dimension of human existence.

What we are here concerned with is not so much new dis-coveries as the re-discovery of what was known long ago to ancient cultures and peoples – knowledge that was simply al-lowed to slide into oblivion as a result of the predominantly rationalistic development of the Western world. It is our task, as the Swiss cultural philosopher Jean Gebser likewise saw it, to rediscover those links and integrate them into the musical consciousness of the twentieth century.

Our present age of upheaval and new initiatives is, in a sense, a pioneering age, with all the attendant risks which such an epoch entails. Nevertheless the increasing popularity of spiritual music, as I personally have experienced it with a wide variety of groups and audiences (or participants), suggests that we are on the right path. What drugs failed to achieve – the creation of a genuine, lasting intensification of awareness – becomes possible through this new experience and appreciation of music.

After many performances of my compositions and of improvisations by our ensemble *Between*, after concerts and seminars devoted to Indian music, as well as self-awareness groups, it has always been painfully obvious to me that, whether on the subject of musical meditation, of the East-West encounter, of harmonics or of intuitive improvisation, there exists in German hardly any literature that the musical layman can understand and put to practical account. Hence my decision, as a musician, to write this long-overdue book myself. It is not written primarily for the practising musician or for the specialist in comparative musicology. Rather is it intended for those readers who are prepared to try *all* types of music, for the many people who are intimately affected by the encounter with the orient and interested in group-activity (including the comparatively new fields of breath- and music-therapy), as well as for all those who are looking for help along the way and wish to gain some general insight into basic principles, methods and practical exercises. In no respect does the following presentation lay claim to being totally comprehensive: nor, on the other hand, has it been possible to avoid going into occasional technical detail – as in the case of the description of Indian and Tibetan music, which is fundamentally different from that with which we are familiar. Readers who are not interested in such explanations can quite happily skip the passages in question.

In view of the fact that many of the texts essential to the theme are scattered among scarcely-obtainable, as yet untranslated or no-longer available books and programme-notes, I have quoted extensively from these sources and cited directly the words of certain musicians on their specialist spheres.

I owe special thanks to musicologists Prof. Dr. Gerhard Nestler of Baden-Baden and Prof. Dr. Wolfgang Burde of Berlin, as also to music-editors Walter Bachauer of Berlin and Joachim E. Berendt of Baden-Baden, who have made available their manuscripts and articles for examination. My gratitude extends also to the Indian musician Dr. B. V. Patekar, of the Hindu University of Benares, for his advice on the chapter devoted to Classical Indian music, to Prof. Ilse Middendorf of Berlin for permission to reproduce special breathing and voice-exercises used by her school, to the sound engineer Ulrich Kraus of Munich for his critical perusal and specialist advice, and to lecturer Dr. Susanne Schaup for her help and support during the book's preparation.

Munich 1976   PETER MICHAEL HAMEL

1 Old and New Paths in Western Music

ON CONTEMPORARY MUSICAL AWARENESS

We are surrounded by music. The radio brings us light music, background music, Beat music, opera, operetta, dance music, light Classical music, serious music, chamber music, orchestral music, Romantic music, Classical music, Baroque music, early music, ancient music, modern music, virtuoso music, refined music, avant-garde music, electronic music, traditional music, Pop music, Rock music, march music and so on. We are inundated with music. Music for driving, shopping, eating, celebrating, conversing, getting up, going to bed, having breakfast, making love . . .

But do we listen to music? Hardly ever. Yet away it plays – on television, in the cinema, at the shops, at the office, at work, at the football stadium. On and on the music plays, and we are no longer aware of it. It has become part of the décor, an unconscious conditioning, a mechanical background to everyday life. Carl Maria von Weber's complaint of 1802 (!) is more justified today than ever: 'Times are getting harder for the composer. There is so much music-making nowadays: from its youth up the public is over-accustomed to music, so that its sensitivity to it constantly declines. That very piece of music which leaves people unmoved today because their ear is sated with music, would affect them greatly if they had heard no music for a whole year.'*

A producer of radio-programmes for motorists, himself possibly a lover of flamboyant Pop music, would never choose it for his programme, simply because 'unusual' music is held to be distracting for drivers at peak listening-times. So it is that, with

* *Gespräche mit Komponisten*, Zürich 1967, p. 61.

few exceptions, the music which is broadcast is precisely that which does not impinge on the listener's awareness, music which simply 'plays'.

But on German radio – unlike television – there is another, alternative programme: twice a week, late at night, one hour of modern Jazz, of avant-garde or non-European music for the initiates, for the minority. The gramophone-record industry too, with its saturated market, observes the same proportions: only a minute proportion of its output consists of musical performances that demand concentrated listening or evoke any response other than a conditioned one.

Classical music is produced for a particular public that is already familiar with operas and concertos; Rock music is produced for a particular public that already knows the groups concerned; Beat music is produced for a particular public that likewise recognises its own stars and interpreters. For the most part the listener is in no position to alter his musical 'class-affiliation'. Even Classical music is quite often produced for commercial reasons only. Sheer economic pressures on a gramophone-record concern flatly rule out artistic idealism as a motive for music-publishing.

The overwhelming majority of the civilised population of the West (America and Europe), then, is no longer consciously aware of music. It is an interesting fact that the majority of cinema-goers simply fail to register the film-music at all. Neither in the supermarket nor in the restaurant is there any awareness of the acoustic background, not even – and perhaps especially not – if it is particularly loud. Our ear is impaired; the noise of our environment renders our hearing dull and insensitive.

On the other hand, or perhaps for that very reason, a super-technique for reproducing music has sprung up – stereophony, quadrophony, earphones, hi-fi, surround-sound stereophony. There is a mass-market for tape recorders, record players and cassette recorders. We hear whole masses of music, but we still listen to it, if at all, in fixed categories. Our listening-capacity is conditioned. The notes are perceived externally, registered in superficial categories, or identified with pre-formed, pre-conditioned, pre-fabricated feelings and states of mind. We know, for the most part fairly accurately, the distinctive 'trade-marks' or style of our favourite music, and by identifying it we then immediately adopt a social standpoint. 'It's Rock for me' – 'Actually I prefer Beethoven's Seventh' – 'Give me John Lennon any time'. There is no doubt about it, each of us 'listens' to his music, is more or less familiar with its characteristics, has his accepted taste and links the pieces he knows with given emotional, mental or even unconscious associations. The musical idiom with which we identify ourselves is often an index of our inner condition.

The question 'Why music in the first place?' seems superfluous to most people, and many will reply that music exists for relaxation, for aesthetic enjoyment, for relieving boredom, for spiritual uplift, for passing the time, for edification. Nevertheless there is no denying that there is also a spiritual power to be felt in great works of the classical repertory. Whatever their style and tendency, they contain noble strains. Such music may well lead the individual into whole new worlds of experience if only the necessary conditions are first created – namely true receptivity, a favourable climate for relaxed self-absorption and above all an understanding of the spiritual significance of music. Indeed, in all earlier world-cultures music stood at the service of ritual, of the holy cult, of consciousness-expansion and the deepest in human experience. The intuitive understanding of this significance would be a precondition for a new auditory consciousness, capable of being applied to all today's varieties of music – whether Classical, Pop, Jazz, avant-garde or non-European.

The Far-Eastern cultures, the magic rituals of Africa, Asia and South America and all the shamanistic rites and cults possess a knowledge – for the most part unconscious – of some primal force that may be summoned up by musical means. We too might submit to its powers of stimulation. But it would be our duty not merely to allow such powers to exert their magical influence upon us, but also to experience them consciously, so that they might become familiar to us, stand at our service, help us to become complete people, in the sense of having achieved an integrated Wholeness. Were we to get to know more intensively, more sensitively and more clearly those musical processes created – whether in the course of millennia or merely over the last few years – to promote self-experience in the listener, we might attain 'participation in the All', as the Swiss cultural philosopher Jean Gebser put it in his essay *Ueber die Erfahrung* ('On Experience'): 'It is possible that the gaining of this conscious participation is the goal of human life. It embraces even the invisible world which, as such, is ineffable and inexpressible – the unimpartable secret.'*

That such an experience can be gained merely through playing or listening to music may seem highly unlikely. Certainly, it is capable of being perceived only by an 'integrated' auditory consciousness that can 'experience the vitality of the magical, perceive the psychic form of the mythical and grasp the structure of the mental.'† This 'total' mode of hearing might finally lead to a 'transparent state' of perception which would not be timeless, as in the case of magical experience, but would, in Gebser's words, repose in a state of 'freedom from space and time'. Certainly there exists today hardly any music that corresponds fully to this state of holistic awareness. But the first signs of its development can be detected in many exotic musical cultures, as well as in those twentieth-century Western musical works that display sympathies with the archaic and magical/mythical forms of music of Asia and Africa.

For in the view of Jean Gebser (who, with Sri Aurobindo and Teilhard de Chardin, has offered the most convincing formulation of this holistic world-view) rational-mental Western man must now re-discover and re-experience the magical-mythical well-springs of human consciousness if he is to achieve the leap which this measure of integration implies. Since our discovery of the unconscious and our penetration of the world of the molecule and the inner atom, we can now be sure (suggests Ronald Steckel, one of the most outstanding spokesmen of the growing movement towards a counterculture based on a holistic view of man) 'that the decisive events which underlie all human experience, all actions and all material phenomena take place at a level of which we know next to nothing and which we cannot see with physical eyes. Behind the visible face of the world is hidden an invisible one.'‡

Our available links with the invisible, according to Steckel,

* J Gebser: 'Ueber die Erfahrung,' in *Ein Mensch zu sein*, Munich-Bern, 1974.
† Compare J. Gebser: *Ursprung und Gegenwart*, Munich, 1973.
‡ R. Steckel: *Herz der Wirklichkeit*, Judie-Taschenbuch, Wuppertal 1973, p. 11.

are the organs of perception and feeling, which lend sharpness
and colour to our experience, penetrate beneath the surface of
that which is experienced and release that which it conceals.
Yet Steckel is here describing the very function of the music of
our time. For the living knowledge of the unity of visible and invisible, of physical and spiritual, has today undergone a dichotomy. 'Our time has been distinguished, more than anything
else, by a drive to control the external world, and by an almost
total forgetfulness of the internal world ... By "inner" I mean
our way of seeing the external world and all those realities that
have no "external", "objective" presence – imagination, dreams,
phantasies, trances; the realities of contemplative and meditative states, realities that modern man, for the most part, has not
the slightest direct awareness of.'*

This knowledge 'which in almost every known historical culture has been summed up in the person of the shaman, the
medicine-man or the cult-priest' (Steckel) might conceivably be
integrated into a holistic consciousness for modern man through
the deep experience of musical self-awareness. It is precisely
through the energies of musical works that we may discover
within ourselves the road that leads to the regions of the soul
and spirit – especially so in these times when new dimensions of
awareness are being opened up on every side 'through the electronic media and experimental electronic music, through the
Folk-Rock music with which the younger generation have loudly proclaimed their dance to freedom, as well as through countless individual experiences of the magical, mind-bending drugs
used by foreign and ancient cultures' (Steckel, p. 84). European
and Asiatic cultures today rub shoulders: the Christian world-
view walks hand in hand with the cosmologies of Hinduism,
Islam and Buddhism: of recent years meditation-centres and
religious *ashrams* have been established all over Europe and
America, concerts of exotic music from India, Tibet or Bali are
filled to overflowing, and at the same time we are being inundated with 'paths of wisdom', yoga-systems and religious teachings passed down via foreign cultures.

As a result it is today easier than ever to grasp the common
core of all exotic religions, and to break through the walls of
ideology and dogma. 'Once we no longer see through the spec-

* R. Laing: *The Politics of Experience*, Penguin 1967, p. 115.

tacles of prejudice, once our over-stretched nerves have found repose and our sensibility resonates in all its fullness, then it is as though somebody had said "Open sesame". In that moment we partake of the hidden treasures, the very well-springs of human realisation, which constantly irradiate the whole substance both of our environment and of our inner world – hidden, veiled, apparently drowned by the inane, obsessive activity, the purely mechanical phenomena and cerebral skills of everyday life' (Steckel, p. 95). If, on the other hand, a person's class-affiliation, environment and upbringing conspire to make him a martyr to the 'inane obsessive activity' of Pop music, the 'purely mechanical phenomena' of distorted electronic sounds, or the 'cerebral skills' of avant-garde confections, recourse to the quieter music of the inner world will presumably become possible for him only when he has rediscovered his own subconscious. For, to Carl Gustav Jung, 'the Western psyche seems to have an intuitive knowledge of the dependence of man upon some dark force whose co-operation is essential if everything is to go well. If and when the Unknown declines to co-operate, he immediately finds himself in difficulties, even with regard to his everyday activities. It may be a failure of memory, of co-ordination, of interest or of concentration; yet such a failure may be the cause of real distress, or even of some fatal accident. It may lead to a professional or moral breakdown. In earlier times people would have said that the gods were unfavourable : today we call it a neurosis.'*

It is a fact that the way to individual self-discovery often leads through suffering, through the 'dark night of the soul', as though painful experiences were being specifically set as a task *in order that* the next step might be made possible and the unseen Reality experienced. Graf Dürckheim writes on the subject : 'When this ultimate crisis of being descends inexorably upon us, annihilation threatens us, meaninglessness and guilt cast us into deepest despair, or in our ultimate loneliness breath finally fails us – when, in short, there is no way out – that is the very moment when the possibility arises of a sudden explosion from within ourselves of that which is "totally other" ... the sudden surfacing of a strength, a meaningfulness, a security of unknown ori-

* C. G. Jung : tr. from preface to W. Y. Evans-Wentz's *Der Geheime Pfad der grossen Befreiung*, Weilheim, 3rd Ed., 1972.

gin, welling up from out of those depths whose workings are beyond all reason, beyond all rational expectation, beyond all reasonable hope.'*

The extent to which music can supply an image of such phases of ultimate crisis and serve as bearer and vehicle of a spiritual message from the 'totally other' – such is the theme of this book. We shall be concerned here not with the enumeration of all the significant spiritual works of musical history – such as Bach's choral or organ-pieces, the late works of Mozart and Beethoven, the chamber-music of Schubert and Schumann, the operas of Wagner or the compositions of Gustav Mahler – but especially with compositions of our own century that have incorporated mystical-magical, spiritual, metaphysical and even non-European elements. Some of those concerned – those musicians and explorers of the inner world – are not internationally renowned composers, or at any rate that status is disputed. Nevertheless they have contributed considerably to the integrative encounter with the Far East and to the shedding of acoustic light on man's esoteric knowledge. They could be the founding fathers of an entirely new form of world-music, now in its earliest infancy.

APPROACHES TO COMPOSITiON

If we apply to the appreciation and development of music the various modes of consciousness defined and illustrated by Jean Gebser (magical, mythical, mental and integral), then the mainly rhythmical, unison-melodic cult music of the shamans of the former north-European and African cultures, the chanting of South American and Mongolian native priests and the heterophonic gamelan-orchestras of entire Indonesian villages correspond exclusively to the *magical* mode of consciousness. All of these primeval, yet for the most part highly sophisticated forms of music are closely bound up with dance and movement, and nearly always fulfil an initiatory function.

The ancient Greek *musike*, the plainsong music of the early Middle Ages which reached its zenith in Gregorian chant, the Persian *dastgah* music with its modal *maqam* scales, and the

---

* Dürckheim: *Erlebnis und Wandlung*, quoted in *Religion und die Droge*, Stuttgart 1972, p. 108.

raga-improvisations of northern and southern India – all these reflect the *mythical* mode of consciousness that is common both to Eastern and to early Western traditions. Here speech and music are still closely associated; both the Greek *musike* (a term which applied equally to speech and song) and the Vedic chanting of ancient India had as their theme the oldest myths of man.

European Musical Culture

In around the fifteenth century the *mental* mode of consciousness gradually came into its own, with its three-dimensional view of the objective world. Alongside the development of perspective in painting came polyphony in music. The composition of polyphonic music demanded techniques of construction, organisation and notation. The great Western musical tradition was able to arise: fugue, sonata-form, the laws of harmony and modulation, tonality (in its functional harmonic sense) and, by the same token, the use of tempered intervals.

In Asia, on the other hand, the music of Japan, China and India continued along its purely melodic, 'mythical' way, revealing the subtlest tone-colours and psychic resonances, an enormous number of tone-rows ('modes') and the use of the finest micro-intervals. The 'magical' music of Africa and Indonesia, for its part, still lingered amid the unconscious regions of its archaic rites, its timeless rhythmic formulae and its primeval chants.

The 'mental' consciousness of Western musicians now began to explore the workings of nature, the physical laws of music, the psychological effects of sounds. But at the same time the invisible, mystic and esoteric powers of music, unknown as they were to those who wielded them – the magical-mythical cultures – were gradually laid bare: an alchemical understanding of music developed in esoteric circles, mixed with a whole range of occult, speculative and pseudo-scientific thought. The 'mental' consciousness was intent on understanding the working-methods of its magical-mythical forebears, even at the risk of reverting to a former stage of consciousness. A tradition of musical esotericism, manifesting through Rosicrucian and other cabbalistic, Pythagorean and alchemistic groups, runs right through the music of the Middle Ages and up to our own times.

At around the beginning of our century major composers were showing greater and greater enthusiasm for the ideas current in these circles. The Russian Alexander Scriabin (1872–1915) developed a mystical scale which is very close to the chromatic scales of the orient, and from which he derived, in his numerous piano-works, harmonic clusters that were literally unheard-of in his day. His compatriot Sergei Prokofiev (1891–1953) drew inspiration for his *Scythian Suite* from the ecstasies of the Scythian shamans. Scriabin, too, wrote an orchestral piece called *Poème de l'Ecstase* – an attempt at a comprehensive ritual-mythical art-form. In his gigantic Eighth Symphony of 1906, the great late-Romantic composer Gustav Mahler (1860–1911) set to music the Whitsun hymn *Veni creator spiritus* and the final song of *Faust* Part II, suggesting that here the whole universe should break forth into song with its 'circling suns and planets.'

During the Paris world-exhibition of 1898 Claude Debussy (1862–1918) experienced for the first time the sound of a Balinesian gamelan-orchestra, Indian theatre music and Japanese pieces for harmonica whose 'music of the spheres' (as Gebser puts it) prompted many of his innovations in tonality. In his *Bolero*, Maurice Ravel (1875–1937) used magical monotony to produce what the conductor Hermann Scherchen called a 'time-static' – i.e. a timelessness typical of the magical. And both of them, Ravel no less than Debussy, were strongly influenced by the 'arch outsider' Erik Satie (1866–1925), who belonged for some time to the French Rosicrucian Order.

Two less well-known British composers must also be mentioned here. Cyril Scott (1879–1971) delved into Theosophy and the secret teachings of the orient, and wrote deliberately mystical compositions. Gustav Holst (1874–1934) devoted himself intensively to astrology and wrote a suite for orchestra entitled *The Planets*, which was increasingly to acquire the status of a standard concert-work. The seven movements are named after the planets and are fascinating for their eclectic musical language, especially at the close – a cosmic vision of 'Neptune the Mystic', with its distant choir fading away into eternity.

It seems that, to a man, the great musical innovators of the twentieth century have all at some time concerned themselves with archaic folklore, esoteric teachings, Pythagorean wisdom or the oriental traditions. Arnold Schönberg (1874–1951) became immersed in Swedenborg's Christian mysticism and with Old Testament thought (*Moses und Aron*). His pupil A. von Webern

(1883–1945) studied cabbalistic number-symbolism. The other inventor of twelve-tone music – and one who saw it not merely as a new technique but as a form of cosmic spiritual knowledge – was the Viennese Josef Matthias Hauer (1883–1959), an initiate of the Rosicrucian Order. He arranged the twelve notes of the tempered octave cyclically and saw given groups of these notes ('tropics') as having actual spiritual effects by virtue of the way in which they were arranged. His work is currently being carried on by the Munich anthroposophist Fritz Büchtger (b. 1903), who sets to music gnostic texts (*Das Gläserne Meer, Das Gesicht des Hesekiel* etc.) with the aid of a 'cosmic' twelve-tone technique of his own devising. 'I believe', says Büchtger in an interview, 'that music is a reflection of a higher order of reality ... an inner world of spiritual being which each man inhabits in the depths of his unconscious ... The composer is distinguished by the fact that he retains, even in the waking state, a certain memory, a consciousness of musical experiences at a spiritual level.'*

Even the otherwise reserved Paul Hindemith (1895–1963) concerned himself at the end of his life with the 'Harmony of the World', as the titles both of his last opera and of one symphony put it. In these works, Phythagorean secret teachings of ancient Greece are reflected in the life of Johannes Kepler – teachings which have recently been brought back into our Western awareness, under the title of *fundamental research into harmonics*, by the Swiss harmonics-expert Hans Kayser, who has expanded them to cover analogous phenomena in the scientific sphere. (See Part 2.)

American Composers

In the western United States, too – which has moved nearer towards the Far East than Europe – music was to gain access to man's inner depths. Witness the brilliant sound-pictures of Charles Ives (1874–1954), the legendary Sunday-composer, who alongside his job as an insurance-salesman composed pieces such as *Three Places in New England, Central Park in the Dark* and several symphonic collages which are counted among the most impressive of American musical works. Colin McPhee (1901–1964), another American composer, lived from 1931 to 1939 on

* NMZ (Neue Musikzeitung), February-March 1973.

the Indonesian island of Bali and allowed Far-Eastern sounds and intrumental colours to influence the Western orchestral language of his otherwise traditional music.

A younger, and perhaps in this connection the most significant, American composer is John Cage (b. 1912). He was one of the first and most intensive students of the essential philosophy of music, of the social preconditions for acoustic communication and of the Far-Eastern musical cultures. Cage ventured to the very limits of music and beyond. In Germany he is chiefly known, and revered by certain minorities, as an anarchistic iconoclast, a notion resulting from what are often uninformed realisations of works written during only one of his many phases of development. How the terse but highly complex performance instructions of John Cage are put into effect always depends on the quality of the performer, for Cage sees 'music' as a process of consciousness and as a vehicle for philosophical insights. It is not unknown for groups with totally opposing ideas to claim his banner for their own.

As early as the nineteen-forties Cage met the great Japanese Zen-Master D. T. Suzuki, whose lectures in San Francisco he attended for several months. Perhaps they find their strongest echo in his programme-works *Silence* and *Empty Words*, and in all those of his works that simply attempt to make silence audible. As Cage puts it, 'What Zen teaches is: if something bores you after two minutes, try it for four. If it still bores you, try it for eight, sixteen, thirty-two and so on. Eventually you discover that it's not boring at all, but very interesting.'*

Even before that, from 1938 onwards, John Cage was experimenting with the 'Prepared Piano' and writing pieces such as *Amores, Music for Marcel Duchamp, Sonatas and Interludes* and *She Is Asleep* for voice and prepared piano-notes. The 'Prepared Piano' is still regarded as an arch, avant-garde device, and yet its purpose is quite otherwise. Very early on Cage had made the acquaintance of the gamelan-music of Indonesia with its small metallophones and gongs giving out a whole variety of overtones (see Part 2, page 83). With the aid of a minutely prescribed inventory of erasers, wires and other utensils which are

* J. Cage: tr. from a paper entitled in German *Ueber das Unbestimmte,* quoted from Wolfgang Burde's SFB Berlin radio script on the American avant-garde.

inserted between the piano-strings, a sound remarkably similar to that of gamelan-music can be produced. Each note – each of which generally has two or three strings – is 'tuned' by the insertion of small pieces of rubber etc., so that at the top end of the keyboard notes similar to those of bells and percussion-instruments are produced, while at the lower end, where the gaps between the individual strings are wider, preparation with soft, thick rubber erasers produces predetermined overtones and gong-like note-combinations of extraordinary harmonic effect. The musical notation for the hands can then be arranged simply and traditionally (only a limited number of notes is used since, of course, not all the strings have to be prepared) as if it were a piece of native folk-music with a traditional rhythmic structure.

To this extent Cage's scores resemble those of the percussion-pieces he devised with Lou Harrison, but they also bear similarities to the specifications of an American constructor of original musical instruments, the visionary Harry Partch. Before his death in 1972 he had invented extraordinary giant xylophones with fascinating sound-effects, and he can be counted among the self-taught musical geniuses of America.

Bartók and Orff

Decades previously, two of the greatest European composers were already reflecting that continent's elemental music and its primal rhythmic forms: Carl Orff (b. 1895) and Bela Bartók (1881–1945). After composing initially in the tradition of Claude Debussy and Richard Strauss, Bartók began a scientific exploration of the folk-music of his native Hungary and the neighbouring regions of Bulgaria. He was aware that the music of the gipsies, far from being a Hungarian folk-art, was an independent, nomadic musical language. Bartók travelled with his colleague Zoltán Kodály through the remotest villages of Southern Europe noting down tunes and rhythms, and found in the so-called 'Hungarian' minor scale the influence of the Far East, of the Saracens and of the Mongols, who had formerly penetrated as far as Hungary. 'Hungarian Minor' is a scale whose abundant half-tones make it sound very strange to the Western ear, while displaying considerable affinities to the musical scales of Asia.

But Bartók also discovered that the 'odd' rhythms (such as 7/8 and 5/4) were natural elements of his native folklore. Under the influence of what he had assumed to be truly Hungarian, but which was in fact Asiatic in essence, he composed a number of masterpieces which represent an integrative encounter between Eastern and Western cultures. A professed atheist, Bartók died in September 1945, having emigrated to the USA, after completing the *Andante religioso* of his Third Piano Concerto. The theme, a Hungarian folk-melody, could equally well have been of Far-Eastern origin. Bela Bartók, a composer of great brilliance and crystal-clear intellect, was able to write music capable of reaching the primarily magically-orientated listener just as deeply as it did his emotional or intellectual counterpart. Several pieces from his works can be held to have achieved the leap to a transparently integral musical sound: parts of the slow movements of his piano concertos, his Violin Concerto of 1938 and the *Music for Strings, Percussion and Celesta.*

Bela Bartók's works bear both considerable similarities and dissimilarities to those of Carl Orff. Both followed completely independent paths which did not reflect the musical fashion of their time. Both Bartók and Orff delved into hidden treasuries of forgotten music that were waiting to be re-discovered. Both to some extent returned to source – in Orff's case to the very beginning of our own cultural epoch, the ancient Greek drama. Both likewise placed musical education very much in their debt – Bartók with his masterly piano-pieces for children, Carl Orff with his universally known and practised system of musical education.

This method of musical self-discovery aimed to stimulate the young person to make his own music, improvising and composing for himself. For the initial stages Orff uses purely rhythmic instruments, both indigenous and exotic; then melodic and basic harmonic instruments are added. Xylophones, metallophones and glockenspiels were developed that were to some extent derived from medieval and exotic instruments. There is of course a striking similarity here to the Indonesian gamelan-orchestra, and Carl Orff confirmed in a personal interview that he had indeed listened to orchestras from Java and Bali in the nineteen-twenties.

After fruitless experiments with Asian wind instruments, the main melodic instrument chosen for Orff's musical-education system turned out to be the recorder – now well-known once again, but until then little more than a museum-exhibit. Suitable models for improvisation were discovered in native and foreign folk-music, though in reality the music is intended to be put together by the players themselves, as Carl Orff was repeatedly to point out. The special techniques of improvisation are meant to arise out of the music itself, as actually happens in Japan and Africa among groups using Orff's system. Only in Europe – and above all in Germany itself – are the printed examples commonly misunderstood by poorly-trained music-teachers and therefore incorrectly applied. This is not to criticise the idea itself, but merely the old-fashioned, uninspired way in which schoolteachers are wont to apply it.

On the subject of his system of musical training, intended to give the young person an early experience of self-made and self-composed music, Carl Orff offers the following explanatory note :

> Elemental Music is never just music. It is bound up with movement, dance and speech, and so it is a form of music in which one must participate, in which one is involved not as a listener but as a co-performer. It is pre-rational, has no over-all form, no architectonics, involves no set sequences, *ostinati* or minor rondo-forms. Elemental Music is earthy, natural, physical, capable of being learnt and experienced by anybody, child's play ... Elemental Music, word and movement, play, everything that awakens and develops the powers of the soul builds up the humus of the soul, the humus without which we face *spiritual soil-erosion*. When does soil-erosion arise in nature? When the land is cultivated in an unbalanced way, when the natural hydrological cycle is disturbed by over-cultivation, when forest and hedge are sacrificed on utilitarian grounds to the drawing-board mentality – in short, when the balance of nature is undermined by one-sided encroachment. And in the same way we face *spiritual* soil-erosion when man estranges himself from the elemental and loses his balance.*

No wonder that Orff's system is better understood and practised in those countries whose peoples still retain a natural residue of elemental/magical consciousness.

* From : *Gespräche mit Komponisten*, Zürich 1967, p. 296.

Carl Orff's work has a quite different and perhaps even greater significance in the operatic sphere. If he had already discovered medieval poetry for himself, working on it from as early as 1937, he was later to turn more and more to the great classical sources, which he left in their original form. In his last great work, *De Temporum Fine Comoedia* (The Play of the End of Time), Orff seems to be signalling the end of our age of mental-rational consciousness. Certainly the mental consciousness-level, and with it our whole Western culture, has its roots in the great thinkers of classical times and has had its fruition in the last five hundred years. In his *Comoedia*, Orff represents the words of the 'Sybilline Oracles', the Anchorites and the Last Men, and celebrates the approaching destruction, world-conflagration and time of dread: 'Ubique daemon, ubique daemon, the Devil's abroad, the Devil's abroad ... till the end of time, till the end of time! – When shall time end?'

The programme notes for its first performance in Salzburg in 1974 explain: 'In the first section the words are placed in the mouths of the nine Sibyls, those mysterious prophetesses of the ancient world ... In the work's second section, too, original Greek verses are to be found in the Orphic hymn to the god of dreams. This divinity is adjured to reveal to the Last Men the end of time in a prophetic dream. The hymn is placed in the mouths of the Anchorites, those early Christian hermits ... who hurl an impassioned 'No' in the face of the prophecy of the Judgement of the Nations. For the purpose of the world cannot be the horror of the Last Judgement, but the return of the wicked to the ways of righteousness, the final redemption of the universe as a creation limited in time ... From the three intertwined speech-layers of Greek, Latin and German there arise gigantic necklaces of sound, rolling reverberations and circling spirals of words.' Orff makes use of the magical effect of timeless, endless repetition in order to bring the hearer into a state of severance from all accustomed, everyday experience, in which he no longer needs to shrink from death and the end of time but, led safely through the midst of the final dread, can hope for liberation. *Kalón thanathein!* goes the call: 'It is beautiful to die!' – a statement which may also be taken as referring to an esoteric death, namely the death of the 'I'.

An initiation always leads, in the first instance, through darkness, and the gates of the underworld, *portae inferi*, open with a terrifying noise before the initiatory message rings out: Lucifer, symbol of the dualism of good and evil (*lucifer*, interpreted, means 'light-bringer', being the one who, through his own darkness, makes light apparent), returns in repentance to God the Father: 'Pater peccavi'. Whereupon 'all is spirit' – *Ta panta nous* – for 'the end of all things will be the forgetting of all guilt', as the first page of the score has it. This great work of the mature Carl Orff will eventually contribute more to the deeper understanding of the primal powers of the spirit than is yet realised today. The concluding part of a personal interview with Orff about his ideas testifies to his great and knowing humility: 'It is as with everything that one passes on: one has oneself had it passed on somehow from elsewhere – it is not one's own. Far be it from me to imagine that I am turning the world upside-down with great new ideas. On the contrary, nothing could be older, I believe, than what I keep saying.'

Music as a Mirror of Angst

Meanwhile Orff is not the only one who uses music as a symbol of destruction, of dread, of fear – as well as of oppression – or who sees such things as a necessary step along the road to self-knowledge, spiritual awareness or enlightenment. As has already been indicated, initiation ceremonies the world over lay down as a condition that the candidate shall successfully pass through the darkest night. Thus, in the mystery-initiations of all the world's mythologies, the neophyte must always undertake a journey through the underworld or a descent into hell.* This is perhaps best symbolised in music by the ordeal by fire and water in *The Magic Flute* by Wolfgang Amadeus Mozart, who is known to have been a member of the Order of Freemasons. From the latter, moreover, come the words on the overcoming of death which Mozart felt to be the key to true bliss: 'Since death, properly regarded, is the ultimate purpose of this life of ours, I have over the past few years made myself so familiar with this true, best friend of man that its mere portrayal no longer holds any terrors for me, but does contain for me much that is soothing and consoling.'†

* Compare Erich Neumann: *Ursprungsgeschichte des Bewusstseins*, Munich, 2nd edition 1974, p. 133.
† Quoted from Bruno Walter: *Vom Mozart der Zauberflöte*, 1955.

Yet alongside this blind faith there is also the terrifying reality of the demons which accompany any experience of near-death, mind-shattering as that experience is. Clara Schumann's diary-entries bear heart-rending witness to the archetypal visions of the great Romantic composer Robert Schumann (1810–1856):

> On the night of Friday 10th/Saturday 11th (February 1854) Robert's hearing was so terribly deranged all night ... He kept hearing one and the same note and with it at times another interval too ... He says it is such beautiful music, with marvellous-sounding instruments such as have never been heard on earth ... We had not long been in bed when Robert got up again and wrote down a theme which, so he said, the angels were dictating to him. He firmly believed that angels were hovering about him, granting him the most beautiful revelations, all of it expressed in wonderful music ... Morning came, and with it a terrible change. The angelic voices were transformed into demonic voices, with horrific music ... He was screaming in pain (for he told me they had pounced on him in the form of tigers and hyenas to seize him) and two doctors, who fortunately arrived in time, could scarcely hold him ... On Monday 20th Robert spent all day at his desk listening to the angel-voices ... At the same time his face had a look so blissful that I shall never be able to forget it, and yet this unnatural happiness cut me to the quick as much as if he had been possessed by evil spirits.*

As we know, Schumann shortly thereafter threw himself into the Rhine, was rescued, and died in the sanatorium at Endenich. The Munich composer Wilhelm Killmayer (b. 1927), a pupil of Carl Orff, has written a gripping work, most reticently and tenderly expressed, which is much concerned with Schumann's destiny: *Schumann in Endenich*.

The world of inner dread has been a theme treated by many composers of our day, and for this they have brought into the foreground a particular family of instruments whose function was formerly mere accompaniment, in order to portray the world of sheer noise, of de-personalisation and of the dark powers themselves. Carl Orff, in his *Comoedia*, brings into play a hun-

* *Robert Schumann*, Zürich 1967, p. 340.

dred varied percussion-instruments drawn from all the world's cultures. Edgar Varèse (1885–1965), pioneer of percussion music and creator of the *Poème Electronique* for the Brussels World Exhibition of 1956, took processes drawn from the world of technology as a basis for his percussion piece *Ionisation*.

The formerly well-known Italian composer and committed Communist Luigi Nono (b. 1924) adds to his expressive choral sounds tape-recordings of the earsplitting noise of a factory in order to denounce the oppression and acoustic violation of the under-privileged. The Korean Isang Yun (b. 1917), now resident in Germany, who composes on the basis of strongly-held Buddhist spiritual views (he has set to music the Tibetans' *om-mani-padme-hum* and written an opera of Taoist inspiration), has also written works in which sharp, shrill notes representing his own personal experience of political imprisonment figure directly alongside the sounds of his native Asia.

The Swiss composer Claus Huber (b. 1924) was inspired to write his large-scale work, ... *inwendig voller Figur* ..., for choirs, large orchestra and tape-recorded sounds (1971) by a vision of Albrecht Dürer's. It was in 1525 that Dürer dreamt a terrifying vision of the end of the world, with water falling down from the sky 'with such speed, rage and fury'; so afraid was he, in fact, that when he awoke his whole body was trembling. Dürer thereupon drew his vision, and Claus Huber points out that the resulting water-colour anticipated the atomic mushroom-cloud of 1945 by 420 years.

Of his composition Huber writes: 'In this work of mine I am attempting to express humanity's primal fear of the end of the world through the medium of music – *my* music ... I still believe that it is legitimate for music to concern itself with levels which are the very stuff of religion and belief ... If I write this music, this expression of primal *Angst*, it is because I want to rouse the individual – us all, in other words – from a foregone conclusion that is little short of schizophrenic, namely our acceptance of the possibility that humanity may destroy itself, and with it all life on earth ...'*

So it is that our own times have seen the development of a type of music which can leave a terrible impression on the conventional listener, but which fulfils a necessary function as a language for the concerns and needs of the contemporary world.

* From the text accompanying the published recording, wergo, Mainz.

Messiaen and Stockhausen

Olivier Messiaen (b. 1908), possibly the greatest living French composer, was to discover his inspiration, in all rational clarity, in Christian/Gnostic mysticism. It was in 1943, in Görlitz concentration-camp, that he wrote his *Quartet for the End of Time*, in which he gives musical expression to another, spiritual world – that circumscribed by the words of the Christian revelation. Meanwhile he was also delving into Indian music, and by 1939 was already making use, in his organ-work *Les Corps Glorieux*, of Southern Indian rhythms and raga forms – the equivalent of the Gregorian church modes. His *Les Couleurs de la Cité Céleste*, first performed in Donaueschingen in 1964, owed its inspiration to five quotations from the Revelation of John. It was the last of the five quotations, which speaks of the City's radiance, that gave him the idea of using colour concepts in his composition. The numerous percussion parts are allocated chiefly to the marimbaphones, of which Messiaen makes frequent use, and for which he himself developed a modification of the Indonesian gamelan. The typical rhythmic motifs, borrowed from the world of the birds, alternate with snatches of a very meditative, almost mantric 'harmonic theme', composed according to the technique of *modal harmony* – which is to say that Messiaen, instead of using his harmonies for functional harmonic reasons, develops them out of the basic material of a given mode or scale.

Messiaen himself testifies to his spiritual, religious credo : 'I believe in the Creator of all things visible and invisible ... The term "invisible things" made a particularly deep impression on me. Does it not embrace everything? Does it not speak to us of the world of the stars as of the world of the atom, of the world of the angels as of the world of the demons, of the world of our own thoughts as of the world of all that is unknown to us, and above all of the world of possibilities, which is known only to God?'*

The influence of Messiaen on the avant-garde of the fifties was, however, based on his intellectual description of his composition technique at the time (*My Musical Language*) which, along with Anton von Webern's twelve-note technique and the theories of the latter's pupil René Leibowitz, was to become the basis of so-called Serial music.

* From the musical periodical *Melos*, Schott's Söhne, Mainz 1958.

A leading representative of this school at the time was Karlheinz Stockhausen, who also studied under Messiaen. As few others he then passed through all the different phases of composition, leaving his mark on each. Stockhausen (b. 1928) was one of the first to explore the possibilities of electronic music, composed 'punctilist' and 'concrete' music and also invented the 'cluster-technique' which was to be developed further by Györgi Ligeti (b. 1923) in his static, purely harmonic pieces (*Atmospheres, Lontano* etc.) and by Krzysztof Penderecki (b. 1933) in his striking post-Serial works of Christian inspiration. Penderecki applies this technique in his *Lukaspassion*, for example, where he stacks up all the semitones of the octave – and even smaller intervals – on top of each other, with merest hints of the simplest motifs from early Christian chant.

Finally Stockhausen developed yet another method of music-making, though one which had admittedly long existed in similar form : *intuitive improvisation*, of which we shall have more to say later. For the first time the duly instructed interpreters of Stockhausen were to be heard playing intuitively, inspired by short meditation-texts (*Aus den Sieben Tagen*) and unrestricted to particular styles, in contrast to the limits imposed on Hindu musicians or performers of Free Jazz. Admittedly, though, Stockhausen himself retained over-all control and moulded the whole performance along the lines of his own intuition.

'We have steadily been opening the skilled and rational side of music-making to the intuition as never before,' reports Stockhausen, 'and I write this *after* experiencing authentic improvised music in Spain, India and Mexico, and having just returned from extensive "listening-tours" in Bali, Japan and Ceylon ... The crass duality between "old" and "new", "traditional" and "modern", "primitive music" and "sophisticated music" – indeed, even between "Asian" and "European" music – has been dissolved. What today is viewed with disfavour by leading music-critics and most of my fellow-composers (with deprecating overtones of : "He has allowed himself to be influenced by irrational, Far Eastern, Japanese and Indian ideas") will come to be seen as one of the most important events : the beginning of a real "symbiosis" of European, Asian, African and South American music.'[*]

* Stockhausen: text of the Darmstadt holiday-courses in New Music.

Further important aspects of Stockhausen's work involve *tone-colour* and the *harmonic series*. The physical fact that virtually every note possesses many harmonics, by whose permutations its tone is determined, is discussed in detail in Part 3. Stockhausen's achievement has been to bring this natural law far more to the notice of contemporary composers, and thus to deepen their understanding of the inner laws of sound.

In his composition *Stimmung* his work on 'tone colour melodies' (a concept of Schönberg's) reaches its culmination in what is called 'spectral-harmonics' or the formant-modulation of a single note and its harmonics (see Part 3, page 100) : for seventy-five minutes, in Stockhausen's *Stimmung*, the notes of only a single harmonic series are sung in exact tuning. The piece owes its title to the various meanings of the word 'Stimmung' in German : 'The tuning of the series, in which the vocalists sing the second, third, fourth, fifth, seventh and ninth harmonics against the bass-note (bottom B); the "tuning in" of a singer during the performance, each time he starts to bring a new sound-pattern into play . . .; and (not least) the German word "Stimmung" also conveys the meaning of "atmosphere", of "mood", of "spiritual attunement".'*

With his works *Mantra* (at whose first performance he cited texts concerning the Indian *guru* Sri Aurobindo) and *Inori* (Adorations) – both of them based on the teachings of the Sufi Hazrat Inayat Khan on the seed-syllable *hu* – and many other works (above all the 'Fourth Region' of his *Hymnen*), Stockhausen has made important contributions to the spiritual experience and understanding of music. 'For Stockhausen it is quite clear,' writes the Berlin musicologist Wolfgang Burde, 'that all revolution, every social change in the individual, has to begin *from within*. There has been no shortage of caustic comments dismissing Stockhausen's particular life-style as nebulous or individual. And indeed it is undeniable that Stockhausen's constantly paraded prophetic attitude and his hardly-concealed sense of mission have at times tended towards the purest banality.'†

Despite his controversial personality, a large number of avant-garde movements have had their origin in Stockhausen's work,

*Excerpt from the text accompanying the recorded edition of K. H. Stockhausen (Deutsche Grammophon).
† 'Philharmonische Blätter', programme of the Berlin Philharmonic, 1975.

and from his circle have come a great many young musicians who have developed even further the process of free improvisation.

In the sixties a whole range of such groups sprang up in Europe and America, freeing themselves more and more from the conventional stylistic categories. The creative era of Pop music made possible a progressive *rapprochement* between Jazz, avant-garde Rock, electronic music and the world's folk-music. Classical Jazz, whose chief ingredient was in any case improvisation – the free, creative embellishment of a predetermined pattern – and which, as the music of Black America, had always had a natural connection with musical self-expression, opened itself increasingly to the world's musical movements. Ornette Coleman and Cecil Taylor were making 'free music' long before it was discovered by the avant-garde. John Coltrane (1926–1967), the founder of America's new spiritual music, was the first to attempt a 'music of the great synthesis'. For him music, even in his own lifetime, was nothing if not intuitive improvisation.

An integral world-music, with its rudiments and spiritual progenitors coming from within 'Classical' music, requires as its precondition an intuitive spontaneity such as must have been present in various of the composers of the last few decades, but which comes to creative expression above all via the process of intuitive improvisation. Many a Western musician – be he the greatest virtuoso – finds it quite impossible to improvise without the aid of a score. Yet precisely this improvisatory process has of recent years brought many a musician to a deeper state of self-awareness and provided the first step along the road towards musical integration.

GROUP-IMPROVISATION AND INTUITIVE MUSIC MAKING

'Three-quarters of mankind needs no written music and knows no written music.'

So says Carl Orff, to whose elemental improvisation method for children we have already referred. In the case of the early human historical cultures certain rhythmic forms and melodic patterns grew up among the world's tribes and peoples, each passed on from father to son. Naturally the performers of this

music themselves derived the greatest pleasure from it – a fact
which disturbed nobody, for everybody took part. There were
no listeners.

That communal music-making entertains only the players is
nowadays the chief reproach levelled against pure improvised
music, which has been practised as such in the West for some
ten years now whilst, in the writing of musical scores, the most
complicated forms of notation have been in process of development. The most influential advocates of so-called collective improvisation have regarded themselves as providing a counter-
weight to the established and institutionalised business of
experimental New Music. The impulse came initially from the
politico-social freedom and youth movement in the U.S.A., and
also from the committed Jazz scene, which had developed very
free forms of collective music-making. This creative, noisy and
chaotic period, characterised by musical self-discovery 'ceremonies', gave birth to a form of Pop/Rock music, which also derived from American Country and Folk music. At the disposition of the groups involved there was a vast technology of ampli-
fication and loudspeaker-systems to help them spread among
contemporary youth their thunderous message of freedom in
giant halls and at great open-air festivals. There, tens of thousands of young people bore witness to the powerful drive towards collective self-experience.

Experimental Music

Apart from the groups of Jazz and Rock origin who started
out as the mouthpiece of the Underground Movement and not
infrequently finished up in the big business of the entertainment
industry, many avant-garde composers too have concerned themselves with improvised music. Years after Cage and Stockhausen,
who here too had provided the first impetus, the trombonist and
composer Vinko Globokar (Yugoslavia) and the Argentinian
pianist and composer Carlos R. Alsina embarked on free group-
improvisation with French Jazz musicians and interpreters of
the New Music. The Englishman Cornelius Cardew wrote a
whole book of improvisation instructions (*The Great Learning*)
for *Scratch Orchestra*, in which as many as thirty or forty
amateurs and professionals would come together to make music
in English villages with only the simplest resources for 'scrap-

ing', drumming and singing. In Italy, as well as *Nuova Con-sonanza*, *Musica Elettronica Viva* had already been founded by the American pianist and composer Frederik Rzewski. These groups used what were, in those days, all new electronic instruments and devices for sound-modulation. At that time, at the beginning of the sixties, the sounds of so-called Live Electronics had not yet been taken up by Pop-music and the various Beat and Rock groups.

Later on a whole range of such Live Electronics groups grew up in Germany too, often from experimental beginnings. From the late sixties onwards the German 'occasional composer' Josef Anton Riedl (b. 1929) started to collect around himself the most heterogeneous group of musicians, among them the American percussionist Michael Ranta, who subsequently went on to Taiwan to study Chinese Taoist music. In the course of his mega-lomaniac 'Multi-Media-Environments', Riedl had these performers react spontaneously to his own previously-prepared tape-cues in order to realise his filigree pieces, which were often provided with poetic plant-names. The German composer Dieter Schnebel (b. 1930), who in many of his pieces stretched the acoustic capabilities of the human voice to its very limits, created a whole series of acoustically abstract musical improvisation-stimuli for educational use (*Schulmusik*). The Frenchman Luc Ferrari (b. 1929), well-known as the composer of 'acoustic snapshots', and who incorporated sounds tape-recorded at sunrise on the seashore in his sensitive *presque rien* ('next-to-nothing'), worked with the German Rock-group *Amon Düül*, whom he had improvise against a musical background produced electronically. Other intuitive and improvisatory forms of a more meditative nature ('minimal art' and 'periodic music') will be described in more detail later on.

But more important than any further enumeration is the improvisatory process itself, for what is at stake is not so much the musical/aesthetic evaluation of such activities as their psychological significance and the opportunity they provide for collective experience-patterns such as arise from exercises in group-dynamics and sensitivity-training. It remains a remarkable fact that musicians who are fully trained in the Classical sense are not generally capable of extemporising freely on a melodic or harmonic figure, or even of idly improvising on their instrument. This incapacity results from their lop-sided training which concentrates solely on playing from the fixed score, so that, even in the earliest stages of learning, the notes are merely transferred mechanically from eye to hand. With few exceptions, the idea of playing music by ear, in an improvisatory way, is almost always ignored in traditional music-teaching.

So it comes about that technically ill-versed musicians are the more easily able to improvise – or rather, lacking suitable training, they often wallow in all manner of improvisatory clichés until they acquire certain acoustic tricks of the trade by virtue of imitating various models. Anyone who undertakes free group-improvisation with other musicians from a whole variety of backgrounds soon learns to recognise the patterns that keep recurring, and also learns the golden rule of all free group-improvisation – listen to each other.

In order that the following report on the gaining of self-experience through group improvisation may be an authentic one, I propose to draw on my own personal experiences as a member of the group *Between* – a group which has counted among its members interpreters of Classical music and South American folk-music, as well as experimental composers and black American percussionists.

In the course of free improvisation, occasional passages come together to give an effect similar to that of composed music. But 'uncomposable' harmonic effects also arise, providing fascinating acoustic experiences for individual players. The young composer Ulrich Stranz calls this 'being among the good stuff'. One is quite prepared to take a chance on having a badly-proportioned shape to the piece, on producing 'hiatuses' or over-long modulations, and even frequently runs the risk of an unconvincing ending, with each player 'bailing out' in turn. Yet the listener can find the experience of being present at the creative process most fascinating. 'The unforeseeables are too many for words, but that is precisely where the enjoyment lies, holding much delight in store for the alert listener. The situation is precisely the same as in Classical Jazz; there, too, the first hearing, the actuality-experience of each original musical development was more interesting than anything a repeated re-hearing on tape or disc could ever offer.'*

In order to avoid this occasional falling-off of quality in a

---

* F. Muggler on 'Experimentelle Ensembles', *Neue Zürcher Zeitung*, 25/2/72.

tape-recorded improvisation, while nevertheless being able to retain the spontaneity of the inspirational process, there remains the possibility of 'cleaning up' longer sessions by editing out (through cutting and fading) the abortive parts and generally organising the recording. This procedure is admittedly eschewed by improvisation-purists even when, thanks to the efforts of a qualified sound-engineer both during and after the performance, the artificial 'joins' cannot be heard. They have, after all, a compositional purpose and make possible the repeated enjoyment of particularly effective improvisations. At all events, constructions of fascinating complexity can often arise during the course of a group-performance – constructions created in the absence of any pre-arranged melodic material or harmonic schemes, and purely on the basis of random communicational circumstances (even if an element of common purpose, or even of 'conjuration', may be said to have been present). But there are also rare moments, captured by tape-recordings, that arise out of a common, supersensory intuition on the part of the players – instants that are neither 'feasible' nor repeatable and which, but for the tape-recorded 'note-banks', would remain the blissful secret of the musicians. Such instants can be appreciated just as deeply, even on tape, by sensitive listeners. The secret reveals itself directly one is listening in a relaxed and open state similar to that in which the musicians, perhaps unconsciously, also found themselves, if perhaps only very briefly.

The *modus operandi* of this rendezvous at archetypal level is as yet unresearched, and seems to resemble that of the mind-bending drugs – the short-circuit flashes of clairvoyant awareness typical of the state of complete self-opening. These intuitive states, well-known to many non-European musical cultures who see them as the whole purpose of the exercise, are learnable. However, when one has practised intuitive music-making alone for some time, encountering many obstacles and trials of patience on the way, one comes to realise how difficult such a process must be for a group of *several* performers. And indeed there are next to no discs of group-recordings of such music, which is essentially *each individual's own secret*. The quality and intensity of meditative music also depends upon the number of performers who are improvising. The more performers taking part (however used they may be to each other's playing), the less deep the resulting musical experience. A further important factor here is the personal relationship of the players to each other, for in improvisation there is a direct meeting of minds, a question and answer situation, a love-hate relationship. No-one can keep his skeletons of prejudice or aversion in their private cupboards. I personally have not experienced any satisfactory performance of intuitively-based music with more than three evenly-matched players taking part. It is not without good reason that in Asian and Arabic countries the typical arrangement that has evolved is that centring around an expert soloist, a Master-musician who leads the performance and is merely accompanied by the other musicians.

Improvisation-models

Many improvisation-groups realised early on the need for intensive interpersonal contact and therefore congregated in country farmhouses or communes. This permitted a more intimate personal and musical contact. Each member learnt to recognise the others' peculiarities and typical reactions. Some groups made it a rule always to start each session 'from scratch' – i.e. to get down to work each time without prior discussion. From such a procedure the most astonishing results emerged, especially among groups of amateur musicians – a form of communication that 'worked' because the participants knew each other. On the other hand these groups often stagnated after some time and went into liquidation : they had nothing more to say to each other and so the participants went off in search of new stimuli.

Other groups, for whom the anarchistic, magical-unconscious (and not infrequently egoistic) liberation-aspect was less to the fore, and who preferred to develop musical architectonics gradually, deliberately and consciously, evolved a series of agreed and previously-discussed *improvisation-models*, based on their earlier experience of structures spontaneously arrived at. For this, one particular technical aid was of the greatest significance : a simple tape-recorder, set to record, as a 'control', every spontaneous acoustic happening regardless of quality. With the aid of this objective observer and its 'transcript', the participants could then join in analysing and consolidating their efforts, and in formulating conclusions.

In this way a number of absolutely basic communication patterns were discovered, such as could help in group music-making without compromising the creative element. One noteworthy improvisation model of this kind was formulated for the group *Between* by the American oboist Robert Eliscu. Four players each have three different notes placed at their disposal, so that, in all, a twelve-note scale is produced. These three notes should have no particular harmonic connection, but should stand in a dissonant relationship to each other. Each player then develops such motifs as are permitted by his three notes at a variety of octave-pitches.*

The music and art historian Gerhard Nestler writes of experiments of this kind in his *Entwurf einer Geschichte der Klangfarbe*:

> Of significance today are attempts by freely-improvising instrumental groups to build connected structures out of the musical material itself. A note, an interval, a given tone-colour are the building-bricks with which the instruments operate, all of them continually exchanging rôles. The construction modules can be used back-to-front or upside-down. Indeed, the basic material can even consist of a twelve-note row, with three notes allocated to each of four instruments, each of which then improvises simultaneously with the others on the basis of its own material. In this way everything goes with everything else – as well as with the ideological and spiritual outlook of the players. Any alteration in one aspect brings about an alteration of the whole.†

In addition, the search for a basis for intuitive improvisation led players to take up once again the modal scales of the Middle Ages, the technique of *organum*, the use of a constant bass-drone or bourdon, and the Indian raga-forms. Signals were developed – so-called 'call phrases' – to warn the improvising musicians that a section was about to end; a regular rhythm was once more 'allowed', though not so much a mere metric *ostinato* as a rhythm with a particular effect, borrowed from the magical world of Africa or South America. And so there developed a

---

* These performance-instructions form the basis of the piece *Memories* (LP entitled *Einstieg*, wergo 1971).

† From the unpublished work of the now 75-year-old Dr. Gerhard Nestler.

form of music without any particular plan, and yet within which a theme, a shape, a rhythmical accompanying figure or a modal scale is identifiable – improvised music that could scarcely have been any different had it been composed.

Music of this sort has of recent years come to be known as 'meditative' or, better still, 'intuitive' music. Karlheinz Stockhausen used the term in connection with the musical realisation of his spiritual-attunement texts *Aus den Sieben Tagen*: 'By the term "intuitive music",' he writes in an introduction, 'I wish to indicate that it proceeds as directly as possible from the intuition – which, in a group of musicians playing intuitively, adds up to more than the sum of the individual "ideas" on account of the process of "feedback". The "direction" of the performers, however – I call it "attunement" – is not arbitrary or even negative (i.e exclusive of all musical thought along certain predetermined lines), but is merely concentrated by my text, which summons forth the intuitive in a particular way.'*

The text of one of these pieces, entitled *Unbegrenzt*, concludes as follows:

'A note lives, like YOU, like ME, like THEM, like IT.
Moves, stretches and contracts.
Metamorphoses, gives birth, procreates, dies, is reborn.
Seeks, stops seeking, finds, loses, marries,
loves, tarries, hurries, comes and goes.'†

The intuitive factor in music-making is in any case not programmable, even when a group is following a spiritual path, whether individually or communally. Among brilliant interpreters of Classical music, too, the process of intuition always comes as a gift of grace, and not on demand. Nor is it easy to spot those moments of supposed intuition which are in fact only imagined to be so, for true intuition is very easily contaminated, whether by intellectual concepts or by design. 'We should erect a protective fence around our intuitive "feelings" in order to preserve the intuition from being undermined by our doubts.' So says the Sufi Hazrat Inayat Khan, who was himself a great

* Accompanying text of the record-album *Aus den Sieben Tagen*, Deutsche Grammophon.
† K. H. Stockhausen: *Aus den Sieben Tagen*, Universal Edition, Vienna 1968.

musician. His thoughts on the intuition reflect the convictions of many improvisatory musicians: 'Intuition is something that lies beyond man's personality and above his knowledge of ways and means. Intuition comes at those times when a person has become passive, and when all knowledge, conscious or unconscious, is suspended ... Intuition is something much higher and more wonderful than mind-reading or traffic with the spirits, because it is pure. Besides, it is our property, belongs to our real selves. From within we receive the knowledge that is much more precious, much greater, much higher.'*

PSYCHEDELIC MUSIC

For many musicologists at the end of the sixties the turning of the young generation to spiritual and Far-Eastern music, their discovery of the wells of human intuition and the wave of musical meditation were all an enigma. The increasing materialism and automation of the West were recognised to be the underlying cause of the 'Asian invasion'. They were the reason for the attempt to escape from a reality deemed to be inhuman into the fantasy-dreamworld of music, which in the exotic cultures was capable of opening up man's inner universe. Finally the connection started to become evident between 'Underground Music' and the mind-bending drugs to which the young people of America and Europe were increasingly turning. It was an open secret that almost every member of these musical groups, both improvisatory and Rock, had experimented with hallucinogenic drugs or at least with hashish or marihuana. The new movement called itself *psychedelic*.†

Now particular substances, hitherto unknown to Western society, started one by one to be registered as dangerous drugs, declared taboo and banned: the Black Market could start up. Nevertheless other drugs had long since quietly penetrated, and become accepted in, the everyday life of civilised societies. But by now life would have been unthinkable without them. The chief difference between these drugs was not appreciated: pills and alcoholic intoxicants have a conditioning and consciousness-

* Hazrat I. Khan: tr. from *Aus einem Rosengarten Indiens*, Munich 1954.
† 'Psychedelic', a recent loanword-formation from Greek, means 'that which expands consciousness'.

limiting effect, while the plant-drugs of the young people, on the other hand, bring about a consciousness-*expansion*.

Consideration of the drugs – both legalised, taboo and illegal – of Western industrial countries makes it clear that our society may justly be described as suffering from a general drug-addiction: television as a drug, alcohol as a drug, nicotine as a drug, sport as a drug, sex as a drug, narcotics as drugs, pills as drugs. In West Germany alone the yearly consumption of alcohol and tobacco amounts to ten billion pounds' worth, of barbiturate sleeping-tablets over thirty million packets, of pep-pills two million packets, of sedatives more than fifty million.* In the working-class districts of Berlin fourteen-year-olds get high on the fumes of chemical adhesives because they have no money for hashish. Irreversible medical damage shows up in the glands within a few months. In 1969 it was estimated that there were 600,000 alcoholics in West Germany, by no means all of them of working-class origin. Meanwhile tax-revenues on alcohol for the same year amounted to eight hundred million pounds.

In such a situation it is understandable that music too has become a mere commercial drug. On the one hand we have the sentimentality of the tear-jerkers in the bars, on the other the aggressiveness of the mindless Rock music in the 'drug-dives'. The identification-mechanism linking music to listener is, as I indicated at the outset, clearly recognisable: most music reflects and bolsters up the state of its clientèle, their inner chaos, their private insecurity and loneliness. While the greater part of Pop music is produced under the influence of drugs, many so-called 'session-musicians' of the Beat music industry are alcoholics. For in our society some drugs are turned into bogeymen, while others are treated as harmless. The distinction between the poisonous, addictive chemical drugs and the plant-based, 'natural' drugs is continually blurred. The TV-cliché of smoke-ridden narcotics parties and the increasing number of Black Market offences arising from blanket-prohibitions are mutually productive of each other.

In Western Europe there is no more hashish; with inflation it has come to be 'eked out' with all kinds of substances, and the LSD-trip, irresponsibly adulterated with so-called 'speed'

* Compare J. vom Scheidt: *Innenweltverschmutzung*, Munich, Zürich 1975, p. 39f.

(Amphetamine), ends in the purest horror. The young 'dealer' of the Pop-scene has long been playing the same double-standards game as his parents. As a result of the illegal, outlaw status of drug addicts in the younger, ill-informed circles, the number of those who cannot cope with 'getting high' and who have 'changed horses' onto the addictive poisons ('fixers') has increased. Many of the 1960 generation will inject and swallow absolutely anything to escape from their grey surrounds into a fantasy-world. One needs to consider here not only the physical, but also the spiritual dependence on drugs which derives from the incompatibility of the real world with the drug-experience. For drug-addicts, our society's competitive principle breaks down, and therein lies the real reason for the turning of drugs into bogeymen.

Just recently the drug scene has undergone a shift. The situation is analogous to what happened with the 'flippers', the American gaming-machines; by the time working-class youngsters started using them, the intellectuals had already ceased to do so. Lacking proper guidance, today's commercial cannon-fodder have for the most part no inkling of the serious self-analysis and self-realisation experiments that can be undertaken with the aid of hallucinogenic drugs and psychedelic music. This is regrettable, for it was precisely at this point that drugs were starting to have a considerable significance in the context of creative musical experiences, while psychedelic music was assuming a communicative rôle in group-analysis. The decline of this creative period is described by Rainer Kranich in a collection of essays, with the collaboration not only of former representatives of the drug-scene, but also of two of the spiritual fathers of the new, integral consciousness – Lama Anagarika Govinda and Jean Gebser:

> This process can be very clearly traced in Pop-music – though only if one listens carefully, for outwardly its success is now at its greatest, this music being virtually the only aspect of the subculture that still survives. But if one listens, for example, to the first LP-recording of the group *Pink Floyd*, which still conveys a feeling of open joy; then the second, in which the spaceflight-sounds start to come in; the third, their swansong *More*; and finally the most recent discs, which gradually

adopt more and more extravagant and pompous, if clumsy, forms – then one senses something of the changes that have occurred during these years.

This trend also shows up in the way in which the musical names have changed : *Underground*, in which the idea of common experience still resonates, and which, after commercialisation had set in, came to be mentioned only with embarrassment; the great goal of *psychedelic music*, a followup of early psychedelic successes; *Pop*, the final relapse into commercialisation, wherein lies almost the whole subsequent history of the group. In the individual sphere of music-listening the same process occurred. I can remember that a few years ago listening to music was a quite central, purposeful experience, a process of common communication involving happenings which are even today spoken of in hushed tones, and which involved a penetration to the heart of the music as it hovered in the ether, no longer fixed in space, time or meaning, creating a powerful attunement-experience.*

Reflections on the relationships between drugs and music will be found in a subsequent section devoted to the effect of drugs on music-making and musical appreciation. That there is hardly any literature available on the subject may be due not merely to the fact that drug taking was in any case customary only in those musical circles where little value was placed on analytical theories and explanations; but also to a frequent inability to achieve any real subsequent recall of the acoustic experiences undergone while 'high'. There has been a tendency to report the quantity and intensity of an experience rather than its quality and its potential for conscious assimilation, for it is the function of the hallucinogenic drugs to lead the musician precisely to those magical-mythical planes of consciousness in which no real conscious thought can occur without a deliberate effort of the will.

While playing under the influence of the hemp-plant cannabis, the performer soon ceases to make any clear distinction between what *he* is playing and what the others are playing. He observes the whole dynamic from within, and identifies himself

* R. Kranich in *Trug der Drogen*, Siebenstern Taschenbuch, Hamburg 1974, p. 30.

with the entire 'happening', rather than setting up his own 'happening' in contrast to the performance of the others. A group that is improvising without any prepared schema can easily get carried away by hackneyed phrases, and the conventionally-derived harmonic categories are re-experienced as a great new discovery. Prepared scores or pre-arranged systems seem unimportant. Rather is one open to spontaneous sound patterns that have ostensibly never been experienced before. If the individual wishes to perform consciously throughout, he finds himself on the threshold between a fantastic sense of overall perspective on the one hand and total confusion on the other – in which case the latter need not be allowed to express itself negatively, but can be savoured as a state of ego-less, dream-like activity.

Group music-making under the influence of marihuana can seem to the individual less collective and thus more sophisticated, and his sense of time is drastically changed, even though he may not always be aware of it. The result is generally less lively, but more concentrated and cheerful. It can also subsequently be re-experienced by the players if it is tape-recorded at the time. Many a tape can turn out to be an important witness to collectively-experienced states, having captured downright hallucinatory sounds, newly-discovered harmonic and melodic figures and archaic twists – things which would have been equally detectable to a 'dispassionate' outsider.

The criteria for judging drug-influenced music-making are admittedly relative ones, a fact which also applies where communication with the listener is concerned. For if one thing is clear, it is that listening to music under the influence of drugs also has to be learnt, for normally the paths to a person's deeper levels of awareness are blocked. In this auditory state, however, even the sounds of nature or the noises of the environment suddenly acquire hitherto unperceived connections with each other, thus opening up unsuspected vistas of musical interrelationships. One's appreciation of a sound can become sharper, even Classical works are suddenly re-experienced as though for the first time, and one reaches a state in which one registers and perceives music no longer as outside oneself, but as inside one's own body. One can even retain this way of listening to music as a sensitised form of perception that can be applied thereafter without external aids – a way of listening that is in fact normal for many sensitive music-lovers and that can also be learnt *without* drugs.

And at this point the process known as synaesthesia sets in: sounds beget pictures and associations, the intellectually orientated listener undergoes physical experiences, and notes hitherto perceived outwardly, structurally or pictorially take on a spiritual aura. What goes for hallucinogenic drugs themselves goes also for music under the influence of drugs: what comes to light in intensified form is what was already there in germ.

However, the musical LSD-trip was able to help many a previously mindless note-spinner to achieve a pitch of self-knowledge that was to influence his whole subsequent output. A prolonged note would be heard across a new and much greater range of overtones. The harmonic series would reveal itself to the sensitised ear like some secret message. A whole universe of the finest microintervals was perceived and translated into music. Suffused by an overpowering sense of joy, one could submerge oneself in one's music, experience a grace and an almost holy awe. With other musicians one felt a marvellous oneness, while retaining nevertheless the feeling of one's own identity amid the whole. This experience, which one could almost call mystical, culminated in spontaneous, deep insights into the relationship of man to the world of sounds.

The great and specific importance of music for psychedelic sessions is affirmed by Hans Carl Leuner, who as a professor of psychiatry has developed 'psychedelic therapy' in Germany. This therapy for chronic alcoholism and serious psychic disorders has three phases: first, bringing into awareness the patient's life-problems, his past and present, his goals, pretensions and frustrations. The next phase is the preparation and psychedelic session itself. Finally, in the third phase, the material of the psychedelic session is thoroughly studied – a process which can take months or even years.

An important element in the success of phase two is the patient's surroundings, the design of the 'treatment room'.

Professor Leuner reports: 'Especially for this kind of hallucinogenic effect the setting is of the greatest importance. It should be a quietly situated room, preferably sound-insulated ... Flower arrangements are brought in, pictures which radiate a harmonious and soothing influence ... A candle can be left to burn during the session. In addition, various forms of stimula-

tion are used, above all music broadcast over a stereo-system,
preferably via a stereo-headset – classical music (such as Bach),
semi-classical or the like. To start with, particularly soothing
music is recommended, while later on the music rises to a peak
of ecstasy – as in the Requiems of Mozart and Verdi, the Ode to
Joy in the fourth movement of Beethoven's Ninth Symphony etc.
Detailed researches into the influence and choice of music in
psychedelic therapy have been carried out by Gaston and Eagle.
The person concerned is asked to lie on a comfortable couch,
relax and listen to the music.'*

On the patients' own feedback-forms, which Leuner appends
to his report, the extent to which the music promotes this self-
knowledge by way of the deepest chasms and most violent fears
is vividly portrayed : 'The music carried me away ... the music
screamed at me ... the music swallowed me up ... I was one
with the music ...'

Admittedly, mystic drug-experiences cannot be programmed,
any more than can intuitive states. But with the help of a doctor
trained in psychology, or of an experienced friend, good results
are invariably achieved. Yet a mystic experience always comes
to the drug user 'as a special and unforeseeable mercy. He can
only long for it. Moreover the way to it via the psychedelic trip
not infrequently leads "through hell", through an "agonising
catharsis". The experience of terror often precedes the state of
bliss ... Mystic experiences, however they are arrived at, cannot just be "consumed". They bring awe and trembling in their
wake and have far-reaching effects at a deep level on the course
of "real" life.'†

Anybody who has taken part in such a process will also have
come to realise that it is specifically music that has this capacity
not only to heighten concentration and sensitivity, but to open
up the individual through suitably-chosen sounds. Music can
make him aware that he *has* an inward side, help him switch off
his thoughts for a while and then go on to planes of which he is
aware only in dreams at best. The effect of such experiences
often comes as a sort of rebirth, and no narcotics are necessary
for it if one is prepared to learn over a period of time to tread a
spiritual path towards inner self-realisation.

---

* *Religion und die Droge*, Stuttgart 1972, p. 40.
† Ulli Olvedi: *Buddhismus – Religion der Zukunft?*, Munich 1973, p. 28.

The Drug-Fraud

The worst cases of drug-poisoning, and the recognition that only those already in touch with spiritual values have really benefited from mystic drug-experiences, have meanwhile tended to silence the champions of the legalisation of certain drugs. In the sixties, before his early death, Rudolph Gelpke was already pointing to the risks and dangers of drugs:

> The possibility of psychological self-injury is of course undisputed. The truth remains: the more extroverted (in the broadest sense) a person's life has been, and the less conscious he has become (outwardly at least) of his own being, the greater the risk that the sudden confrontation with his inner reality – which he can no longer dodge – will prove too much for him, even, in extreme cases perhaps, bringing him to the point of collapse ... It is expected of our psychiatrists and psychologists that they should either fit the individual, and specifically the 'difficult cases', back into the complicated mechanism of our technical world, so that they 'function' smoothly within it, or isolate them as mental patients. Whether, and if so how, this task can be squared with actual experience I do not know. But it is clear beyond a shadow of doubt that drugs, regarded by Indians and orientals generally as the key to the gates between the Here and the Beyond, can reactive the normally dormant, but potentially usable, mystic capabilities even of modern man to a degree that has not hitherto been thought possible.*

The extent to which this key of hallucinogenic drugs can open the doors to a *lasting, integral* knowledge is described in the following account of a psychedelic self-realisation experience intensified by religious music, written by the great Dutch psychologist Arendsen Hein (b. 1912):

> Following my insights gained during psychedelic experience, I had made extensive efforts to cultivate my spiritual life through suitable reading, conversations with friends etc. about these blissful memories. It turned out, however, that under the influence of auto-suggestion, I had merely been using the

* R. Gelpke: *Drogen und Seelenerweiterung*, 4th edition, Munich 1975.

'delights of the spirit as a refined form of self-gratification'. Also involved was, among other things, a partial refusal to recognise the bad side of my life, together with an idealisation (rather than a realisation) of myself, other people and circumstances generally – which of course alienated me from a good proportion of earthly reality. That was when it became clear to me that even the psychedelic/religious experience of oneness with transcendental reality does not free man from subjection to the errors of his existence in this world, and that existence means being no more and no less than one really is.*

The 'pioneers' of the former psychedelic music scene are to-day scattered to the four winds. Many finished up in the awful trap of injections and addiction, a few 'joined the big time' while their reminiscences of psychedelic inspiration became ever more sterile, others have disappeared, perhaps to live in the country, perhaps to the Far East or into the intellectual glasshouse of rational self-prostitution. A few Western European electronic groups, disciples of the drug-prophet Leary, had a go at founding a new musical movement – 'Cosmic Music' – but expressed their psychedelic experience only in the titles of their pieces and in their commentaries, and achieved no further musical self-development.

Many, however, and their numbers were considerable, began systematically to study the music of Asia and Africa. They learnt exotic instruments, Indian chants or African rhythms – not so as to escape from incompatibility with present reality, but in order consciously to re-encounter the submerged magical/mythical levels of their own consciousness. Now they are looking for a 'sound' capable of serving as an acoustic aid which will make recourse to a 'fix' unnecessary and will develop into a kind of music that will create the preconditions for becoming inwardly quieter and less self-willed, for remaining aware, being patient, and moving nearer, step by step, to the realisation of a new consciousness.

* A. Hein in: *Religion und die Droge*, pp. 103 and 106.

2 Encounter with Non-European Music

The non-European countries were already being explored in the fifties and sixties, and even before, by those tired of the West, by the Hippies and by the more original ethnologists. More and more young people from America and Europe were following the newly-discovered routes, returning in exotic clothes and bringing back with them Arabic, Indian, Javanese, Japanese, African or South American music as evidence of having undertaken the Great Journey. Accidentally or otherwise they had encountered cultures that were magically and mythically aware. The Jazz and Pop-musicians appeared in long African robes or oriental shirts and presented themselves as 'different'.

For many years now the West Berlin Institute for Comparative Musicology has been arranging events which until only a short time ago were regarded as *recherché* activities for initiated specialists. Nowadays, whether they be a dancing-troupe from Bali, an Arabic lutanist, virtuosi from northern India or musicians from Turkey, Korea or Japan, these events are sold out as soon as announced. During the Munich Olympics in the summer of 1972 the exhibition entitled 'World Cultures and Modern Art' presented highly-qualified representatives of the Classical music of every continent. The Munich composer J. A. Riedl engaged the services of African and South American rhythm-groups and presented a cross-section of international folk-music, while Joachim E. Berendt organised, among other things, a concert entitled 'Africa Now', in which celebrated American musicians appeared alongside ensembles from Africa and the Middle East – among them the percussionist Art Blakey, who had already performed with African drummers.

In 1976 it was even arranged for a complete Balinesian village, which comprises at one and the same time an opera-group and gamelan-orchestra, to spend several weeks in West Berlin and demonstrate its culture. African and Japanese musical groups were likewise invited. But these cultures are not being stripped of their very essence in the colonial fashion (as happened during the unthinking 'empire-rush' of former centuries) and patronisingly classified as 'folklore'; instead, the very thing which most threatens to disappear from these ancient cultures is being impressed upon them as being of quintessential importance – their access to the collective unconscious via music.

The great musical encounter had begun in the sixties with the celebrated 'Jazz-Meets-the-World' movement, which in Europe was led above all by Joachim E. Berendt, the Jazz-specialist and radio-producer. He it was who arranged the meetings between a Tunisian Bedouin music-group, saxophonist and flautist Sahib Shihab and violinist Jean-Luc Ponty, and between American clarinettist Tony Scott and Japanese and Indonesian musicians; and he put on the first 'Jazz-Meets-India' concerts, in which the world-famous Indian *sarod*-player Ali Akbar Khan collaborated, as also did the well-known trumpeter Don Cherry.

The 'exotic' trend achieved popularity through the Beatles, who committed themselves to the 'Transcendental Meditation' of the Maharishi Mahesh Yogi and learnt to love and honour the *sitar* virtuoso Ravi Shankar. The 'India-trip' reached its first highpoint when Ravi Shankar played with Yehudi Menuhin and was 'discovered' by a big recording-company and sent on tour with much publicity. Commercial as this undertaking may have turned out to be, a wider public suddenly gained access to Indian music. The *sitar* was 'in'. However, the trend lasted only a year or so.

For businessmen and publicity-agents the fashion soon started to lose interest, yet only after this juncture did the real 'homework' start to be done on this important encounter: young American composers and musicians now began to visit India, Indonesia or Central Africa for several months at a time, in order to study the exotic musical traditions in depth. One would concern himself with the Voodoo-rhythms of the Ghanaian medicine-men, another would learn to play the little metallophones used in gamelan music, and most went to study under the countless great Indian musicians. Suddenly it was realised that Ravi Shankar was only one among many outstanding *sitar* virtuosi,

and not by any means 'the best', and that in the heart of individual countries the world over a host of humble musical
treasures were waiting to be discovered by the West. For the
young, eager Western musicians were managing to reach Asia
and Africa just at the very moment when the indigenous musical
cultures were in the process of dying out under the influence
of technological civilisation. The native peoples had begun to be
ashamed of their own cultures, and it is a particular miracle of
cultural interchange that through a few Western students and
musical ethnologists a part of these dying acoustic treasures will
survive – as a vital aspect, oddly enough, of contemporary and
future Western music.

Now the greatest musicians of the Far East started to make
their way here. The broadcasting stations of West Germany put
on festivals entitled 'Encounter with Japanese Music', 'Encounter
with India', etc. Ali Akbar Khan and the great Pandit Pran Nath
have their own music-schools in America; in Amsterdam there
is a gamelan-ensemble with Western players; in West Berlin the
Indonesian composer Paul Gutama Soegijo is teaching the rudiments of Javanese music; and in Berlin in 1974 the music editor
Walter Bachauer, too, organised 'Meta-Music' weeks with
Vilayat Khan – perhaps the greatest Indian musician of our day
– with the fabulous *sarangi* player Ram Narayan, and with a
troupe of Tibetan monks. In addition, seminars on Indian Classical music were held by the Masters themselves: Imrat Khan,
brother of Vilayat Khan, Pandit Patekar (the Hindu teacher from
Benares) and many others, who are coming to the West because
their music is becoming less and less valued in their homeland.

Seen from a purely sociological point of view, this trend towards the non-European cultures may seem suspiciously like
'mystical escapism'. As some are only too eager to point out, the
great Far Eastern cultures have either collapsed or are dying out,
and so the question naturally arises as to how useful they are
likely to be to us. A further objection concerns the fact that in
the Far Eastern cultures – as also in Europe until the eighteenth
century – music was monopolised, almost up to our own day, by
the feudal overlords, and that therefore in our pluralistic, demo-
cratic society there is no room for what is in fact an anachronis-
tic extravagance. In reply one might point out that this music
is a living art-form which is not bound up with any particular

kind of society, and that today those Asian and African musicians who still possess and embody the power of man's primal magical-mythical depths – the very ones who are most sought after by the 'musical pilgrims' – are not infrequently completely forgotten, or even laughed at, in their own homelands. The non-European upper classes have long preferred their Western 'sound'. The old wizards of music, the bearers of sound's secrets, often live poorer and less highly regarded lives than the simplest villager. On the other hand it is observable, if one has the luck to meet one of these musicians, that these inconspicuous Masters have their circles of pupils, and that these not infrequently come from the West. If one further considers that, because of the driving of the Tibetan people into exile in India, Europe and America, a centuries-old secret religion of the greatest sophistication is gradually taking root in the West, cultivated not only by scholars but also by growing circles of spiritual seekers, then it becomes clear that the outward westernising of the orient is going hand in hand with a still largely invisible orientalisation of the West.

At this point we shall go on to consider the music of India in more detail, as this music is the easiest for the Western listener to grasp inwardly. A description of Tibetan sacred music comes next, followed by an over-all look at the shamanic, magic and ecstatic aspects of African, Arabic, Indonesian music and so on. This survey of non-European music will in no sense be exhaustive. But even these brief notes are sufficient to indicate the perspectives that constantly recur in every ancient musical culture.

INDIAN CLASSICAL MUSIC

In his travelling-diary of 1921 Graf Hermann Keyserling wrote the following on the music of India:

> This music could neither be reduced to the framework of a melody, nor be related to particular harmonies, nor analysed in terms of a straightforward rhythm; even single notes varied in shape. Nevertheless every pretended whole did seem to have a real unity – a unity of mood, which lasts until another mood takes over. The theory – one might almost call it a

mythology – of this music is quite extraordinary. From the earliest times, given sequences of notes have corresponded to given artistic themes: for each theme the connoisseur knows the corresponding raga. And each raga corresponds to a particular time of year and may only be played at particular hours of the day. There are ragas for each hour of the day and night ...

It is not easy to explain in words what Indian music means, for it has so little in common with ours: it is basically of a mind with Indian dance. No aim, no previously-sketched shape, no beginning, no end; a rushing and surging of the ever-flowing stream of life. Hence a like effect on the listener: it does not tire one, could go on for ever, for nobody ever has enough of life ... In no way does it reflect Time, but the circumstances of life, projected against the background of Eternity ...

A French artist once remarked of Indian music: 'C'est la musique du corps astral'.* That is *precisely* what it is (in so far as there is an astral realm corresponding to the traditional concepts): a vast, unmeasurable world in which states take the place of circumstances. One experiences nothing definite, nothing tangible while listening to it, and yet one feels most intensely alive. While following the cadences of the notes one is in reality listening to one's own self ...

The quintessential point about Indian music is that it lies in a different dimension to ours ... By comparison with ours, this music is monotonous; often a long composition covers only a few notes, and often it is a single note that is the vehicle of a whole mood. The essence of this music lies elsewhere; in the dimension of pure intensity; there it needs no broad surface layer. Indian metaphysics, too, is monotonous. It speaks continually of the One, without a Second, in which God, soul and world coalesce, the One that is the innermost being of all diversity.†

If, fifty years after this encounter of a European with Indian Classical music (at Calcutta, in the house of the Tagore family),

* 'It is the music of the astral body.'
† Graf Hermann Keyserling: *Das Reisetagebuch eines Philosophen*, Darmstadt 1921, Vol. I, pp. 398–403 selected.

one reads reports of the starvation catastrophes in the interior
of India and the slums of Calcutta, it becomes evident that India
is an underdeveloped country. At all events, anybody who
spends some time living in India and considers the history of
this continent, will recognise that India has *become* underdeveloped and in need of aid. The demon of materialistic, selfish
thinking is taking over; British colonial rule taught the Indians,
it seems, above all the diseases of its own civilisation. As we pass
through the poor-quarters of Calcutta, Bombay or Delhi we
easily forget, to start with, that we are visiting this country to
study its great culture and its music.

India is haunted by starvation, epidemics and natural catastrophes. Economic development is crippled by the population
explosion, political unrest, corruption, nepotism, antiquated in-
stitutions and the Black Market. India is in a state of permanent
crisis. The typical city, whether Hindu or Muslim, has traded in
its beliefs – figuratively speaking – for transistor radios and fixed
its sights on an industrialised, Western standard of living – which,
however, few actually enjoy. The caste-system, which has lost
its religious basis and original purpose and is officially suppressed, while still surviving *de facto*, is becoming more and more of
a social horror. The average – and particularly the well-to-do –
Indian is coming increasingly to despise his own culture, his own
style of dress, his own religion, his own music.

The countless musicians of India are now imitating for the
most part the trivial light music of the West, and the result is a
bastard form of music that is excruciating to our ears. But they
have to survive and feed their families, and so 'Hindi-Film-
Music' (as this mixture much-loved by the Indians is called) is
produced and brings in a certain amount of money. Those more
significant Classical performers who are still able to retain something of their inner spiritual energy live – unless they are
counted among the handful of virtuosi and celebrities – for the
most part in seclusion, poverty and social oblivion. Among them
are many far greater musicians than the Classical performers
known to us here through broadcasts and big concerts, who cast
their pearls before privileged and moneyed dilletantists at élite
concerts in well-to-do circles.

A few of these greater figures are also known in the West:
Ravi Shankar and Ali Akbar Khan, or the brothers Imrat and

Vilayat Khan. Most of them hail from musical families of long standing, have from childhood learnt nothing but their own particular instrument, have often been unashamedly drilled to play it. Later it sometimes happens that they cannot cope as people with their musical greatness, and incline to alcoholism or take on airs of princely or kingly vanity. And they know that whatever personal objections may legitimately be levelled against them will have disappeared *after* their concert-appearance. For they are very well aware of the power and magic of their music, even if they are unable fully to appreciate its *modus operandi*.

While the music of northern India became overlaid with Arabic and Persian musical techniques and concepts as a result of the Muslim invasion, the music of southern India remained strictly Hindu, and thus exclusively a form of religious devotion. The form of each piece was more strictly laid down – even to the extent of being composed – and there was less room for improvisation. Again, even today, religious chanting and the playing of the *vina* takes pride of place, whereas in the thirteenth century the Persian *sitar* was introduced into northern India by Amir Kushru, who came to India in the wake of the princes and moguls. The music acquired a worldly aspect, and musicians were allowed more scope for improvisation. Whereas all singing and playing had previously been for God alone, the Islamic courts were more interested in the supernatural powers that could be evoked by a singer or player through the medium of music. There are reports of almost unbelievable prodigies that are alleged to have been produced through the agency of music.

Of Tan-Sen, the greatest north Indian Master and court-musician of the Mogul emperor Akbar, it is recounted, for example, that as a result of his chanting a candle began to burn and the sunrise occurred an hour early, and that through his playing clouds and rain-showers occurred outside the monsoon-period. On being questioned as to the teacher from whom he had learnt such arts, Tan-Sen answered the mighty Akbar that the former would not appear before him, since he sang only for God. Akbar is then said to have gone in ascetic garb with Tan-Sen to the latter's guru and, on hearing his voice, to have fallen into a divine trance.

Today such musical wizards are apparently extinct, but in the subtler sphere of music's psychological effects there are still

experiences of the greatest profundity. Yet it is a rare slice of
luck actually to meet one of these musicians who still has complete command of the strict rules of ancient Indian music, who
still manifests its religious principles in his own life, and who
still holds total sway over the powers of the spirit. An essential
precondition is a willingness and surrender on the part of the
listener such as is, for the most part, quite foreign to Western
man. None the less a few concerts involving Indian musicians
have taken place in Europe and America which have not merely
conveyed an impressive perfection and an exotic flair, but have
opened the inner ear of many people both young and old and
set in train, so to speak, a spiritual awakening through the
medium of sound. This had more than a little to do, in those
days, with the psychedelic drugs, which encouraged an aban-
doned, relaxed form of listening: soon it became fashionable to
listen to Indian music while 'high'. In the 'Underground', in the
many new spiritual communities that have grown up in Europe
and America over the years, Indian music is enjoying an ever-
growing popularity. For those people who are involved in yoga
or meditation, in Hindu or Islamic mysticism, or who are studying Sufism or in some other way gradually learning to increase
their awareness of their own inner selves, Classical Indian music
– the southern, *karnatic* form just as much as the *Hindustani*
music of the north – can prove itself a marvellous vehicle for
the journey into the sub- and superconscious.

I first discovered for myself the music of northern India
through the recordings of Ustad Vilayat Khan and through meeting Ustad Imrat Khan, his younger brother, through the good
offices of his German pupil Al Gromer. Without much theoretical
knowledge – a lack which in no way detracts from one's listening, as any Indian will confirm – but with great enthusiasm, I
attended Imrat Khan's second concert in Germany in 1972 at the
Berlin Academy of Arts. One year previously he had already
appeared in Berlin, and the legend that this *sitar*-player could
send one 'on a trip', even without drugs, preceded him to the sold-
out concert at Bachauer's music-festival. Two performances were
envisaged – the first late at night in the concert-hall, while the
second one, on the following afternoon, was to be relayed from
the large exhibition-hall to the sunny quadrangle of the academy
via an excellent amplification-system.

While this second performance was to attract hundreds of

listeners, who wandered about, sat meditating in the long grass or assembled in mass-concentration in front of the players (the *sitar* was accompanied by Fayaz Khan on the *tabla*-drums), many of those present at the evening-concert underwent a magical sensation such as they had never before experienced. If very little can be said about this experience, it is because the whole thing is coupled with a state of subjective enthusiasm and waking ecstasy into which only a person who has undergone similar experiences can really transpose himself. Then a key-word suffices, and the other immediately remembers. Imrat Khan's music was at once urgent, hesitant and flowing, now robust and austere, now innocently merry, and finally sweetly romantic. At certain moments I found myself trembling, and it was as though gold-dust were trickling over me – an image that others present were to confirm. In the end the playing of Imrat's *sitar* became so moving that many began to weep. Imrat Khan himself was weeping too, and he told us later that these powers had been summoned up not by himself but by his School, his guru and his teachers' teachers. He saw himself merely as the medium of this music, which was why he always had to follow the same programme : in the middle of it is a solo on the larger, deeper-sounding and, for many, even more powerful *surbahar*, an instrument that comes very near the sound of the *vina* of southern India. At the end, a raga of tender, devotional and detached character is played – while the opening section comprises an often hour-long raga which displays all the arts and skills of the virtuoso.

By contrast with the *Hindustani* music of northern India, the *karnatic* music of southern India is even less well-known – and unjustly so. Anybody who has explored southern Indian *vina*-, violin- or drum-music, or who has had the luck to hear the unique female singer Subbulakshmi from Madras 'live', or even on disc – with her incredibly gentle and yet at the same time powerful voice – will know that it is really here and not in the north that the true source of Indian music is to be found.

Southern India has at least 5831 ragas, each with its own name and exact performance-instructions. At the basis of each lies a fixed composition which is the nucleus of the performance. Today's southern Indian concert-life is extraordinarily tradition-conscious, and relates itself – as does the Western tradition to its triple constellation of Haydn, Mozart and Beethoven – to three composers who were similarly active in the eighteenth century,

and who were also poets and singers. But then such Indian concerts need to be differently pictured from our own: in their
great, colourful, festively-decorated halls things are already
under way as early as 4 p.m., performances of as long as two
hours succeed each other (song, flute, dance, *vina* and violin),
and such a programme can last a good twelve hours.

The criteria for judging a singer's or *vina*-player's quality
are so subtle as regards microintervals and the making of the
finest distinctions of tone and colour – criteria all of which are
objectively laid down by tradition – that one can scarcely speak
of criteria for judging 'the best', but rather, perhaps, of the qualities that identify a musician as *one* of the best.

To Western ears all Indian music initially sounds somewhat
alike – even possibly monotonous and alien. We are accustomed
to listening to music pictorially and at a surface level, and are
often aware only of its most superficial outward shape, which
therefore has the more effect the more it is constantly subjected
to drastic and sudden change. The sound of a single, prolonged
note, or of a continually recurring sequence of notes, is more
likely to make an exclusively mentally-orientated person edgy
and irritable than to exert a calming or pleasant influence on
him. Indian music, which springs directly from the mythical
consciousness, requires a relaxed letting-go of oneself, an ex-
pectationless perseverance, the ability passively to penetrate
those levels where unceasing thought and reasoning have no
more power. All the delights of rational Western listening – such
as the complexity of a syntactical form or the intermingling of
different parts and sequences (the result of a process of continual
refinement ever since the age of counterpoint) – are in Indian
music sacrificed in favour of a 'primitive', ever-constant form:
it begins with the slow, meditative *alap* to establish the mood,
a gradual rhythmic pulsation sets in (*jor*), there follows a theme
with solo variations (*gat* and the *taans*), and the performance
finishes with the culminating virtuoso conclusion called *jhala*. In
southern Indian music the form is even simpler: the *alap* (initial
improvisation) is shortened, then the composed piece is presented, between whose sections improvised solos are inserted, and
the whole piece nearly always ends with an extended virtuoso
drum-solo on the south Indian *mridangam*.

For Indian music, as for the performer himself, it is much
more important that the public *should be able to listen with the*

heart, rather than observe the musical development or 'appreciate' the music critically and dispassionately. In the West this attitude is commonly confused with 'emotionalism', and much pompous misrepresentation is associated with it. This 'listening with the heart' is nevertheless a very aware condition requiring both receptivity and the faculty of conscious, discriminating perception. Once one has 'got the feel of' Indian music, its monotony suddenly becomes so colourful and full of nuances that its riches start to spill over into deeper dimensions. The almost infinite distinctions of quality which this improvised music admits become just as audible as the diverse effects of individual styles and schools, and of the various basic scales themselves.

The basis of all Indian music, whether of Hindu or Islamic origin, is the human voice, the sung recitation of the Holy Books – the Vedas and the Koran. Just as in the ancient Greek culture, no distinction was made in earlier millennia between singing and recitation. The *musike* of the Greeks, already mentioned earlier, corresponds to the chanting of the *Samaveda*, the oldest book about the links between music, man and cosmos. The mythical origins of Western and Indian/Chinese culture have a great deal in common. The ancient peoples were, so to speak, quite content with a single note, intoned interminably and communally during the rites of the Egyptian temples or in the tents of the Mongolian steppes. The Vedas were sung (and still are today) on three notes – the tonic (or basic) note and the two notes one whole tone on either side of it. This also corresponds to the way in which the Homeric texts were recited (*Odyssey, Iliad*). In Indian musical language these notes are called Sa – Re – Ni; in the West we call them Doh-Re-Ta, or C-D-B flat, where C is the tonic.

In the course of its development Indian music has remained unison/melodic. That is to say, everything constantly relates to a basic note or drone which is never varied: there is no accompaniment in the form of harmonic chords or changing bass-notes, but instead the *tambura* (or *tanpura*) – the instrument commonly used for accompanying – is given the job of continuously sounding the tonic (Sa, or Doh) and its first two overtones (octave and fifth) as a kind of drone or bourdon. This was also the case in medieval Western culture, and the church-modes used in Gregorian chant all have this same relationship to the tonic.

On the basis of this bass-drone there developed in early Greece, as in India, so-called *tetrachords* of four notes, covering the interval of a fourth. Two of these basic note-groups put together made up a seven-note scale: in India the lower interval from the tonic to the fourth is called *purvanga*, while the higher interval leading up to the octave is called *uttaranga*. Within this octave various arrangements of half- and whole-tone intervals were then arrived at. The Indians did not have the Pythagorean – and later the tempered – system of tuning, which divides the octave into twelve notes, but instead they developed a system of twenty-two *shrutis* – much subtler and more sophisticated for melodic purposes – which provides half- and whole-tone intervals of a variety of sizes. The finer intervals have no equivalent subdivisions in Europe (with the exception of the quarter-tone music of the Czech Alois Habá, 1893–1973): they arose not mathematically but out of their psychic awareness and an ear more subtly attuned to the needs of melodic music. The complicated subject of micro-intervals has been convincingly covered in the musical-ethnological works of Alain Daniélou, whom we also have to thank for the publication of the UNESCO gramophone-record series on non-European music.

Raga

The scale of a *raga*, as played, consists (like the various medieval modes of the West) of a selection of seven basic notes and five modified ones. There are also ragas which consist of only five notes, or whose upward scale has only five or six notes, while their descending scale uses all seven. In many ragas it is even permissible to add richness by introducing further intervals, subject to certain rules. If we think of C as the keynote or tonic, then either D or D flat will be the second note, E or E flat the third, F or F sharp the fourth; G (the fifth) is always constant (or is omitted), A or A flat will be the sixth note and B or B flat the seventh.

Our major scale C – D – E – F – G – A – B – C is reflected in the Indian scale Sa – Re – Ga – Ma – Pa – Dha – Ni – Sa, just as in our minor scale C – D – E flat – F – G – A flat – B flat – C. There are ten basic raga-forms – the so-called *thats* – in northern India and 72 basic ragas in the south, each one comprising a different application of one of these basic scales. To mention here only those which correspond to the old Church modes:

C – D – E flat – F – G – A – B flat – C (Dorian)
corresponds to the *that* of the Raga Kafi;

C – D flat – E flat – F – G – A flat – B flat – C (Phrygian)
corresponds to the *that* of the Raga Bhairavi;

C – D – E – F sharp – G – A – B – C (Lydian)
corresponds to the *that* of the Raga Yaman;

C – D – E – F – G – A – B flat – C (Mixolydian)
corresponds to the *that* of the Raga Khamaj;

C – D – E flat – F – G – A flat – B flat – C (Aeolian)
corresponds to the *that* of the Raga Asawari;

C – D – E – F – G – A – B – C (Ionian)
corresponds to the *that* of the Raga Bilaval.

On the other hand there are also scales with extreme intervals which are generally unknown in our music and which therefore sound 'typically oriental' :

C – D flat – E – F sharp – G – A flat – B – C (scale of the Raga Bhairav)

C – D flat – E flat – F sharp – G – A flat – B – C (scale of the Raga Todi)

C – D flat – E – F – G – A flat – B – C (scale of the Raga Purvi)

C – D flat – E – F sharp – G – A – B – C (scale of the Raga Marwa)

In northern India several hundred ragas are based on these scales, each of them differing in choice of notes, tone-quality, mood and significance. Two or more such ragas can even have the same scale and yet differ from each other in the minutest of details. Indeed, more than 5,000 ragas are currently identified and analysed in southern India – though not all of them are in actual use today.

By contrast with the fixed notes of our own scale, the transition from one note to the next is often a sliding one in India. To emphasise the essential qualities of a raga, there are innumerable forms and embellishments of this *glissando* – so-called *meends* – and the singing-technique, which involves jumping hither and thither among several notes, sounds extremely odd to our ears (*gamak*). In fact the notes of a scale are never laid down in the same rigid way as on our own piano. They can be approached initially by the singer, according to certain fixed rules, from above or below, and it is here that the great art lies – always sounding in each *glissando* only those notes that belong to the corresponding raga. These varieties of *glissando* and of virtuoso vocal ornamentation come across in a particularly vivid and affecting way, and it is in this that the truly deeper qualities of an Indian musician find expression. Since all string and wind instruments derive from the imitation of song, they too are so built as to permit the production of such micro-intervals and small alterations of pitch, in this case by stretching the strings or by slow variations in wind-pressure. It is above all in the *taans*, the singer's guttural jumps, in the successions of short phrases or the impetuous leaps and runs, that these characteristics come into their own, and particularly in the *alap* which introduces the raga at the beginning of the performance.

The well-known German *sitar* and *surbahar* player and musical ethnologist Michael Manfred Junius sums up the peculiar character of Indian music thus:

> The music of India belongs to the modal systems. Modal music has less to do with the historical and dynamic perception of time than with the quest for objectivisation and standardisation of the modes, whose psychic content is more important than their historical setting. The basic psychophysical conditions that determine the expression of the intervals are seen and felt to be objective – they are conventions. It is to the connection between interval and psychic perception that the artist can relate. Each mode creates a unity, a musical colour. The comparison between the minutely refined modes of Indian music and the concept of colour is an apt one, for 'raga', the designation for these modes, means 'that which colours the mind'.

A raga must have the keynote Sa (the tonic); each note is heard as much in relation to this keynote as to the other intervals. The keynote is therefore constantly audible during the performance, often in the form of a chord comprising bass-note, octave and fifth, played on a particular accompanying instrument. In addition a raga must have a so-called *vadi*-note – a 'speaking-note which beautifies the whole raga as does a

ring the hand.' Moreover a variety of embellishments are
proper to the presentation of each raga. Every raga has its
special affiliation: the time of year and the various festivals
are taken as much into account as the hours of the day or
night, the various gods and the moods of the human psyche.
A raga must have the ability to cast a spell on man; it must
colour his mind. The ragas have also inspired poets to write
verse, and even in painting we find pictorial representations
of the ragas.*

In the course of its development Indian music remained
purely melodic, a fact which also indicates the persistence of a
mythical awareness of polarity (in this case, of interval and keynote). Music provides a good picture of the differing cultural and
awareness-levels of Western and Eastern man. In the West all
aspects of music have always been in a continual state of further
development; forms, systems, styles have constantly changed; it
has been progress, progress, all the way. The Classical forms were
superseded by musical 'expressionism', programme-music, late
Romanticism, twelve-tone technique, Serial music, electronic
music, *musique concrète*. How odd it is that precisely those
Western musicians who have themselves gone through this
whole development in speeded-up form are the ones who now,
through their encounter with Eastern music, are taking a new
interest in the old 'objective' drones and bourdons.

In India, on the other hand, a form of music lives on that for
centuries has been born anew every day, has retained its original,
strictly-regulated form and preserved its spiritual basis. This
basis is reflected in its purely melodic nature and in the melody's
relationship to the keynote. For it is precisely from the playing
of a single note, or from the heterophonic playing of pairs of
notes by two instruments in canon (as in southern India on a
pair of *vinas*), that a hitherto unrealised wealth of tone-colours
can arise, throwing open to the Western listener a whole new
world of sound: the tone-colour comes to be experienced as the
vehicle of the spiritual, as the musicologist Nestler puts it.

It is also worthy of note that there is no fixed pitch in India:
the drone and the intervals from it are based on an individually-

* From: *Einführung in die indische Musik*, programme-booklet of the
Meta-Music-Festival 1974, Berlin.

determined tonic. This 'subjective tonic' is determined by the range of the singer's voice and by the construction of the instrument. For the most part the keynote is D flat/C sharp, (or, for female singers, around A flat) because the instruments are so constructed that their string-tension emits the best sound at around this pitch. The strings are stretched across a slightly rounded, ivory bridge. At the exact point where the string touches the bridge a thin wire is attached which, when correctly installed, causes the string to emit a 'tinny' sound. The harmonics thus resonate to better effect, or rather the fact that they are now reinforced makes it easier to hear them.

The raga is thus designed as a function not merely of a 'single' note, but of the whole harmonic series that each note possesses thanks to the laws of physics. The character of the raga is determined by its relationship to the harmonic series, a fact which is particularly evident in the *alap*. For mystically-inclined musicians, for the old holy-men of India and the remote gurus who perform music only for the Almighty, the *alap* is the most vital part of their music. From the profane point of view, however, one can also say that the *alap* presents the analysis of a raga, clearly introducing its peculiarities and its particular choice of notes. At this stage, then, one can find out which notes are characteristic of the raga, and often the performer spins out each of the characteristics at such length that it can be a long time before the listener knows which raga is being played. For often there is only the subtlest of differences, each of which has to be presented according to very precise rules and developed in certain systematically-constructed ways. Thus many ragas, for example, start with the same musical material, and if the player fails to make it clear in the course of his musical fantasising which raga he is about to play, he can hold a musically knowledgeable audience in a state of breathless tension for minutes on end. Once the decisive note is reached, or a specific turn of phrase appears, finally making it clear which raga is involved, the tension releases itself in an audible sigh of relief and relaxation on the part of the audience. And it is noteworthy that people of *all* social classes can appreciate such fine distinctions.

In a concert the *alap* can take up the greatest time, and it is precisely in the *alap* that it becomes apparent not merely whether the musician is a virtuoso, but whether he has *bhav* – which can signify spiritual power, religious devotion or musical magic. 'If you had heard an *alap* by the late Bade Ghulam Ali Khan, you would have broken into tears and forsaken your family,' an Indian musician assured me in a conversation on the 'true' music of India ('one who forsakes his family' is an ascetic or monk). The tradition of the great *alap*-singer is certainly lost for ever. It was intimately bound up with the powers we mentioned earlier on in connection with Tan-Sen.

Rasa

The character of a raga is determined essentially by the type of feeling to which the raga is assigned. For centuries Hindu culture has distinguished a certain number of basic moods which are expressed in the *sangeet* of every art-form. These nine *rasas*, which take in the whole gamut of basic human feelings, are represented in chanting, in music, in literature and in dance – in fact in all the various art-forms that at one time were indivisible in India. Ravi Shankar, the first significant *sitar*-player to visit the West, has described this division of musical states into nine different mood-concepts in his book *My Music, My Life*:

> Each *raga* has to have its own psychological temperament in relation to its tempo, or speed. Many of the heavy-serious *ragas* such as *Darbari Kanada* or *Asavari* should be sung or played in slow tempo. Others, such as *Adana* or *Jaunpuri*, which express a lighter mood, are best rendered in a medium or medium-fast tempo.
>
> The performing arts in India – music, dance, drama, and even poetry – are based on the concept of *Nava Rasa*, or the 'nine sentiments'. Each artistic creation is supposed to be dominated by one of these nine sentiments. The more closely the notes of a *raga* conform to the expression of one single idea or emotion, the more overwhelming the effect of the *raga*. This is the magic of our music – its hypnotic, intense singleness of mood. It is now generally agreed that there are nine of these principal sentiments, although some scholars number them as eight or ten.
>
> In the generally acknowledged order of these sentiments, the first is *shringara*, a romantic and erotic sentiment filled with longing for an absent lover. It contains both the physical

and mental aspects of love and is sometimes known as *adi* (original) *rasa*, because it represents the universal creative force.

Hasya is the second *rasa*, comic, humorous, and laughter-provoking. It can be shown through syncopated rhythmic patterns or an interplay of melody and rhythm between singer and accompanist, or between sitarist and *tabla* player, causing amusement and laughter.

The third *rasa* is *karuna*, pathetic, tearful, sad, expressing extreme loneliness and longing for either god or lover. (Hindus tend to elevate mortal love into a divine love, so the beloved can be an ordinary human being or often a god, such as Krishna, or Shiva.)

Raudra is fury or excited anger. This *rasa* is often used in drama, but in music it can portray the fury of nature as in a thunderstorm. Musically, it can be shown through many fast, 'trembling' ornaments, producing a scary, vibrating effect in the low tones. (But such *rasas*, far from frightening an Indian, excite in him a solemn reverence for the Divine in nature – PMH)

Veera expresses the sentiment of heroism, bravery, majesty, and glory, grandeur, and a dignified kind of excitement. If it is overdone, it can turn into *raudra*.

Bhayanaka, the sixth *rasa*, is frightening or fearful. It is difficult to express in music through one instrument (though a symphony orchestra could do it easily) unless there is a song-text to bring out its exact meaning.

Vibhatsa – disgustful or disgusting – is also difficult to show through music. This *rasa* and *bhayanaka* are used more for drama than music.

The eighth *rasa*, *adbhuta*, shows wonderment and amazement, exhilaration and even a little fear, as when one undergoes a strange new experience. It can be expressed by extreme speed or some technical marvels that, in certain kinds of singing or playing, provoke amazement.

The last *rasa* is *shanta rasa* – peace, tranquillity, and relaxation.

Some people mention a tenth *rasa*, *bhakti*, which is devotional, spiritual, and almost religious in feeling; but actually, this *rasa* is a combination of *shanta*, *karuna* and *adbhuta*.*

* From Ravi Shankar, *My Music, My Life*, London 1969.

Tala

Another important aspect of Indian music, along with the ragas and rasas, is its rhythm – the *tala*. This derives ultimately from two basic elements – the double beat and the triple beat. The double beat arises, as in all musical cultures, from the rhythms of walking and of the human heartbeat. The triple beat derives from the rhythm of breathing, which in India is analysed into three time-components. Every *tala*, then, is a combination of these basic components (e.g. 2 – 2 – 3; 3 – 3; 4 – 4 – 4). The *tabla* or *mridangam* player learns to speak these rhythms in a fixed 'alphabet' corresponding to the various tones of the drum. Every given beat, whether with the finger or the heel of the palm, has its identifying syllable. In this way the player learns all the important forms and variations like a language, which he then transfers to the instrument itself. All the *talas* are arranged cyclically – that is to say, there is a dynamic rhythmic sequence followed by a return to the beginning, called *sam*. The best-known *tala*, which to Western ears bears a relationship to the blues scheme, is *teental* (4 – 4 – 4 – 4): every beat has a different weight, being either heavily or lightly struck, and some are even omitted entirely (*khali*). These omitted beats indicate the point of return, or the extremity of the circle.

The *sam*, the conclusion of a group-variation, is the most important orientation-point both for melody-instruments and for the rhythm. Within each cycle the original *tala* may be freely improvised upon, whilst at the same time the original form of the *tala* has to be kept constantly present in the performer's mind as his guiding pattern. The rhythmic improvisations are apt to be so complex and sophisticated that the subdivisions and superimposed syncopations can be followed by the Western listener only after long practice.

Nevertheless *tabla*-accompaniment is nowadays attracting much attention in the West, for many people today appreciate music primarily from the rhythmic point of view. And the dialogue between *sitar* and *tabla* particularly, in which the *tabla*-player has to keep pace with the most complex improvisations, is enjoying great popularity. This question-and-answer format has the purpose of bringing about mutual inspiration and encouragement, so as to bring the player into a state in which spontaneous creativity is combined with the most extreme precision. The

Indian rhythmic patterns and *taanas* (the elaborate sequences and musical figures) that have been noted down by Western ethnologists could never be practised or performed in terms of 'notes' as we in the West understand them.

Indian Musical Studies

The form of instruction used in Indian Classical music is *imitation of the teacher*. To start with the instruments are tuned by pupil and Master. The *sitar* has two playing-strings and a whole collection of strings resonating in sympathy, which have to be tuned to the scale of the raga. If a given note is now played, the corresponding 'sympathetic' string sounds with it, whence the characteristic *sitar*-sound. The *vina*, the southern Indian prototype of the lute, has only a few of these 'sympathetic' strings while the *sarangi*, the Indian bowed instrument, and similar to the medieval *viola da gamba*, has up to forty of them. In southern India our own violin is also in use. It is often differently tuned though (in fourths), and is played in such a way that the left arm of the player (who sits on the ground) rests on his thigh, while the hand moves up and down the strings almost independently of the arm.

When all the strings have been tuned and the movable frets of the *sitar* are subdividing the octave at the correct points for the scale in question, the teacher begins to play the first phrases of the *alap*, and the pupil repeats them in short sections, using the same tone-colour. At this stage not only are the various note sequences imparted to the pupil, but also the details of each individual note of the raga. During this process hardly a word is exchanged: it is entirely a matter of listening and repeating: how the important *vadi*-note is distinguished, which note is played only from above downwards, which note is approached only from below, and so on.

Singing-instruction proceeds in exactly the same way: the *tambura* is tuned, the teacher commences whichever bass-note, or *Sa*, sits most naturally for the voice. Even while the instrument is still being tuned one must immerse oneself in the sound of the *Sa*. The Indian singer Pandit Patekar of Benares always stresses that one should go on to further exercises only when the *Sa* is sounding inwardly: 'Visualise your *Sa*, take the *Sa* as your guru, become wholly *Sa* ...' Then the relationship is estab-

lished between the keynote and the corresponding scale, though
the notes should not be treated as though they are notes on the
piano. It is much more a matter of 'flowing' through the scale,
yet still always alighting on the exact pitch of the next note.
This 'flowing' technique is extremely unfamiliar and difficult for
Western music students, but there is a range of exercises designed to 'make the stiff voice elastic' as Patekar put it (in
numerous conversations when I was his pupil in India.)

For each style and school there are particular *taanas* and melodic pieces (*ghats*), and in the *Khyal*-style there are composed
songs, based on the form of *antara* and *stahi*, the constantly-
recurring refrain-type motifs of the rhythmic cycle. These simple,
immediately accessible melodies are learnt by heart, as well as
being written down in the symbolic notation used for the Indian
note-names, and the *tabla*-player can now join in, to start with
adding only the simplest rhythmic patterns. One gradually ac-
quires a feeling for the *tala*-cycle and from then on learns to
return almost automatically to the *sam*.

In the course of time it becomes clear to the pupil that through
imitation of the teacher he has gained other, deeper musical
qualities. The *alap*, and certain specific turns of phrase that are
in fact capable neither of notation nor of being learnt by heart –
because they lie on too subtle a level – have been transferred
by the teacher into the pupil's subconscious. To start with he is
unaware that he has suddenly mastered this or that phrase.
True, he was previously capable of playing it correctly in dialogue with the teacher, but within a short time he had thought
it lost again. It is often months later, after intensive practice,
that he rediscovers his Master's own expressive depths in his
own playing or singing.

These quite powerful vibrations can also be relayed to the
listener to Indian Classical music, provided that he knows how
to listen to it properly. The art of listening properly to Indian
music, even without theoretical expertise, is explained by Pandit
Patekar in the following notes:

The highest aesthetic joy is attained when the artist and
the audience stand in a harmonious relationship to each other.
The following is a list of the rules of conduct that are absolutely essential for becoming a good listener:

1. Temporarily release yourself in thought from the usual way of thinking and concentrate on the higher, spiritual aspects of life. Music offers the best means for such concentration.

2. Place the universal in the forefront of your contemplation, and endeavour to lay aside or to forget the habit of looking at partial aspects only.

3. Immerse yourself in a mood of meditation and contemplation. For this the *alap* of a raga is most suitable. The *alap* is the quiet, meditative exposition of the musical idea.

4. Establish a link with the supernatural aspects of reality. This can be attained as much through the notes of a raga as through its rhythms.

5. Leave aside all inner preconceptions.

6. Try to think your way inside the artist. In other words, try to feel with him and to become one with both artist and theme.

7. Be still and spiritualised – both inwardly and outwardly. Om Shantih.*

A Singing Sadhu on the Ganges

To conclude this chapter on Indian music I propose to recount a musical experience which speaks for itself:

I had read and heard that certain notes produced by India's musical 'magi' can open up the inner psychic centres. Many musicians also said that they declined to use drugs because their music brought about a purer state of inner awareness without artificial aids and without intoxication, but solely by means of musical vibration. Many reported that they could recall their divine past by singing religious *kirtan-* and *bhajan-*songs for hours at a stretch, and that Krishna and Sri Ram had appeared to them.

Through the cosmic songs of Paramahansa Yogananda I already knew the five levels of singing: 'Singing aloud, whispered singing, mental singing, subconscious singing, superconscious singing. Subconscious singing becomes automatic when the mind effortlessly repeats a melodic phrase while at the same time thinking or doing something else. Superconscious singing starts

* Retranslation from the German of the original English version written on the occasion of his European tour during the early months of 1975.

when the inner vibrations of the singing are transmuted by one's understanding and when one's attention is directed unceasingly to the very real vibration of the cosmos itself – to OM or AUM – and not to any imagined or outward sound. That is when super-conscious singing begins.'*

In the book I have already cited by Ravi Shankar, I read:

> These great musicians were not just singers or performers, but also great yogis, whose minds had complete control of their bodies. They knew all the secrets of *Tantra*, *hatha yoga*, and different forms of occult power, and they were pure, ascetic and saintly persons. That has been the wonderful tradition of our music – and even today, though such miracles may not be performed, one can see the immense impact on the listener and, as many put it, the 'spiritual experience' the listener feels.†

Now everywhere I went on my Indian travels, I kept asking where such a *sadhu*, ascetic or magician was to be found, and whether such people really did still exist. Whereupon people would smile and tell me that I should find one as soon as I was ready for it; he would already be awaiting me ...

Naturally I didn't take this too seriously, and as I had the chance to meet the Indian holy-woman *Ananda Mayi Ma*, I quickly forgot my musical *sadhu*. In order to see 'Ma' in her ashram at Agarpara, to the north of Calcutta, I took one of the antediluvian Indian buses to this forlorn spot which, by virtue of its position hard by the Ganges, imposed on one the most awful ordeal by mosquito and test of human patience during the always-humid hot season.

The conversative ashram grants the 'unclean' foreigner only a limited stay within its walls, so that I had to set out in search of somewhere to stay and some way of getting meals. I was soaked with sweat, tired and irked that the ashram had turned me out. On top of that, it appeared that 'Ma' was not expected until a few days' time. So I walked along beside the Ganges, refreshed myself in its brown flood, and looked for a shady spot against the heat of midday. Then at some distance, by the side of

---

* Retranslated from the German version of *Cosmic Chants* (Introduction), Self-Realization Fellowship, Los Angeles.
† From: Ravi Shankar, *My Music, My Life*, London 1969, p. 29.

a mud hut, I saw a seated figure who seemed to have been watching me for some time. As I drew nearer I could hardly believe my eyes: the man had long, matted, white-grey hair, an enormous beard, and nothing on but a tattered strip of cloth around his waist.

He had to be either a yogi, a loafer or a tramp, I thought, or all three at once, and I simply made to pass him by. But at that moment his gaze flashed at me oddly, and I felt intensely unnerved. It is well-known that countless pseudo-gurus wander around India, conjuring up black mischief with the aid of powers gained through yoga – mesmerising one, for example, through eye-contact, and evoking sympathy to the point where one hands over all one's cash.

I had no wish to encounter his *siddhis* (mental powers), and did not have the impression that he would know where I might find lodging – let alone a hotel. I was already past him when an indescribable voice called out behind me: 'Hallo, my friend!' I stood rooted to the spot. 'I'm happy to meet you'. He smiled invitingly. 'Very hot season now . . .' His English sounded typically Indian and almost incomprehensible. Moreover it consisted of only a few scraps of conversation, as I soon established. 'Come in'. He indicated his hut, which was very primitively erected atop a few hunks of rock. Now I realised for the first time how near it was to the water. During the monsoon the spot was inundated – obviously a 'summer-residence' only. I was too worn out to refuse the invitation, and in addition a force radiated from him that affected me more than I cared to admit. Above all I found that I was incapable of looking into his eyes, even though he seemed to keep trying to provoke this very thing. He had a decidedly penetrating gaze.

In the hut there was nothing but an old teacup, a mat and . . . an enormous, black *tambura*. I sat down on the floor; at last the sun was no longer burning my head. After a period of silence, during which the *sadhu* gazed at me unflinchingly, I said (simply by way of something to say): 'Very nice place – very nice instrument,' and indicated the *tambura*. Then his eyes met mine, and I felt an extraordinarily powerful emanation of goodness. 'Music', was all he said, but much lay in that one word. He continued merely to sit there looking at me, as though it was quite normal for me to turn up at his house. Then he pointed at

me, laughed, and again said, 'Music!' I nodded: he nodded.
'Vocal music – *bohut adsche* (very good) – I will teach you.'

For me it was not by any means all such a matter of course.
Could he know, then, that I was studying Indian vocal music?
And as though in answer to my inner question came the striking
sentence: 'I know everything about you.' I must have looked
pretty sceptical at that. 'Yes, I know everything about you.'
He nodded. 'On Holy you go to Benares.' But this was inexplic-
able: back in Calcutta I had indeed got myself a railway-ticket
to Benares for the 8th March, which fell on the Holy Feast-day.
I was nonplussed and helpless, and simply said, 'Very hot.'

Then the *sadhu* carefully reached for his *tambura* and almost
whispered, 'Tori – very good for this time, do you know Tori?'
Gathering that he meant the Raga Todi, I nodded somewhat un-
certainly. He smiled and began to play the *tambura*, re-tuning
it somewhat as he did so. What a sound! The instrument had
six strings – which is very rare – and to my ears was tuned in
a completely strange way. (Later I learnt that Todi is sung without a fifth, and so the seventh note – the *Ni* – resonates with the
bass-note).

He looked at me, cleared his throat a few times and started
to sing – slowly, deeply, almost under his breath. Now nobody
could say that the fellow had a 'beautiful' voice – in fact if
anything it was rather rough and primitive. Yet it had a mysterious undertone, a vibration that one could only feel. To my
astonishment I felt myself more and more as though surrounded
by a cool breeze. I ceased to sweat and felt refreshed. Yet, fully
conscious as I was of everything around me, I could not detect
the slightest movement of air. The cool, fresh feeling was somehow coming from inside me.

During his powerful and yet very gentle song he looked continually into my eyes, and his *tambura* sounded so beautiful and
many-toned that I let go of myself and eventually was able to
withstand his gaze. It seemed to me as though the hut was opening up on all sides, and as though I could see into the far distance.
A radiant face beamed at me, with deep, earnest, loving eyes,
and soon all feeling of time had dissolved. This feeling, at best
hinted at under psychedelic conditions, was so strong that, under
the circumstances, tired and worn out, I could not resist a blissful, pleasant feeling of tiredness – and fell asleep.

When I awoke I had no idea where I was, and the hut was empty. Only now did I notice how skilfully the roof was thatched. The *tambura* lay beside me on the floor, and behind it my shoulder-bag. Immediately I became aware again of the intense heat and recalled my experience. When I looked outside, the *sadhu* was busying himself with a small hearth, making tea. So many questions arose in my mind: how and what did my host eat? Why were there no mosquitoes in his hut, when every other shady nook was swarming with them? What was all that about the Raga Todi?

The *sadhu* came with the tea and immediately 'answered' my unspoken questions: wherever he went on his pilgrimage, everywhere there would be somebody who would look after his physical well-being. And he was not very keen on mosquitoes ... I could stay with him for three days and learn something about his music. By then Ma would be back. I had told him nothing. On the subject of the Hindu holy-woman he merely said, 'Ma!' and beamed: at the word 'ashram' he made a disparaging sign with his hand. After tea he passed me the *tambura* – that is to say, he simply placed it before me. I had never before seen such a large instrument. 'Two hundred years' he said, obviously referring to its age.

After he had let me play the instrument a little, he started his actual instruction: *Nada Yoga*, the technique of human self-realisation through inner sound. The *sadhu*'s appearance kept altering. At one stage I thought he must be around seventy. Later he struck me as being a robust forty-year-old. His true age remained a secret. Nevertheless I did learn a little about him. His teacher had been Abdul Karim Khan, whose importance was unknown to me at the time. At his death in 1937 he was reckoned to be India's last great musical genius and singer. My *sadhu* too – who, questioned as to his own name, would offer only a beaming 'No name!' – had apparently given some celebrated concerts, but now he sang only for Lord Shiva, as he reverently put it.

Each morning he was up before dawn, singing in extraordinarily long, deep tones. I was able to follow him with my own voice once I had woken up, but only when he had reached my own vocal range. His deepest notes remained unforgettable for me. Each morning and evening, sometimes in the afternoon too, one or two young lads came by with two plates of simple food – rice and Indian vegetables – and a pot of fresh water, which they presented with a reverent bow. How the lads had learnt of my presence, so that they looked after me too, is a puzzle to me. On one occasion the *sadhu* was visited by a number of better-dressed Indians and presented with garlands of flowers. Apparently he is revered as a guru – though this fact tended if anything to confuse me, for as far as I was concerned these few days were a strenuous course of instruction with a fatherly, natural friend who merely wished to share with me as much as possible of his knowledge.

Every day we went for a walk, he generally taking me by the hand. We visited a little temple to his lord Shiva, the creator and destroyer of the universe. And just as I was beginning to get used to this timeless, primitive way of life he indicated to me that our time together was at an end. He accompanied me to the nearby ashram of Ananda Ma. A seething crowd of Ma's admirers and hangers-on suddenly invaded the lonely district. At the gate of the ashram garden he bade me farewell. As he embraced me, he simply said '*Jai Ma*' (Long live Ma!) and indicated his bare chest.

He had declined to accept the money for some ointment that he needed fairly urgently for a painful wound. But I slipped it between the pages of his English exercise-book, in which I had to write my name. This exercise-book full of notes was the only thing he possessed – apart from his *tambura*, of course. There would be only one chance of ever meeting him again : every 26th October in Bombay, where the annual remembrance-concert for his teacher takes place.

This unexpected encounter with a true Master had shown me what powers operate within the traditional Indian teacher-pupil relationship. The *sadhus*, who in reality embody a spiritual mission, live such withdrawn lives in India today that they seem to have disappeared. And yet they live on, in secret; on the banks of the Ganges, on the slopes of the Himalayas, in caves and in huts. I have also undergone profound experiences with musical Masters in the north of India, where the Tibetan refugees have built up their little settlements. There in the humblest accommodation, some of them in huts of corrugated iron, live the Tibetan monks, who often possess nothing more than their ritual implements. These include a bell, a little drum and a wind-instrument

made from a human bone. Compared with the songs and notes of
the Indians, the chanting of the monks has an even more powerful effect: it derives from the primal magical powers of the
Tibetan culture.

TIBETAN RITUAL MUSIC

When, a few years ago, a record of music from Tibet was broadcast by a radio station for the first time, there was a flood of
telephone-calls from people who were so unnerved by this music
as to be in a state of near-panic. This music is indeed strange
and unfamiliar to our Western ears, and even within the Buddhist cultures it is unique and unmistakable. Even for those
familiar with this music, of which there exist a few gramophone
records, a personal encounter with the living Tibetan sound can
prove an uncanny experience, as the following report of an experience in the Tibetan refugee-village of Dharamsala makes
clear:

> The quiet walk was suddenly violently interrupted. Out
> from the temple, and away over the sagging ridges of the
> mountains on which the village stands, there rang out the
> strains of the monkish orchestra – the note-sequence admit-
> tedly superficially familiar from gramophone-records, but now
> in the flesh so unexpected an effect, such primal and shatter-
> ing power, that my inner composure was dealt a staggering
> blow.
> The mighty, powerful tones of the giant tubas surged like
> the breath of primal magic against the mountain walls, broke
> and rolled thundering into the valley – sounds from another
> world, that penetrated into deep levels of one's consciousness
> and received from them a burning reply. Thus, inwardly and
> outwardly exposed to sound-frequencies that I had never be-
> fore experienced, or at most had received hints of in deep
> dreams, I stood breathless, stunned, yet involuntarily submis-
> sive to those gigantic vibrations.
> When the high wind instruments with their whirring tone
> joined in, my nerves seemed to be stretched to breaking-point,
> until finally something in my head burst with a kind of flash
> and my hearing was no longer burdened with the feeling of

'receiving' the sound, but instead allowed the sound through, vibrated in sympathy, seemed to become one with the very notes themselves – the unearthly sound of the tubas, the shrilling of the cymbals, the joyful little notes of the horns. Something decisive had happened – so at least I was to realise during the next few hours. The primal might of this ancient music had hacked great breaches in the walls of my consciousness, had violently ripped it open, and now I found myself in an exposed, bewildered, vulnerable, over-sensitive, yet at the same time wonderfully receptive state, that subsided only slowly as it oscillated between deep insecurity and electric euphoria.*

This primeval music can be understood only in the context of Tibetan-Buddhist esotericism, for it is intimately bound up with the history of this religion, not only as regards its sound-effects, but also as regards the symbolic significance of its instruments. Not a note of it has its roots in human feelings or in the human dimension at all. Rather is it the expression of the shamanic and animistic aspects of the original Bön-religion of the Himalayas, a belief that was integrated into the Tantric form of Mahayana Buddhism. That the ancient power of this old tradition has been preserved in so pure a form is due to the fact that Tibet is shielded from the outer world by its mountainous inaccessibility and was cut off from all contact with other civilisations for many centuries.

Only through the Chinese invasion did this old magical tradition leave 'the roof of the world'. Here, where loneliness and stillness reign as on the highest mountain peaks, where man's conscious thinking has not covered up all deeper experience of the invisible world, a form of music could develop that is the perfect expression of elemental natural phenomena, and that builds a bridge over into the world of the spirits and the demons.

Lama Anagarika Govinda, one of the greatest Buddhist scholars and experts on Tibet, states on the subject:

Tibetan Buddhism regards man not as a solitary figure but always in connection with and against a universal background. In the same way Tibetan ritual music is not concerned with

* Ulli Olvedi, authoress and translator, from her unpublished diary.

the emotions of temporal individuality, but with the ever-present, timeless qualities of universal life, in which our personal joys and sorrows do not exist, so that we feel in communion with the very sources of reality in the deepest core of our being. To bring us in touch with this realm is the purpose of meditation as well as of Tibetan ritual music, which is built upon the deepest vibrations that an instrument or a human voice can produce: sounds that seem to come from the womb of the earth or from the depth of space like rolling thunder, the *mantric* sound of nature, which symbolise the creative vibrations of the universe, the origin of all things. They form the foundation as well as the background from which the modulations of the higher voices and the plaintive notes of the reed instruments rise like the forms of sentient life from the elementary forces of nature.*

The Instruments

Only wind and percussion instruments are present in the Tibetan monks' orchestra. The wind instruments used include horns, which are often marvellously decorated and sometimes used in pairs, together with trumpets made of bone, silver and other metals, oboe-like instruments, and finally long, tuba-like instruments of copper up to fifteen feet long. The bone-trumpet was formerly fashioned from a human thigh-bone and appertains to the 'household utensils' of every monk, who also always possesses a handbell and a hand-drum: this was likewise formerly made from two human skull-bones and for that reason is also called a skull-drum.

Two kinds of cymbals are included in the orchestra, as are a large drum with hide stretched across both sides of it and many small drums with clappers. These small *damarus* likewise belong to the ritual paraphernalia of every monk. They are shaken to and fro by the right hand while the other is ringing its handbell. Every instrument has its deep symbolism: in Tibetan Mahayana Buddhism there are two types of deity – those of the one type being merely the fearful aspects of the others, who are represented as full of goodness and mercy. In any case, the aggressive gods are in no way malicious beings, but rather the

* Govinda: *The Way of the White Clouds*, London, 1966, pp. 29–30.

protectors of the faith against the demons. It is to the peaceable gods that the oboe, the horn and the large cymbals are dedicated, while the short trumpets and the shriller cymbals correspond to the fearful deities. The deep *rag-dungs* – the yards-long tubas – and the drums can be assigned to either kind.

The composition of the orchestra can vary and is not always subject to strict rules. Where necessary the lamasery will use all the instruments available. One peculiarity, which is also found in old Arabic traditions, concerns the breathing technique used in playing the instruments. The performer breathes in through his nose without any break in his playing – a feat which is made possible by the use of the mouth as a wind-reservoir. Apart from a slight darkening of the tone, the sound can be prolonged without interruption more or less indefinitely.

Before we come to discuss the most important 'instrument' in Tibetan music – the human voice – it would be as well to explain briefly the nature of the musical material. There are a number of basic sound and note patterns that can be combined and varied at will. To each instrument is assigned a range of such short, fairly clearly laid down melodic and rhythmic patterns. The way in which these basic elements, proper to any one group of instruments, are combined with the basic patterns of the others depends entirely on the course of the ceremony or on the exigencies of the performance itself. Now the basic material consists, not of predetermined notes, themes or rhythms, but of directions expressed in relative terms as to the length and 'character' of the notes to be played. A *dor*, for example, is a very deep note, a *dor-haa* the same note, but somewhat shorter, followed by a higher note. *Shung* signifies a prolonged note of medium pitch and *ti* simply means 'high note'.

In Tibet there is also a form of musical notation, which is not, however, played at sight but serves purely as an *aide-mémoire* for certain rarely-played passages. Above all, of course, it is the endlessly-prolonged chants that are written down. Alongside that for the countless recitatives, another, quite special notation has been developed for one particular type of choral chanting – but this in any case reveals slight differences in each monastery. This kind of chanting is called *tantric* and is without doubt the vocal style most peculiar to Tibet. Developed by particular tantric schools, it is also dubbed the *yang*-style.

Chanting

The *yang*-style is a phenomenon that has become known in the West through the appearances of the lamas of Gyoto lamasery in Berlin and other European cities. As the music critic of the *Süddeutsche Zeitung* put it:

> Even if one has no idea of the former Gyoto lamasery, no inkling of the mystical concepts underlying the ceremonial chanting, no understanding of the text, this music radiates more than mere exotic charm. With only slight, occasional variations, the chant centres around one single note – but what a note! The six monks intone their litany-like phrases – a Ghiaurov or Talvela could well be envious of them – at sepulchral depths (for pedants, BBB), their performance being punctuated during the first section of the two-hour ritual only by small hand-bells and a wooden percussion instrument, later joined by drumbeats and the mighty sound of a Tibetan alpenhorn.
>
> What is fascinating about this chanting is not merely its resonant depth, but a special voice technique that accentuates certain overtones so strongly as to give the impression that the monks are singing in harmony. But the deeper, mystic links between the proportions of the cosmos, of the human body and of the harmonic series (each perceptible pitch is connected with a particular part of the body – between solar plexus and forehead – which is its seat) are not, admittedly, something that can be grasped at the drop of a hat.*

These links with tantric meditation are not fully understood by uninitiated Tibetans either. In fact 'foreign' syllables have been purposely inserted into the texts in order to conceal their esoteric content. These consequently 'veiled' texts are disguised even further by the singers' unnaturally-modified voices. 'The *yang* vocal style serves for communication with the gods, which may explain its peculiarities, for one does not "speak" with the deity in the same way as with men.'†

This method of singing cannot be 'produced' in the sense of a virtuoso technique or of voice-control, but requires a completely

---

* D. Polaczek in *Süddeutsche Zeitung*, 15/10/74.
† Publication of the Institute for Comparative Musicology, Berlin 1975.

relaxed body, free breathing and a capacity for self-absorption. The sepulchrally deep bass-notes arise from a complete relaxation of the vocal cords, which have consciously to be allowed to resonate at the octave *below* the note as normally sung. After a lengthy period of practice this deep note eventually 'cuts in'. A grumbling-noise underneath the actual note sung by the vocal cords, it takes the form of a kind of undertone or sub-resonance : the whole body vibrates strongly in sympathy with this exaggerated resonance, and the resulting overtones are varied by slightly altering the shape of the mouth. A few Western musicians have also started to learn this powerful way of chanting, using it for meditative improvisation and their own personal *sadhana* (spiritual exercises).

Not all monks practise this tantric form of singing : there are only a very few schools that carry out these partially-secret rites and ceremonies. The others sing their mantric formulas and prayers, if not in Tibetan then mostly in Sanskrit, in simple, sometimes very beautiful motif-like phrases. The chanting centres around a single bass-note in constantly recurring variations based on given modes. Such a 'mode' usually comprises no more than three or four notes and, as sung by a single monk, sounds in its 'pentatonic' way very similar to Tibetan folk-music, which is of Chinese-Mongolian origin (see Appendix, Musical Example No. 1).

These simple chants, in contradistinction to the magical, tantric, 'multivoice' technique, have a soothing inner joyfulness about them which is typical of all Tibetans. The chanting of the monastic community is decorated in the most varied ways according to personal taste – above all with *glissandi*, which can be very prolonged as they slide upwards or downwards from note to note. To start with, this individual free improvisation during the course of their often hour-long celebrations (*puja*) tends, to Western ears, to produce a harmonic and rhythmic chaos; but gradually, by entering the same state of contemplative self-absorption as that of the monks, this is heard to resolve itself into a fascinating, inwardly unified form of communal singing.

After a given interval the symphony fades, leaving the single, deep voice of the *umdze*, the precentor, who is also generally the chief lama present. Thereafter a new, slow rhythm marks the beginning of the next part of the liturgy. At those points

where particularly significant mantras are recited, an accompaniment is provided by all the ritual handbells and hourglass-
shaped *damarus* together. If there is an orchestra present, it
usually joins in with the multifarious bell and drum sounds, and
then itself performs the middle section with its oddly-rotating
cymbals, its yards-long *radongs*, its bass-drums and its various
wind-instruments.

> Just as the bass-voice of the precentor forms the basis of the
> choir, from which the liturgy starts ... in the same way the
> huge twelve-foot *radongs* form the basis and the starting-
> point of the orchestral music. They are always in pairs and
> are alternately blown in such a way that the sounds of the
> one merge into the other without breaking its continuity and
> at the same time producing the effect of gradually swelling
> and ebbing tides of an ocean of sound. And on the surface of
> this ocean the breeze of individual life creates and plays with
> a multitude of waves and wavelets which, like the high-pitched
> tremolo of the oboes, add vivacity and melody to the vastness
> of the ocean, whose sound seems to be that of the all-embrac-
> ing OM, the prototype of all *mantric* sounds ... If the *radong*
> or the human bass-voice represent the primeval cosmic sound,
> in which we experience the infinity of space, the drum repre-
> sents the infinity of life and movement, governed by the
> supreme law of its inherent rhythm, in which we experience
> the alternating cycles of creation and dissolution, culminating
> in manifestation and liberation.*

The music of Tibet thus has its spiritual basis in Buddhist cosmology and is concerned with supernatural levels of being.

MUSIC OF MAGICAL CONSCIOUSNESS

It has already been briefly indicated that some basic elements
of Tibetan ritual music are relics of the former shamanic religion of Tibet. Hence the melodic element, which for the most
part belongs to the mythical level of consciousness, has less place
in this form of acoustic art than the rhythmic element. The latter
is embodied by the various kinds of drums and percussion instruments and corresponds to the magical form of consciousness

* Govinda: *The Way of the White Clouds*, London 1966, p. 30.

which reigned supreme in the animistic Bön-religion. Now it was precisely the great merit of Buddhism that it was spiritually strong enough to combine old magical usages and mythical symbols into a unified cosmogony.

It is the rhythm of the smaller drums, the rolling thunder of the bass-drum, the mighty clashing of the cymbals, that give Tibetan music its unique structure and meaning, for not only the Tibetan, but also every other magical culture, makes quite different associations with the drum and the cymbal from those usual in the West. The significance of the drum, even in the earliest beginnings of Indian culture, is made clear by a comparison of the Buddha's in which he likens the eternal laws of the universe to the rhythm of the drum. And the first thing the Buddha does after his enlightenment is to speak of the 'drum of immortality' that is to ring out across the whole world.

Now it is important to know what enormous significance the self-same bass drum of Tibetan music already held in the ceremonies of the old Bön-rites. For there it was the drum of the shamans, who stood in magical contact with the gods, demons and other worlds. Throughout northern and eastern Asia the drum had a large part to play in the shamanic ceremonies. It had a wide-ranging and deep symbolism, and its tasks were legion.

The Drum of the Shamans

Not only in Asia, Northern Europe and North America, but also in the original South American and African cultures, a shaman or medicine-man without a drum would have been unthinkable. The dancer and conga player Jeffrey Biddeau from Trinidad, who teaches dance and drumming in Paris and was initiated into the magic rites of the Voodoo priesthood in his youth, described to me vividly the rôle of drumming during cult-sessions or dances. All the gods – the gods of wind, of water, of fire and of war – have their own special drum signals, which are almost indistinguishable to the untrained ear. The differences consist of minute rhythmic hesitations, short gaps and pauses between the beats and the minutest gradations of volume. These acoustic signs are detected not by the head – i.e., the intellect – but with the belly, or rather in the human centre of consciousness.

The best-known of these magic rhythms in the West is that of the god Shangó, to whose musical 'secret society' a good many

Black drummers belong: anyone who plays Shangó absolutely authentically belongs to the 'society'. This complicated rhythm, impossible to grasp intellectually, is based on a persistent six-eight bar subdivided into superimposed duple and triple elements. Typically, however, it comes across as a syncopated beat which, if properly executed, has an *immediate* effect on the listener. A fractional rhythmic hesitation settles it and – Shangó is here.

The two conga-drums of the Trinidadian Voodoo-player, who originally brought the ritual cults from Central Africa during the 'emigration' into slavery, are always tuned in flattened thirds. These thirds are somewhat smaller intervals than the tempered minor third of the piano. The left hand plays the lower note on the deeper drum, and the right hand the upper note; and through striking the drum in a variety of ways a whole drum language comes into being. Although the basic rhythmic pattern scarcely varies, it is nevertheless virtually impossible to notate this pattern exactly. The syncopation likewise derives not from a 'notatable', conscious source, but from a magical one. And what is so fascinating today is that rhythm in this way is becoming so attractive to mentally-orientated people.

The Significance of the Drum

As we have already mentioned, the drum rhythm of the shaman appeals primarily to man's centre of magical consciousness. In the early, animistic cultures of Africa this centre in the human abdomen was associated with the heartwood of a tree. The hollowed-out tree trunk was also the original form of the drum, which, as the cult-instrument of various tribes, was never allowed to be seen by the uninitiated. In the (mythical) Buddhism of Ceylon, even today, the drum is used as a means of driving away demonic, subconscious powers.

In Guatemala the drums are dedicated with human blood, while on the islands around Celebes and Guinea drums are attached to the house-entrances as a protection against dark powers. And of perennial fascination for us Westerners are the ecstasies of native peoples which we cannot emulate; as when they stick swords or knives into themselves without bleeding, when they demonstrate paranormal powers, run over glowing coals and thereby display states of trance-like self-forgetfulness.

For the African tribes, as for the Asian peoples of the Arctic, the drum is the voice of 'the One above', the Thunderer, the

Father of All, the Almighty. The drum therefore also represents a means of communication with the underworld. Among the *Koryaks* it is called the 'lake', which the shaman enters in order to reach the underworld, just as the Eskimo shaman climbs down to the *sedna* in the submarine depths of the underworld. For the *Yakuts* and Mongolians 'the drum is the horse', as Mircea Eliade writes in his book *Shamanism:Archaic Techniques of Ecstasy*. On it they ride in their initiation-dreams to the 'centre of the world', to the site of the world-tree, to the Lord of the Universe.

'It is from a branch of this Tree, which the Lord causes to fall for the purpose, that the shaman makes the shell of his drum ... Seen in this light, the drum can be assimilated to the shamanic tree with its notches, up which the shaman symbolically climbs to the sky ... The drum depicts a microcosm with its three zones – sky, earth, underworld – at the same time that it indicates the means by which the shaman accomplishes the break-through from plane to plane and establishes communication with the world above and the world below.'* It is always instruments that establish contact not only with gods, spirits and demons, but also with the souls of the ancestors and the mythical beasts. Not to mention the ascent into heaven and descent into hell of the drumming and singing shaman.

Eliade further points out that the idea of an ecstatic journey also recurs in the names given by the shamans to their drums. Among the *Yuraks* of the northern European tundra the drum is called 'bow' or 'singing-bow'. Among the *Lebed-Tatars* and the *Altays* the bow is the magic, musical instrument which replaces the drum. The bow is used not as a weapon, but exclusively as a single-stringed trance-inducing instrument. The trance-state is attained among the shamans of Siberia by dancing to the magical melody of a stringed instrument called the *kobuz*. It is a form of music based on a single note and its natural harmonics.

Ecstatic Chant in Persia and Mongolia

The finest example of a magico-animistic – and yet free and colourful – musical language is to be found in Mongolia. This cultural region, nowadays ruled partly by Russia and partly by China, was formerly a centre of shamanic power.

* M. Eliade: *Shamanism: Archaic Techniques of Ecstasy*, London 1961, p. 168 ff.

The shamans of Mongolia listened very carefully to the sound of their singing bow. As they bowed or plucked it, they listened particularly – more so than any other ancient culture – to the melody of the single note: the harmonics, the tone-colour melody. Thus the Mongolian was from the earliest times in a position to appreciate the secret of music, the physical basis of sound-production, and learnt to realise vocally this original, archaic phenomenon of the 'monotone'. A whole singing technique was developed for it – *xöömij*, which means 'pharynx' or 'throat'.

With this technique the individual Mongolian is able to sing in two voices at once. He hums or sings nasally a note of medium pitch and alters the volume of his mouth-cavity by opening and closing his mouth, thus varying the harmonic spectrum of this single, long-drawn-out note. Suddenly, at a very high pitch, a shrill melody rings out, though consisting solely of the amplified harmonics of the single bass-note. (The exact notes involved will be explained in the chapter on the world of esoteric sound.) We are already familiar with the 'Jew's harp', whose essence lies in the production of a continuous, humming basic note produced by means of the vibration of a little steel tongue supported on the lip, while its various overtones are brought into play by the player's alteration of the shape of his mouth.

The Mongolians force the air under great pressure through the tensioned vocal cords, as a result of which a basic note is produced somewhat like that of a 'Jew's harp', and rich in overtones – various of which they are able to amplify by varying the shape of the throat. The ghostly and almost supernatural effect of this singing technique makes it easy to understand the tradition that singers able to master such overtone melodies were in touch with the spirits and possessed supernatural powers. It is said that there have been shamans who showed such mastery of this technique that they could be heard loud and clear over great distances. They are also alleged to have succeeded in singing *in three parts*.

Between *xöömij* and the Tibetan *yang*-style there is a clear correspondence, as much in the principle of overtone singing as in the mode of consciousness that lends both types of singing their power of magical evocation. Meanwhile, corresponding to the cult of the shamans in the mythical sphere, we have the mystic ecstasy of the religious believer. It is quite understandable that even within the 'high religions' musical forms should have arisen – based mainly on the human voice – which, though outwardly 'unnatural', were able to release mystic powers of insight and enlightenment not only in the singer, but also in those listening to the ritual office. But of course it is above all the gnostic schools and sects, with their shamanistic cult elements, who have undertaken the journey into the collective unconscious via the world of sound.

In the Persian and Arabic region from Turkey to Afghanistan it was primarily in the mystic secret schools of the Sufis that music was regarded as a means and path to enlightenment. True, many Islamic sects had forbidden not only representational art but also all music, as a result of an over-zealous interpretation of the Koran. But Muhammad's interdict really applied only to worldly, sensual music, with which the chanting of the Sufis was not concerned.

In the Islamic sphere a special technique was likewise developed, in which the voice is altered beyond all recognition. From time immemorial the *muezzin*, who intones the Holy Koran from the minaret, has placed both hands on his temples and sung the call to Allah in an unnaturally high tone with his head-voice, the *falsetto*. The notes, which in quiet areas can be heard miles away, sound in the distance like a soft woman's voice, and only in the vicinity of the singer does one become aware of his exertions in forcing and straining his voice. Here, too, tradition has it that the singer with divine powers is in direct touch with the Prophet's message.

In Sufi chanting this jump into the head-voice has developed even further. In ecstatic moments the singer of the Holy Scriptures brings off a kind of hiccup or very rapid yodel which, as with an overblown flute, switches the voice to a higher harmonic pitch. If one is attuned to this music, this singing-technique can strongly affect the listener – even literally to the point of tears. Via this powerful form of chanting, the mystic message of the texts, or ecstatic prayers, is conveyed to the initiate *by direct means*. A technique which reflects the mystic Islamic combination of austere power and loving devotion.

With most of the communal chanting of the Sufi schools mystical dance is also practised, as brought to Europe by George

Gurdjieff. One of these dances is a swinging circular movement in which all participate, and whose rhythm is taken from that of each individual's breathing. On this rhythmic basis the name of Allah is called out faster and faster and ever more loudly, with some syllables even being sung during the inbreath. Everything rises to a summit of ecstasy which affords the members of this mystical order or school a deep communal spiritual experience. Here again, moreover, most of the practices involved are secret, from which it may be inferred that their roots lie in the magical form of consciousness.

The Instruments of the Islamic Calling

Apart from the original Zoroastrian cultures of the Persian-Arabic area, its music has been influenced above all by the various schools of Islam. In Persian musical ensembles the wind instrument par excellence is the *nay*, for which the position of the player's mouth may be described as half-way between that of the recorder and that of the orchestral flute. Its sweet, ethereal sound is the subject of esoteric symbolism in many Islamic poems. The main stringed instrument is the *kemantshe*, and the chief plucked instrument the *setar*, from which the Indian *sitar* is derived. Another important lute-type instrument is the *ud*, which has become known even in Western Europe through the fabulous *ud*-player Mounir Bachir from Baghdad.

Alongside these, another important instrument deserves mention, one which is also in use in north Indian Kashmir and especially in Afghanistan – the *santur*, generally with eighteen strings. This instrument, a kind of dulcimer played with hammers, is certainly the precursor of the eastern European *cembalo* and thus of our own piano. The *santur* demands immense patience to tune. One has only to consider the fact that for every mode, almost every piece, it has to be re-tuned differently. Hence the oral tradition that one needs half a lifetime to learn to play the *santur* and the other half to tune it. The rapid rhythm-instrument of Arabic music is the *tumbak* (pronounced 'doom-beck') – a drum like a big goblet which is played by the fingers of both hands while held under the right arm. All these instruments, apart from the *ud*-lute and the *nay*-flute, were primarily instruments for accompanying the singer of Persian or Arabic poetry, before they became independent instruments in their own right.

The modal systems of Arabic music – the musical scales – occupy a mid position between the Indian ragas and the old Church modes. These Arabic *maqam* scales (called *dastgah* in Iranian) have an untempered tuning, and sound strange to our ears chiefly because of the 'neutral' third that lies somewhere between a major and a minor third. But once we stop listening in terms of 'right' and 'wrong', and really listen to these unfamiliar intervals for what they are, they are the very ones that impart to us a deep, new experience. For it is often the 'out-of-tune' intervals that first open our ears – accustomed as they are to tempered keyboards and harmonies – to modal music. We have long since ceased to appreciate the fine differentiations of unison/melodic music, and they no longer touch our soul. And when we are suddenly confronted with an 'out-of-tune' interval, to start with we perhaps find it an unpleasant experience; but then we begin once again to listen more deeply to the performance, with its varying relationships between the single-note melody and the keynote.

Nor does this apply solely to the melodic ragas, *maqams* or *dastgahs* of Western Asia, but to all music that has arisen from levels of consciousness other than our own mental one. For there is also modal music that does not make the relationship to the keynote as clear as in Indian music, which supplies a special instrument for that purpose (the *tambura*). In these other cultures the mode or scale is expressed primarily by a heterophonic method of playing. That is to say that several musicians play the same modal figure, the same melodic sequence, at approximately the same speed; yet they do not all start together, but play one after the other, as it were in canon, accentuating alternately the strong or weak beats.

Indonesian Gamelan Music

It is in this same heterophonic way that all the music of the islands of Java and Bali is played – a music which is among the most fascinating produced by any self-contained, magical island-culture. To begin with it sounds completely foreign to the Western listener, yet gradually it becomes familiar to him – in fact he even experiences an affinity with it, for of all the music of the non-European world it is the most impressive acoustic manifestation of the archetypal symbols of that collective unconscious that links us all. The music of Indonesia is primarily orchestral, i.e., the playing in concert of many – thirty or forty – musicians, and not infrequently takes the form of an accompaniment to theatrical presentations.

On the Indonesian islands it is the magical aspect of Hindu religion that is most developed. The *Ramayana*, the great Hindu epic, represents in Bali and Java, above all, the clash between man and the demonic world of the spirits. Here the divine prince Ram, for the mythical Indian the god and guru of personal self-realisation, is (with his wife Sita and his brothers) first and foremost a champion in the shamanic wars and battles against the ape-kingdom, the magicians and the powers of the higher and lower worlds. Furthermore the Balinesians have not been over-careful to stick to received tradition, and have written their own 'operas'. Every village has its own orchestra, dancing troupe and singing ensemble as a matter of course. A master musician – the medicine-man, so to speak – both plays and conducts. The music is worked out and tried out communally, topical allusions are worked in, and each man plays for himself. True, the actors' dancing-masks and the coloured costumes are traditional, but the music is a living thing and has been in a constant state of development right up to the present day.

The Indonesian gamelan-orchestra comprises a whole range of small metallophones which are played like xylophones. There are a large number of gong players, with several deep, boss-shaped gongs, all of which have a single, predetermined pitch. In addition a number of hand drums and flutes are generally available, and singing is added for good measure. The singers are often simultaneously actors and dancers. The result is a composite artwork combining all the various genres in one. Alongside this living music of Bali, daily reborn anew, there is also a Classical variety of gamelan music. It has traditionally been cultivated above all in the royal palace of Java, the Kraton of Djakarta.

The Indonesian modal-heterophonic playing-technique, already mentioned above, has two main modes – two scales – to which the individual glockenspiels (or metallophones) and gongs are tuned. Here, too, both scales have a whole collection of 'out-of-tune' notes – i.e., they subdivide the octave into intervals that are completely different from our own familiar ones. One of these two modes is pentatonic (known as *slendro*) and sounds *almost* like the tuning of the black notes on the piano. Nevertheless none of the intervals is tuned according to the exact note-system of our tempered keyboard.

Each of the five notes of *slendro* has a particular name: the first – let us assume it is C – is called *Barang*: *Gulu*, as the second note, is about one-sixth of a tone higher than D; *Dada* sounds a quarter of a tone higher than E; *Lima* is one-sixth of a tone higher than our tempered fifth, but also higher than the pure fifth; *Nem* is a quarter of a tone higher than A, and even the octave is one-sixth of a tone higher than the pure octave. It is interesting to note that the octave is thus divided into five al-most equal parts and that the fourths between the second and fourth notes, and between the third and fifth notes, are virtually pure ones – i.e., tuned in the ratio 3 : 4. This scale is thus to some extent accessible to our Western ear. But the second main scale of Indonesia, which is called *pelog*, sounds completely alien. It has seven notes; two or them, however, have only a subordinate function.

All the metallophonic and gong-type instruments, then, are alike exactly tuned to these (for our ears) 'unnatural' intervals. Certain structural motifs are taught to every player from his childhood until he achieves an incredible virtuoso mastery of them. The notation for these rhythmic formulae reveals the de-gree of difficulty entailed. Some of the time certain of the 'parts' play only on the weak beats – which means that the player has totally to omit the main beat.

Thus the characteristic form of an orchestral piece has many of the players repeating the same motif-like figure heterophonic-ally, but none the less to large extent in exact parallel; the pat-terns overlap or are superimposed on each other; and at specific signals (generally given by the leading hand-drummer) the pat-terns are intensified – i.e., become louder – suddenly slow down or become faster, and eventually come to a halt. On top of all this, solo singers or players join in with the same patterns in slow form. This musical process, which eventually leads to the formation of a finished piece, is not conducted, and the listener is aware that the communication necessary for its successful execution is only possible if the performers are instinctively following a common musical impulse. This latter is provided by the gestures of the dancers.

The effect of this music, available only on a few gramophone-records from Bali and others of the Djakarta court-orchestra, is comparable to no other state of consciousness evoked by notes and sounds. Terms such as 'waking trance', 'timeless time', 'clair-voyant intoxication' suggest themselves. But as the music editor Walter Bachauer has pointed out (having travelled to Bali to invite a whole village to the Berlin Meta-Music-Festival of 1976), a true impression of this music can be conveyed only through its live performance. That may very well have been the reason why the Munich composer and conductor Eberhard Schoener took his synthesizer to Bali to perform in person with a gamelan orchestra.

Music in China and Japan

To conclude this brief survey of non-European music we shall turn our attention to those musical cultures which offer a particularly 'difficult' acoustic reflection of their meditative and contemplative practices. The religious character of Japanese Zen-Buddhism, for example, is hardly visible outwardly, since the major part of its practice – *sitting* – is carried out in silence, has an inward orientation and lacks outward symbolism. Thus the musical aspect of the Zen monastery can give only an outward reflection of the inner state and goal of *Za-Zen*, or silent, medi-tative sitting. The sung prayers are in many monasteries accom-panied at short intervals by bells and cymbals, as well as by drum-beats and drum-rolls.

The German Zen teacher Gerta Ital reports of a Japanese temple:

> When, after the entry of the monks, the almost overwhelming cacophony of bells, gongs, drums and cymbals announced the approach of the Master, all present were, like me, undoubtedly translated into that shattered condition which, on the one hand, is held capable of preparing man's soul to experience the extraordinary, and on the other of lending the one who is the object of the ceremony (being the centre of this common ecstasy) the strength to attend the sacred proceedings.*

Otherwise, however, the Zen path is pursued in complete silence, in which the acoustic signals of the *Rôshi* strike deep

* G. Ital: *Der Meister, die Mönche und ich*, Weilheim, 3rd edition 1972, p. 217.

into the meditators. These signals consist of a variety of given blows on a small metal vessel that gives out a bright, penetrating sound, and the sharp clapping together of two wooden sticks to announce the beginning and end of a session.

The traditional court music of Japan is likewise born from the state of silence. The wind instrument *shakuhachi* and the zither-like *koto* permit only a very few notes, intervals or *glissandi*. The *glissandi* of the *koto* are produced by pressing the plucked string, thus altering its pitch. The *koto* can also play harmonic music, though everything is subordinated to a specifically chosen modal scale, for the most part pentatonic. The best-known and, to our ears, most typically Japanese-sounding sequence is C – D flat – F – G – A flat – C.

The *koto* has its prototype in the Chinese zither, just as Japanese Zen developed from the Buddhist *Ch'an* of China. The musical system of China is the oldest and philosophically most highly-developed in the whole world. Music in China is alleged to have been born when Ling-Lun met a pair of birds that whistled to him, as the emissaries of God, a few notes which Ling-Lun duly imitated on some bamboo pipes. Thence came the twelve notes of the Chinese tone-system, the twelve *Lü*. In China the philosophy of music is based on the age-old relationship between number, note and cosmos. Anyone who has studied the Chinese 'Book of Changes', the *I Ching*, knows of the significance of two and three, on whose many combinations the hexagrams and readings of the oracle are based. Chinese music, too, has the two and the three as its direct basis. From the numerical ratio 2 : 3 comes the fifth, and from the superimposition of these fifths comes the Chinese pentatonic scale. Nobody today knows which note was originally the bottom note of the Chinese scale, or even which note was considered to be the 'lowest'. However, the note names are:

1. Huang-chung (F)
2. Ta-lü (F sharp)
3. T'ai-ts'u (G)
4. Chia-chung (G sharp)
5. Ku-hsi (A)
6. Cheng lü (A sharp)
7. Jui-pin (B)
8. Lin-chung (C)
9. I-tse (C sharp)
10. Nan-lü (D)
11. Wu-i (D sharp)
12. Ying-chung (E)

The traditional music of China influenced not only Japanese and Korean folk-music, but even that of Mongolia and Tibet. Of its former power the following incident from the books of Liä-Dsi (c 400 B.C.) relates:

> Whenever Gu-Ba struck the zither, the birds would circle above him and the fishes would leap up out of the water. The master musician Wen of Cheng heard it. He left his home and followed Master Siang on his wanderings. For three years he fingered the strings without ever producing a tune. Master Siang said: 'Go back to your home.' Master Wen laid the zither aside, sighed and said: 'It is not because I do not know how to pluck the strings, not for that reason that I have brought forth no tune; what is in my mind has nothing to do with strings; my goal has nothing to do with notes. So long as I have not reached that goal in my heart, I can give it no outward expression on the instrument. That is why I dare not lift my hand and touch the strings. Yet give me a little while and then see what I can do.'
>
> Not long afterwards he came once again before Master Siang. The latter said: 'How is it now with your zither-playing?' Master Wen said: 'I have succeeded; please put my playing to the test.' Thereupon he struck the *Shang*-string during the spring and let the eighth pipe accompany it. And suddenly a cool wind arose, and plants and trees bore fruit. When it was autumn he struck the *Güo*-string and let the second pipe accompany it. And mild breezes came blowing softly, and plants and trees revealed their rich array. During the summer he struck the *Yü*-string and let the eleventh pipe accompany it. And frost and snow fell apace and the rivers and lakes were suddenly stilled. When it had become winter he struck the *Chi*-string and let the fifth pipe reply. And the sunshine became stiflingly hot and the hard ice quickly melted away. Finally he made the *Gung*-string sound and combined it with the four other strings and delightful zephyrs rustled, bountiful clouds floated by, sweet dew fell and mightily roared the fountains.*

Most of the musical magicians of China lived among the Taoists, and today it is hard to find a single artist who has even a basic knowledge of the origins of the oldest Chinese music. However, a few of these old Taoist Masters do still live in

---

* R. Wilhelm: *Das Buch vom quellenden Urgrund*, quoted by Fritz Stege in: *Musik, Magie, Mystik*, Remagen 1961, pp. 185–186.

Taiwan and Korea, and one or two of the pilgrims of world music have succeeded in studying under such Masters. But then the traditional music of China or Japan, not to mention that of Korea or Vietnam, is available only to a relatively small élite of Western listeners who possess the few existing records and tapes and who are familiar with the historical and theoretical background. In the USA and Europe, by contrast, considerably greater sympathy has greeted African rhythm-music. Jazz has integrated the musical ecstasy of the Blacks, has helped it gain popularity, but at the same time has masked it, so that really pure African music now has little, if any, relationship to its commercial adaptations in the field of Pop, Rock and Jazz.

Rhythmic Aspects

If we visit an Afro-American dance-club or listen to the sounds of Black Jazz or Latin-American *Latin-Rock*, the rhythm literally forces us into physical movement. Our magical impulses stir once again into wakefulness, and indeed we sometimes enter a kind of trance-state that is completely foreign to our normal consciousness. 'They're trying to dance,' smiled the Black American drummer Jeffrey Biddeau from Trinidad, as he watched us Whites twisting ourselves into all sorts of 'trance-like' contortions in a Rock-club. And it was fascinating to observe what happened when he joined in the rhythmic efforts of the excellent Rock-group during an unamplified conga. Suddenly the music 'caught fire', the bass-player improved by several degrees, and nobody knew what had hit him: the dance-club was 'ablaze', though the conga itself was scarcely audible.

When rhythm inspires us, the magical consciousness awakes in us. It is of course not foreign to us, but rather asleep in most civilised, rational Westerners, having now been taken over by what one might call the onward march of human history. The danger is that, through music and drugs, we may become so fascinated by the re-awakening of our magical awareness that we relapse into the long-since subdued magical consciousness, and draw back 'by default' (Gebser) from our task of conscious integration, bewitched by the musical 'shamanism' of our own day. That would be mere escapism, a throwback to the pseudo-magic of sheer 'gut-music', the 'music-power' of unconscious irrationality.

Our opportunity consists in the conscious realisation – on the mental-rational plane – of the magical within ourselves, in the simultaneous experiencing of the power of the collective unconscious, and in the mutual harmonisation and integration of both. In this connection we also need to speak of the differentiation of rhythms, for there are also mythical and mental/intellectual rhythmic patterns. So far as I know the differences between these rhythmic forms have nowhere been worked out to date.

The rhythmic structure of the *magical* consciousness is built up out of continuous patterns, indefinitely repeated. These drumrolls and sequences of beats bring the shaman to the 'centre of the world', enable him – in the shamanic ceremonies of the tundra – to fly or to capture the spirits, or help him to concentrate on making contact with the spirit-world. The drumbeat is modelled on the rhythms (perhaps unconsciously perceived) of the heartbeat or of walking (duple time) or of breathing (triple time), each being repeated, as in nature, *ad infinitum*. Sometimes this basic rhythm is continually drummed out or stamped out with the foot whilst another part of the body or a second drum presents the actual syncopated rhythm itself. These variations of the beat come in the form of periodic pauses, significant, continually recurring insertions, or a more or less irrational but always precisely reiterated syncopation. These pauses, insertions and syncopations have a direct effect on the centre of the unconscious, the human being's actual centre of gravity, which lies in the region of the abdomen.

Rhythmic patterns characteristic of the *mythical* consciousness, on the other hand, are *cyclic* ones – patterns which, after going round in a circle, return to the point of departure, as described in the case of the Indian *talas*. The beat itself becomes very sophisticated, and the variations are so arranged as to be subtle metric subdivisions of the beat itself; or else a variation may be based on another beat, but in such a way that they both converge on a single point. This dynamic of rhythmic polarity is felt or experienced by the heart or emotions, as in all Indian or Persian mythical music. Finally, the rationally-devised rhythm of *mental* consciousness is not, in the proper sense of the term, a rhythmic form at all, but a metric, mathematical one. The fascinating, but still consciously-devised rhythmic structures of a work by Johann Sebastian Bach, right through to the minutely interlocking rhythms of the music of Anton von Webern or Pierre Boulez, are similarly a purely intellectual component of their composition.

What can all these briefly described non-European musical cultures offer us? Have they really influenced or enriched contemporary Western music? In the chapter on *periodic music* it will be seen how intensely the percussion music of Ghana, the Indonesian gamelan, the Indian ragas and the deep tones of Tibet have influenced the American and European avant-garde music of recent years. In the more successful cases Jazz and Pop-musicians, performing with African and Asian players, have developed a new, spiritual form of music – a *musical meditation*.

3 The Esoteric World of Sound and Research into Harmonics

Through the encounter with the non-European cultures a re-discovery of the suggestive effects of music has become possible for us in our present over-rationalised age. The knowledge of the magical power of music, for millennia an essential part of cultures the world over, is starting to figure prominently in the interests of many contemporary composers and music groups. Prolonged chants, ecstatic rhythms and ancient melodic patterns can carry present-day Westerners into states of consciousness that bring about a momentary release from the subjective personality and permit experience of the collective unconscious within the human psyche.

Carl Gustav Jung, the pathfinder of the East-West encounter in psychology, contributed materially to the ability of the mentally-orientated Westerner to achieve a deeper understanding of his own inner nature. At the same time, however, he constantly pointed out the danger of succumbing to the fascination of the Far East and of losing one's own cultural roots. Jung places much greater value on the re-discovery of the esoteric symbols of our own Western culture and thus on becoming aware once again of the typically Western images and archetypes.

'Through the activities involved in analytical treatment there arise experiences of an archetypal nature which demand expression and embodiment. Naturally this is not the only occasion when such experiences occur; archetypal experiences not infrequently arise spontaneously, and certainly not only among "psychological" people. In fact, I have often been told of the most wonderful dreams and visions by people of whose mental health the specialist could have not the slightest doubt. The experience of the archetype is often kept as the most private secret, for one feels oneself involved at the deepest of levels. It is a kind of primal experience of the spiritual non-ego, one's inner "opposite number", that demands interpretation.'*

Likewise self-experience via music is, in Jung's terms, not merely concerned with the exotic and magic sounds of Africa and Asia, but requires access to our own Western esoteric musical sources. Significantly, a similar development is taking place among a great many composers and musicians: after leaving behind the deceptive world of drugs, they have turned to the non-European cultures, and then have finally come back to ancient Greece, to early Christianity, to the Middle Ages and thus to their own past.

The significance of music among the ancients was intimately bound up with mythical intimations of the *Harmony of the Spheres*. Music was in those days seen as part of the terrestrial blueprint, as the foundation of the world, even as the world-soul itself, as the musical historian Gerhard Nestler puts it: 'This music was inaudible; only its symbol was audible. This symbol comprised the notes or sounds that man chose from the profusion that the cosmos placed at his disposal. Music arose from the polar tension between the audible and the inaudible. The cosmos could be either a myth or a likeness of the divine, spritual order. It all depended on what man believed. Either he chose the myth and found a symbol for it, or he created that symbol out of the spirit of cosmic order. The unheard substance of the cosmos, the Essential, was in both cases sound and tone. These demanded expression and representation by means of notes and instruments.'†

Since the time of Pythagoras the concept of the *Harmony of the Spheres* has woven its way like a scarlet thread through the history of musical esoterics as a symbol of cosmic world-order. For the musical researcher Fritz Stege, the cosmic symbol of the *Harmony of the Spheres* is the 'idea' of our music, which presents itself to our ear via the mathematical interrelationships of sounds. As early as the ancient Greek era the acoustic proportions had been discovered – laws both of music and of physics.

These so-called *harmonic* phenomena of the secret schools

* C. G. Jung: *Ueber die Psychologie des Unbewussten*, Frankfurt 1975, p. 80.
† G. Nestler: *Die Form in der Musik*, Freiburg 1954, Introduction.

of Pythagoras were re-discovered in the Middle Ages by three distinguished scholars who were concerned with the 'music of the spheres': the Jesuit Father Athanasius Kircher, the English Rosicrucian Robert Fludd and (most outstanding of all) the astronomer, and discoverer of the planetary laws, Johannes Kepler. Kircher enriched contemporary musical thought on the cosmos with his valuable symbolic representation of the World Organ (see opposite) which Fritz Stege explains as follows:

> Kircher compares the creation of the world to the music of the organ. Six groups of pipes, arranged in sacred sevens, represent the six days of creation ... The sixth day shows man and woman by the apple tree in company with the mysterious unicorn, medieval symbol of virginity. All the stops of the organ are pulled out, to show that creation is complete. And under the keyboard there is a minute Latin inscription: 'sic lucit in orbe terrarum aeterna Dei sapientia' – so plays God's eternal wisdom on the terrestrial globe.*

Another symbolic representation is the 'World Monochord' by Robert Fludd (see p. 96):

> The single-stringed measuring instrument with whose aid the Pythagoreans worked out the intervals is anchored to Earth (*Terra*). The latter corresponds to the *Gamma Graecum*, the bottom note of the medieval note-system. Above it lie at intervals of a second the other elements *Aqua*, *Aer*, *Ignis* (Water, Air, Fire – the highest, because lightest, element) – and thus, in fact, the whole material world. We then ascend into the kingdom of the cosmos, from the moon to Jupiter, via the listed planetary signs, whose *meso*, or centre, is occupied by the sun.
>
> The arcs cutting the string refer to the spacings of the notes – on the right the intervals, on the left their mathematical proportions. The interval between sun and earth produces a *diapason materialis*, the Greek designation for the octave, corresponding on the left to a *proportio dupla*, i.e., 1 : 2. Further 'material' intervals portrayed include *diatesseron* (i.e., the fourth), *diapente* (the fifth), *diapason cum diapente* etc. The whole universe is thus divided into a double octave, with the

* F. Stege: *Musik, Magie, Mystik*, Remagen 1961, p. 133.

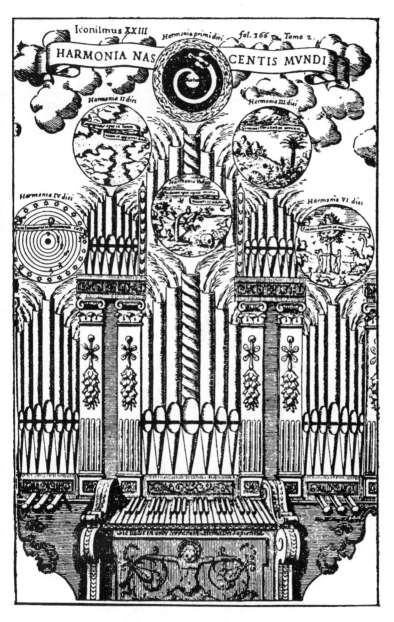

The Harmony of the Creation of the World. Facsimile from
A. Kircher's *Musurgia*.

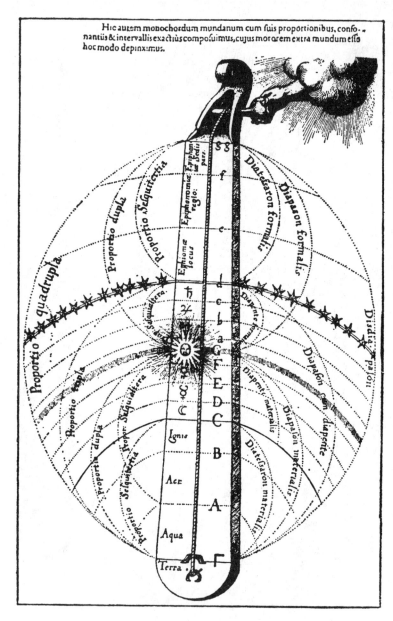

The World-Monochord of Robertus de Fluctibus, from his
Metaphysica, physica atque technica ... Historia, Linz 1519.

sun at its centre ... Examination of the interval system reveals the absence of the tierce or third. The octave and fifth rule the universe as the basis of all our music; and indeed it was only later that the chord of the third entered man's conceptual horizons as a typically 'human' phenomenon. The 'interval-experience' has very largely become lost to us – to say nothing of the experience of the single note. What sidelong glances were directed at the composer Carl Orff, for example, for attributing a special significance to a single note in his opera *Antigonae*, or at Anton von Webern in his orchestral pieces! Yet in doing so they were merely reviving the practice of the ancient Egyptian mysteries – whether intentionally or otherwise is of no significance – in which each single, sustained note, intoned by all present, signified an invocation to a particular deity.*

It is precisely this experience of the single note and the significance of the intervals that are once more of interest in the new spiritual music. Rulolf Steiner was already interpreting the intervals in his day, associating subjectivity and destiny with the 'experience of the third', the discovery of the higher self with the 'octave-experience' and imagination with the 'fifth-experience'. The anthroposophist Anny von Lange went on to explore the esoteric interpretation of the Greek modes and of 'cosmic-ethereal' pentatonism. With her specialist expertise and intuition, she points the way towards a new way of listening to music and towards a spiritual understanding of note-combinations.† More recently, the musicologist Hermann Pfrogner has published a comprehensive, esoteric, and at the same time scientific interpretation of notes and intervals within the cultures of antiquity and of the Far East, as well as researching the cosmic aspect of the twelve-tone system.‡

Alongside these anthroposophist interpretations, *harmonic symbolism* has also found a new form. Its roots lie in the secret teachings of the Greek initiates, of which only sporadic and fragmentary knowledge has been preserved. This was collected together by Albert von Thimus in 1868 in his work *Die*

---

* F. Stege, op. cit., p. 126.
† A. v. Lange: *Mensch, Musik, Kosmos*, Freiburg 1956 (Vol. II 1960).
‡ Hermann Pfrogner: *Lebendige Tonwelt*, Munich 1976.

harmonikale Symbolik des Altertums, while quite recently it has been above all the wide-ranging scholar Hans Kayser who has written significant and complex scientific works on the theme of fundamental research into harmonics.

Experiments with the Monochord

In order to illustrate the laws of harmonics, I now propose to describe the monochord work with the aid of which Pythagoras was already able to discover the acoustic proportions and their mathematical ratios.

A monochord consists of a box-shaped resonance-chamber which has the effect of amplifying sound, and across which is stretched a string, say, 120 cm. in length. This single string is tuned to C – that is to say it reproduces the note C when its whole length is vibrating. Now let us try inserting a small bridge under the exact mid-point of the string, so that the string is divided into two halves, and then pluck the half-string: the *octave* of the former note C is produced – i.e., C′. Thus the ratio 1 : 2 sounds as an octave.

With the slightest movement of the bridge away from the mid-point, or if our eye has somewhat deceived us in placing the bridge, an inexact relationship results which our ear is immediately aware of. Even with an inaccuracy of as little as two millimetres the result is not a precise octave. In fact, then, our ear is a more accurate means of measuring than our eye. This aural facility is of the essence for the harmonicist, who can thus proceed on the assumption that an integration of the intellectual and spiritual spheres, of quantity and quality, is possible via the sense of hearing.

Next, we shall let our ear measure the mathematical ratio 2 : 3. On our 120 cm. string the bridge must be moved to the 80 cm. point – which is not so easy for the eye. Thus it could well be helpful to draw some kind of scale on the wood beneath the string. Once the right spot has been found the resulting sound-ratio will be that of 80 : 120 cm., or 2 : 3, the fifth from the bass-note, or G. For the ratio 3 : 4 the bridge is installed at the 90 cm. point and produces the interval of the fourth, or F. Again, the ratio 4 : 5 produces the major third (E) and 5 : 6 the minor third (E flat). The subdivisions are now becoming smaller, and it is becoming increasingly difficult to find the 'right' position for each note. While most people can tell immediately if the octave sounds 'right', the decision as to when the fifth is in tune is already a matter of fine discrimination and concentration. These tense moments are well-known in Indian music when the *tambura*, the accompanying instrument, is being tuned.

Pursuing further the laws we have discovered, let us now divide the string of the monochord into smaller and smaller parts, corresponding to the fractions ½, ⅓, ¼ ... and so on. The halving of the string, as we already know, produces the octave (C′); the marking off of a third of it produces the fifth of the octave above (G′), since one third of the whole string is the equivalent of two thirds of half of it. A quarter of the string once again produces the note C, though two octaves higher, for we are talking in terms of halving one-half. One-fifth of the string gives E″ – the major third above this second octave – one sixth, the minor third above that (thus, G″), and with one-seventh an even smaller interval results – a flat third. This last-produced note, rather lower than B″, is unusual in our note-system, and is regarded by harmonicists as *eccentric*, or only marginal. The next note, in the ratio 1:8, brings us to the third octave up (C‴).

The spacings have now become so small that for the purposes of practical experiment it is now worth switching to a mono-chord with a string-length greater than 120 cm., so that the spac-ings of the small ratios can still be measured. In Germany two composers and musicians have developed monochord-type in-struments for 'live' music-making, both making use of electroni-cally-amplified strings: the American Rolf Gehlhaar has built a *super-string*, the effective length of whose string can be altered by pressing on it (thus permitting *glissandi*), and the Argentinian guitarist Roberto Détrée has invented a *motocello* which is operated, with the help of a motor, by a crank-like continuous bow, and can be plucked or stopped with the fingers. Both instru-ments – like the electronic instruments of the physicist Dieter Trüstedt – are played with small bars of metal and will re-produce the various mathematical ratios in convincing acoustic form.

Since the large version of the *motocello* has a three-metre-long string it is possible to investigate even smaller subdivisions. One-ninth of the string produces the note D‴ – which lies slightly higher than on the tempered keyboard – one-tenth is E‴, one-eleventh an out-of-tune, 'flat' F sharp, one-twelfth G‴. After that the intervals become smaller still, until within the space of a single tone an infinite number of further notes can be produced.

THE HARMONIC SERIES

Under the terms of the ancient techniques of acoustic self-realisation, the knowledge of these interval-subdivisions of a string took on the rôle of a link between nature and the soul. For these basic laws reveal the connection between notes and numbers: the intervals can be physically experienced, and the ratios correspond to particular feelings. Since these proportions can be detected by the ear, and even at that time were recognised as laws fundamental to all music, musical concepts became central to the ancient Greek view of the world. All the notes discovered by subdividing the string, and now reduced to written musical notation, together comprise the 'natural tone-row' or 'harmonic series'.

Now the physicist calls a vibration without overtones a 'tone', whereas a musician designates anything which has a fixed pitch a 'note'. Such a 'note' is, in physical terms, regarded as a 'sound' consisting of a number of 'partial tones' which normally stand in whole-number frequency ratios to each other – $2:1$, $3:1$, $4:1$ and so on. The musician speaks here of 'timbre' or 'tone-quality', while by 'sound' he often means a combination of several 'notes', e.g., a chord. Since we are not here concerned with giving a purely physical account, but are looking at the physical phenomena from a musical point of view, the various terms will tend to overlap somewhat in our account.

Each note of a Classical musical instrument has a special sound, which derives its particular quality and unmistakable character from a particular arrangement of overtones. The tone-quality of a note is thus dependent on a particular configuration of the harmonic spectrum, in which certain partial notes may be emphasised while others are muted. By no means all resonant bodies have harmonic overtones corresponding to whole-number frequency ratios. When bells, cymbals or gongs are struck, for example, discordant partial tones, frequently sounding 'out-of-tune', often sound at the same time. On a monochord, however, or on any stringed instrument, it is a simple matter to make audible the notes of the natural harmonic series by gently stroking the string at the points described above. They are then known as *harmonics* (in Germany as 'flageolets') as in Example No. 2 : the harmonics of the bottom C-string of a cello. The natural harmonic series can be demonstrated up to the fortieth overtone. Normally, however, only the first eleven are used in harmonic research. The ones which sound harmonious and 'right' to our ear are those corresponding to the simplest ratios, 2 : 1, 3 : 2, 4 : 3 and so on; or expressed as fractions, $\frac{1}{2}$, $\frac{1}{3}$, $\frac{1}{4}$, etc. To start with it is scarcely possible to distinguish individual overtones within a note, however good one's hearing. A quite special form of attention is necessary to detect overtones, which otherwise stay hidden. For all our sense impressions are not just sensations of the nervous system, as the well-known physiologist Hermann von Helmholtz wrote as early as 1857, 'but a special activity of the soul is involved in translating the sensation of the nerves into a conception of that object which gave rise to the sensation.'[*] Listening to the harmonic spectrum, self-immersion in the harmonic series, is in numerous Asian and Arabic schools a form of sound-meditation leading to self-realisation.

The Formants

In present-day physics individual groups of overtones are also termed the 'formants' of a note. Most of the research on the ways in which the formants work has been carried out in connection with the production of electronic musical instruments and musical composition on the synthesizer. As early as 1960 Stockhausen was referring to the harmonic series as 'spectral harmonics' – i.e., the harmonic superimposition of the partial-tones of the harmonic spectrum. It is the configuration of the formants that gives each sound its distinctive life and sharpness, be it produced by acoustic or by technical means, and that lends each instrument its typical tone. But it is not a matter of a broad, continuous spectrum, but rather (as already indicated) primarily of groups of overtones that are either particularly strongly emphasised or muted or suppressed. It is precisely these formants

[*] Helmholtz: *Ueber die physiologischen Ursachen musikalischer Harmonien*, Munich 1971, p. 45.

that give a particular family of musical instruments its characteristic tone. Their pitches are constant and independent of the
basic frequency of the note in question; for the formants are
produced directly by the sound-characteristics of an instrument's resonance-chamber, or of the human head and chest
cavities. For this reason the formants are known by the name
of the vowel in which they are most prominent. The following
table shows the most important frequency-ranges of the vowels:

Vowels	Average Resonance-frequency (Hertz)	
U (Oo)	300 Hz (ca.F^1)	
A (Ah)	500 Hz (ca.B^1)	
Ae (Eh)	1000 Hz (ca.B^2)	
Oe (Er)	1350 Hz (ca.F^3)	and 500 Hz (ca.B^1)
O (Aw)	1550 Hz (ca.G^3)	and 300 Hz (ca.F^1)
Ue (as French u)	1800 Hz (ca.A^3)	and 700 Hz (ca.F sharp^2)
E (Ay)	2100 Hz (ca.C sharp^4)	and 500 Hz (ca.B^1)
I (Ee)	3000 Hz (ca.G^4)	and 300 Hz (ca.F^1)

The frequency ranges given here refer to averages obtained
in the course of statistical researches, where the level of the
resonance-frequency corresponds clearly to a particular class of
vowel in German: in ascending order, U – O – A – E – I. Just as
with the human voice, so instruments too have their particular
formants. And if one wishes to imitate instruments electronically (as, for example, on the organ), particular attention has to
be paid to this fact. What is known as 'attack' also plays an
important rôle. It was discovered very early on that the initial
moments of a note, its attack as it starts to resonate, are part of
the characteristic trademark of an instrument.

Electronic Sound-production

Since any amateur can nowadays produce effective musical
pieces with the aid of electronic musical apparatus and synthesizers, a few observations are appended at this point on
sound-production using electronic instruments. To simplify
somewhat, we can distinguish in electronic sound-production between additive and selective methods of sound formation. Using
the *additive* method, the desired sound is put together from pure
tones without harmonics (in other words, sine-waves) produced
by individual sound-generators. In this way any desired spectrum of sound can be built up. Certain difficulties are involved,
however, in altering the pitch of the combined sound thus pro-

duced without altering the intervals between the individual partial notes. Modern synthesizers nevertheless offer excellent synchronisation between multiple generators.

Selective sound formation is a quite different matter. The raw material generally consists of a sound rich in overtones, whose spectrum is modified by various types of filter that are switched in subsequently. Since the individual overtones come from a single generator, they follow the harmonic series, and the intervals between them remain constant even when the pitch of the fundamental tone is altered. Of the most frequently used filters two of the most important are the *resonance-filter* and the *bandpass*.

With the aid of the *resonance-filter*, individual frequency ranges are amplified and in this way formant effects are obtained. If such a filter is made especially selective, individual frequencies of the spectrum become so strongly amplified that they can be clearly distinguished by ear. In this way very striking sound-modulations can be achieved. The filter is so installed as to make it possible gradually to turn up and down individual overtones.

A *bandpass* is so designed, on the other hand, as to allow through all the frequencies below an adjustable so-called 'limiting-frequency', while all higher frequencies are increasingly muted, or become inaudible. If, for example, one places the limiting-frequency below the first overtone, then all the overtones are muted, and one hears only the almost sine-wave-like basic oscillation.

Filters of this kind are available in virtually every synthesizer, just as a great variety of miniature versions of them are at the disposal of many avant-garde or Rock-groups. Performing with such equipment, which to all intents and purposes can effortlessly prolong any note to infinity and modify it in any way desired, has once again opened many musicians' ears to the laws governing the inner mechanics of the individual sound.

The key word for all this is 'Live-Electronics', if what one means is manually-playable music produced electronically, but not under mechanical or electronic control (such as punched tape or computers) or by tape-recorders. For without direct contact between the player and the notes on the instrument the pre-formed acoustic or dynamic patterns all too easily remain sterile and dead. No drawing-board technique can replace the player's feeling for sound or rhythm, his improvisatory tensions, or above all the rhythm of his breathing as he reacts to the experience. It is not by accident that great composers have often had every detail of their compositions worked out in their heads before ever writing them down, as well as having good reputations as improvisers.

The distinction of being the first composer to commit himself to live-electronic performance on a large scale belongs to Oskar Sala (b. 1910). He had studied under Paul Hindemith and collaborated in the significant acoustic research of the physicist Friedrich Trautwein (1888–1956). With his equally great technical as well as musical expertise he developed Trautwein's 'trautonium' several stages further into the 'mixturtrautonium'. From his first public performances in the year 1930 in pieces by Paul Hindemith for three trautoniums, up to his collaboration in Arthur Honegger's *Jeanne d'Arc* and Wagner's *Parsifal* (until about 1953), Sala took part in many concerts in Europe, in which he exhausted the live-electronic possibilities of his instrument.

Fundamental research into the further development of electronic music was begun by the German-American Robert A. Moog at the beginning of the fifties. His basic idea – that of controlling generators, filters, frequency-modulators and all the other components of electronic sound-production and modulation by means of electrical potentials – opened up new paths and has now become universal. Through the miniaturisation of components it is possible today to get as much electronic equipment into a small portable suitcase as previously into a large, immovable amplifier cabinet. No wonder that today practically every composer uses electronics at some time or other; no wonder, either, that synthetically produced or modulated sound also rules the Pop and Rock scenes. In fact it may be here that many a musician, by dint of careful listening, has encountered for the first time the universal dance of the overtones.

Thus, at the very moment when music could for the first time be produced without the traditional instruments, the basic laws that govern the production of notes and timbres were being rediscovered, or rather newly heard and experienced. This rediscovery led musicians back again to the sources of music, and thus to the monochord, the mathematical ratios and the experience of the harmonic series.

At the same time, however, our knowledge of the harmonic series also permits us to understand the singing techniques of the Tibetans and Mongolians, with all their magical-spiritual effects. The melody of the Mongolian shaman follows precisely the arrangement of the natural harmonic series. In the process he even sings the 'out-of-tune' intervals – which to him sound quite natural and inevitable – the 'flattened' diminished seventh and the 'flattened' tritone: measured from C these would be B flat and F sharp. And the 'flattened' third of the ratio 6:7 is precisely the interval between the pair of African conga-drums. Interestingly enough, the scale that most closely follows the natural sound-laws (namely C – D – E – F sharp – G – A – B flat – C) is known in southern India as the Raga Saraswati, and *Saraswati* is the goddess of music and the sciences. Even the 'mystic chord' of Alexander Scriabin is a combination of the eighth, ninth, tenth, eleventh, thirteenth and fourteenth overtones (C, F sharp, B flat, E^1, A^1, D^2).

Harmonics and Science

The conformity of the harmonic series to natural law appertains on the one hand to the level of esoteric or mystical knowledge and on the other to that of scientifically demonstrable fact. Whereas in the West esoteric research formerly belonged to occultism, it has now been brought into the sphere of the 'real' through the agency of modern atomic physics and relativity theory. From the above description of the monochord experiment, which demonstrates the derivation of the natural notes, it becomes clear that if the spatial variable (the length of the string) decreases, the temporal variable (the frequency-count) increases, and vice versa. Thus, space and time stand here in inverse proportion – a situation reminiscent of the space-time relativity discovered by Einstein. Another basic law connected with the overtones or harmonics of a violin or cello string is clearly related to Max Planck's quantum-theory: 'When the finger is moved up the string, only quite specific notes are sounded ... in other words, nature herself has to make a choice. The notes jump from one position to the next – they are arranged in quantum-fashion and not as a continuum.'*

In his books *Der hörende Mensch*, *Akroasis*, *Harmonia*

* H. Kayser: **Lehrbuch der Harmonik**, quoted by J. Gebser in: *Abendländische Wandlung*, Berlin 1965, p. 116.

Planetarum and above all in *Orphikon*, Hans Kayser demonstrates in rigorous scientific and mathematical terms that, in
chemistry, atomic physics, crystallography, astronomy, archi-
tecture, spectroanalysis, botany etc., there exists an underlying
framework of whole-number ratios such as we hear in notes –
as octave, third, fifth, fourth. The construction of a 'musical'
cosmology, and the harmonic correspondences between the laws
of music and of atomic physics, are thus not just mere esoteric
speculation. Contemporary research has ventured into the field
of 'occult' phenomena and revealed a scientific basis for many of
our intuitive and mystic intimations.* The natural phenomena
of music have thus been once again recognised to be elements
of the basic laws of physics. The *Harmony of the Spheres* is
discussed in relation to Max Planck's law of quanta; the basic
laws of acoustics find their equivalent in the ratios between the
shells of the atomic nucleus. Observation of the radiation-spec-
trum shows that the radiation-quanta released when an electron
jumps from an outer to an inner orbit possess a sequence of
gradation similar to that of the note-intervals.

In the no-man's-land between scientific exactitude and intuitive hunches there stands the researcher Wilfried Krüger, whose
chief work *Das Universum singt* was published privately, as it
was too scientifically specialised for some publishers and too
mystic and speculative for others. Self-taught in the fields of
atomic physics and musical theory, Krüger has succeeded in
constructing a picture of the musical *modus operandi* of the
atomic nucleus. He returns constantly to the theme of the musical proportions governing intervals and notes, proportions which
are to be found equally in the shells of the atomic nucleus.

Thus, in a résumé, Krüger refers to the structure of the major
scale – i.e., the Gregorian Ionic mode – which can be demonstrated in the nucleus of the oxygen atom : 'The eighth atom of
the periodic table, the oxygen atom (O), *the* basis of our breathing, reacts under radiation (heating, burning) with almost all elements. Its nucleus contains eight protons. Our scale has eight
notes. The two notes at each end of the octave coincide almost
exactly, and through their oscillation-ratio create the strongest
resonance.' The 'magic numbers' (2, 8, 20, 28, 50, 82, and 126)

* Compare Bergier/Pauwels: *Aufbruch ins dritte Jahrtausend*, Bern
1961.

for whose discovery Maria Goeppert-Mayer and Hans D. Jensen received the Nobel prize for Physics in 1963, give to the atomic nucleus (e.g., in the case of oxygen, whose atomic number is 8) a special stability. An atom comprises a nucleus and a shell. The nucleus consists of protons and neutrons. The shell consists of inner and outer shells that surround the nucleus concentrically. The inner and outer shells are full of electrons. Wilfried Krüger now compared the spacings of the inner atom with those of the scale, consequently found the structures of both minor scales in the atomic nucleus and finally arrived at the following deduction in respect of the harmonic scale: 'With the harmonic minor scale we face a synthesis between the vertically-orientated forces of the inner atom and the horizontally-orientated forces binding the molecule together . . . In the case of the carbon atom (atomic number: 6) the scale can contain only six notes. The "carbon-scale" is a hexachord.'

Likewise one of the deepest secrets of the Pythagorean secret teachings, the sacred *Tetraktys*, is traced in Krüger's work to the prime elements of organic life, the nucleic acids. This *Tetraktys* comprised the four intervals of the octave, fifth, fourth and second, according to whose governing laws, under the terms of the Pythagorean teachings, the life of the world and creation itself unfolds (see illustration in Appendix, p. 220).*

These brief notes on the work of Wilfried Krüger by no means cover all aspects of his discoveries, but they do make it clear how the esoteric knowledge and intuitions of the ancients can be tied in with today's scientific method. Soon speculative hypotheses and intuitive insights alike will perhaps be seen to be based on safe scientific principles and accepted by modern music-research. Even such obscure concepts as 'objective music' or 'inner octaves', as proposed by the magician George Gurdjieff, could come to be regarded as 'proven' in terms of the harmonic series and its harmonic correspondences in the sphere of microphysics, and thus come to be seen in a completely new light:

Objective music is based solely on the 'inner octaves'. And it can produce not only definite psychological phenomena, but also definite physical phenomena. There can be music that

---

* *Das Universum singt*, Wilfried-Krüger-Selbstverlag, Trier 1974/5, 2 editions.

will freeze water. There can be music that would kill a man
stone dead. The biblical legend of the destruction of Jericho
through music is a legend of such objective music. And it can
not only destroy but also build up. In the legend of Orpheus
there are indications of objective music, for Orpheus used to
impart knowledge through music. The music of the snake-
charmers in the East is an approximation to objective music,
even if a very primitive one. Very often it is only a single
note that is extremely long-drawn-out and rises and falls but
little, but within this one note 'inner octaves' and 'inner-
octave tunes' are continually operative, inaudible to the ear
but sensed by the feeling centre.*

The long notes mentioned here are once again reminiscent of
the chanting of the Tibetan monks and the magic music of the
Mongolians. Other nature-religions too had knowledge of the
application of musical powers which never became an end in
themselves, but always a means of penetrating the esoteric laws
of nature. And they had the ability to manifest their knowledge
quite exoterically and visibly. There is a whole range of sub-
stantiated parapsychological phenomena known to have been
produced by means of sung or inwardly-spoken vibrations.

'In India there is a secret knowledge based on notes and on
the various kinds of vibration corresponding to the various
levels of consciousness ... And since each of our centres of
consciousness is directly linked with a particular one of these
levels, it is possible, via the repetition of certain sounds, to link
up with the corresponding levels of consciousness ... The fundamental notes or nuclear sounds wherein resides the power to
establish this link are called *mantra* ... They are literally vibrations or waves, rhythms that take over those of the seeker, penetrate deep within him.'†

In the absence of a knowledge of physical proportions such
thoughts are 'mere' esoteric knowledge, which many are capable
of appreciating intuitively, without being able to accept them as
experiential fact. But in the light of scientific research into ultrasound and the properties of ultrasonic tones even the legendary

* Ouspensky: tr. from *Auf der Suche nach dem Wunderbaren*,
Weilheim 1966, p. 437f.
† Prem, Sat: *Sri Aurobindo oder das Abenteuer des Bewusstseins*,
Weilheim 1973, p. 171 f.

tradition that the Egyptian pyramids were built with the aid of 'chanted spells and deep tones' seems a little less far-fetched than before.

The first European to study the magical effects of secret sounds and syllables is said to have stumbled upon these mysterious powers through personal experience with Indian mantras. On one occasion Arthur Avalon (actually Sir John Woodroffe) had to pronounce judgement between two quarrelling Indian families in his capacity as a colonial judge. Suddenly his sense of justice became confused: at one moment he found himself sympathetic to one party, then suddenly he was accepting the arguments of the other, having already rejected them the day before. Finally Avalon discovered that he had apparently been systematically manoeuvred one way or the other by both groups by means of mantras and concentrated thought. This obviously black-magic procedure led him to his deep study of the powers of mantra, to which we shall now turn.

THE MEANING OF MANTRA

In order to be able to understand the power of words and syllables spoken inwardly – *mantra*, in Sanskrit – knowledge of the ancient Greek theory of music is necessary. According to the laws of vibration and acoustic proportion, a body can be disintegrated by means of its 'own note' or basic resonance-frequency, provided that this frequency is known in the case of the body in question: 'Each organism exhibits its own vibratory rate, and so does every inanimate object from the grain of sand to the mountain and even to each planet and sun. When this rate of vibration is known, the organism or form can, by occult use of it, be disintegrated'* — or, for that matter, cognised and brought into awareness.

Thus it is the sound of the 'word', the power of song, that can establish a link with the underlying substance of all things and all beings and can react esoterically upon that of the cosmos itself. Song is a means of entering into a direct relationship with the most occult of powers. 'Singing or rhythmical speech is in the deepest sense an active conjuration, a creative act within

* Evans-Wentz: Appendix to the *Tibetan Book of the Dead*, London, 1927.

the world's acoustic foundations ... The power of song, as the first manifestation of thought, created the world, in that the sound of the primal vibration sacrificed itself so that it might become progressively transformed into an upward-spiralling rhythm of ever-higher, newly-formed vibrations, gradually to become transmuted into stone and flesh ... Not only the creation-myths of the primitive cultures, but also the cosmogonies of the high cultures of Africa and Asia refer to a dark, unfathomable sound as the mother of the creator of the worlds.'*

This primal sound, as here described by Marius Schneider, is known to Hindu mythology as *nada*. Played by the god *Brahma*, the creator of the world, on his cymbals, it was from this that the universe arose. The preserver of the world, *Vishnu*, in his incarnation as *Krishna*, plays a flute whose melody symbolises self-realisation, union with the primal sound. *Shiva*, the destroyer of worlds, plays the drum out of which fell the letters of the Sanskrit alphabet, subsequently to distribute themselves as seed-syllables about the various spiritual centres of the human body, where they now provide each of us with a means of encountering, and identifying with, a divinity. The Hindu calls these five (or seven) spiritual centres lotuses or *chakras*. They correspond physiologically to the various physical glands, and are associated esoterically with the five elements.

Each of these chakras therefore has a variety of seed-syllables corresponding to the number of the petals of the lotus in question, and it is these that are whispered by the guru into the disciple's ear as a *mantra* during initiation, arranged into various and (for the most part) secret combinations. Since every divinity to whom the Hindu prays or offers incantations as *Ishvara* (that manifestation of the divine most revered by him) has its own *mantra*, it is possible for the adept to establish through knowledge of this *mantra* a kind of wireless-communication or telepathic link with that divinity, or indeed to enter into total union with it, in the mystical sense.

'As the outer air vibrates to gross sounds, the inner, vital airs (*prana-vayu*) are set in motion and utilized by the use of the sounds of *mantras*: the Goddess first catches up the subtle occult sound, and, in tones of divine music, she causes it to ascend from her throne in the Root-Support Psychic-Centre to one after

* M. Schneider: *Singende Steine*, Kassel 1955, p. 12.

another of the Centres above, until its music fills the Lotus of a Thousand Petals and is there heard and responded to by the Supreme *Guru*. ... Unless the mantras are properly intoned they are without effect; and when printed and seen by the eye of the uninitiated they appear utterly meaningless – and so they are, without the guidance of the human guru. Furthermore, the correct pronunciation of the *mantra* of a deity depends upon bodily purity as well as upon knowledge of its proper intonation. Therefore it is necessary for the devotee first to purify, by purificatory *mantras*, the mouth, the tongue, and then the *mantra* itself, by a process called giving life to or awakening the sleeping power of the *mantra*.'*

This text from the *Tibetan Book of the Dead* reveals how carefully the disciples and initiates have to prepare themselves to perform *mantra-yoga*. Wherever the esoteric knowledge of the inner words has been preserved it has been kept secret as the hidden power of sound or vibration, as the creative germ of all existence. Throughout the ages the secret was well-known to the Masters – to the ancient Hindu *rishis* (seers), living alone in the foothills of the Himalayas, to the Sufis of Persia, to the Adepts of Zoroastrianism, to the priests of the Egyptian pyramids, to the voodoo-magicians and medicine-men of Africa and South America.

They knew then, and still know, that the mantric syllables and words, whether sung or inwardly recited, bring about a subtle inner process that gradually awakens the invisible centres (*chakras*) and leads them to deeper dimensions of their consciousness.

The essence of all beings is earth,
the essence of earth is water,
the essence of water is plants,
the essence of plants is man,
the essence of man is speech,
the essence of speech is the Holy Knowledge (Veda),
the essence of Veda is Sama-Veda (word, tone, sound),
the essence of Sama-Veda is OM.

Chandogya Upanishad

* Evans-Wentz: Appendix to the *Tibetan Book of the Dead*, London, 1927.

The most important mantra in the whole of Asia is OM. It corresponds to our AMEN, the AMIN of the Moslems, the Logos, the Word. In the Upanishads OM is divided into its phonetic components, whereby the O is seen as a combination of A and U, so that OM actually represents AUM. If we pronounce AUM slowly it becomes clear that we open the mouth wide with the sound A, gradually reduce the size of the mouth-cavity to produce the U, and finally close it with the M. Consequently the AUM embraces in a quite practical and concrete sense the whole frequency-range used in human speech.

Lama Govinda is the greatest of experts on Asian mantras, and through his Western origins and spiritual training, he is in a position to interpret for Western man the whole Buddhist tradition, and in particular the deep meaning of *mantra*. In his book *Foundations of Tibetan Mysticism*, which is the primary source for this discussion, Govinda writes: 'Since OM is an expression of the highest consciousness, the three elements A, U and M are explained as three degrees of consciousness – A as waking consciousness, U as dream consciousness and M as the consciousness of deep sleep – while OM as a whole is the all-embracing "cosmic" or "fourth" consciousness which transcends all words, the consciousness of the fourth dimension. In other words, the subjective consciousness of the outer world, the consciousness of our own inner world (i.e., of the thoughts and feelings, wishes and desires that we call our mental consciousness) and the consciousness of undifferentiated Oneness, at repose in itself, are no longer split into subject and object.'*

A *mantra* is spoken inwardly, generally not even whispered. It is visualised as lying literally in a particular inner centre – as a flame, as a white dot, as the Sanskrit sign for OM. Thus visualised, this sound is gradually listened to inwardly and then shifted (for example) from the heart to the forehead or through all the centres in turn. Arthur Avalon describes the various states of the yogi as, after years of practising the inward speaking of a *mantra*, the psychic centres start to open: 'With (the opening of) the third centre one is able partially to remember vague astral excursions, sometimes with a half-conscious memory of flying through the air in blissful delight. With the fourth centre the person becomes instinctively aware of the joys and cares of

* Govinda: tr. from *Grundlagen Tibetischer Mystik*, Munich 1972, p. 11.

his fellow-men, at times experiencing in his own body their physical pains and sorrows.

'With the awakening of the fifth centre he hears voices that bring all kinds of influences to bear on him. Often he hears music or other, less pleasant sounds. Full unfolding leads to clairaudience on the astral planes. The awakening of the sixth centre confers experiences such as half-perceived landscapes and clouds of different colours. When one can bring the pituitary gland into full play, it becomes a bridge to the astral vehicle. The awakening of the seventh centre enables one to leave the body while fully conscious.'*

Personal reports by adepts in *mantra-yoga* continually refer to musical sound like that of cymbals. They see flames that seem to unfold like psychic emanations and the sounds of letters that in the visualisations are tinted in various colours. The *chakras*, which all have their own particular colour, can be brought into communication with various other centres by means of seed-syllables of that same colour.

Syllables and Words

In the case of the mantric symbolic syllables, the minutest vibrations of a sound are of enormous importance. The power of a *mantra* , of whatever materiality or purpose, is intimately bound up with the state of consciousness of its performer. A *mantra* is not a sound-wave phenomenon of the physical sort and has no effect if it is performed by one who is ignorant. True, a *mantra* can be accompanied by a physical sound, but its power is spiritual and cannot be perceived by the outward ear, even if it is perceptible to the heart. Thus the *mantra* is not actually uttered by the mouth but by the spirit, and consequently it has significance only for the instructed initiate.

In Japan a person praying to the Buddha and desiring to become more at one with him says: *gya te gya te hara gya te hara so gya te bo dhi so wa ka*, which in translation means roughly: 'Thou who hast passed, passed over to the other shore, honour be to Thee'. And the Tibetan Buddhist venerates the Enlightened One with: *thayata om muni muni maha muniye svaha*, which means roughly: 'Thou who hast achieved realisation, Silent One, Silent One, Great Silent One, hail to Thee.' The worshipper of

* Avalon: tr. from *Die Schlangenkraft*, p. 13.

the female bodhisattva *Tara*, the merciful protectress of the
Tibetans, inwardly pronounces *om tare tutare ture svaha*. But
many other *mantras* are secret and would never be handed on
to a Westerner. It is quite possible that many *mantras*, for example those of the Tibetan oracle-priests, have never been spoken
aloud or heard by the world at all.

The most celebrated *mantras* of the Hindus, on the other hand,
are also familiar as religious chants and are thus not kept secret
but are often recited for hours and days on end in the Hindu
ashrams. This technique is called *Japa-Yoga*, and one of its best-
known *mantras* begins *hare krishna hare krishna krishna krishna
hare hare hare rama hare rama*. *Hare* or *hari* is the equivalent
of 'Most High', or 'Great God', while *krishna* and *rama* are
Hindu deities. The praises of the divine prince Rama, whose
name derives from the seed-syllable RAM of the heart-centre,
are also sung in the form of the chant *sri ram jai ram jai ram*
(see Musical Example No. 3).

Another important *mantra* peculiar to Hinduism is *hong-so*
(otherwise pronounced *hang-sa*). It is spoken with a nasalisation;
the sound *hang* during the inbreath (also nasalised as *han* or *ham*)
and the sound *sa* (or *so*) during the outbreath. This *mantra* takes
a different form in every yoga-school; Yogananda taught the
form *hong-so*, Sivananda *ham-sa*, and so on. Among the Hindus
what matters is not the 'right 'or 'wrong' form, but the form
which one has received personally from one's *guru*.

A further *mantra*-formula commonly used by Hindus, especially in southern India, to preface every performance, and
whose musical form, intoned for hours at a time, often serves as
a melodic basis for the *alap*, is *hari om tat sat*. One of the greatest
of Indian singers, Bade Ghulam Ali Khan, used to sing this
mantra so uniquely and devotionally – despite the fact that he
was a Muslim – that the whole congregation (it is alleged) used
to weep. *Tat sat* means roughly 'It is so'; in its figurative sense
one could also translate it to mean, 'The Absolute exists in being
so.' *Sat*-gurus are holy-men who are simply 'so', i.e., at one with
all things.

Finally, *tat tvam asi* is a mantric formula that has likewise
been translated and interpreted by many mystics, even in the
West – for example, Bô Yin Râ's 'Thou art that', or 'That is
yourself', which amounts to saying: 'In yourself also resides the

All Highest.' Another *mantra* was brought to the West by Hazrat Inayat Khan, the *Murshid* (Master) of an order of Sufis – the syllable HU, which has enormous significance for many groups of mystics. The Masters of *Eckankar* teach their pupils ceaselessly to repeat the syllable HU inwardly and soundlessly, in other words in their minds. The author's most vivid impression of a mantra intoned aloud occurred when, at the entry of the holy-woman Ananda Mayi Ma into a giant tent near Calcutta, some five hundred women raised a polyphonic chant consisting solely of the syllable HU.

As was mentioned at the beginning, the seed-syllables of the *mantras*, and some of the *mantra*-sounds themselves, belong to the Sanskrit alphabet. Each letter is assigned to an inner lotus-centre, and according to the number of petals in the lotus, an equivalent number of letters is assigned to it.

This raises the question as to whether only Sanskrit has such a meaning. Is there no similar concept within our own cultural sphere, touching the deep secret of speech as such? There are indeed many such instances, for example, in the Greek or Hebrew alphabets, albeit in veiled or secret form. Thus in the Qabalah each letter has a given numerical value, and in a number of Western mystic orders the Greek alphabet has also been construed in various ways. Let us consider, for example, our own vowels, A E I O U. As is explained in more detail later (p. 125), each vowel opens a particular part of the human body when imagined during the inbreath and spoken inwardly. This 'opening' by means of the vowels is to be understood quite concretely, in the sense that the breath penetrates more or less deeply into the region concerned. The U fills the lower regions of the body, the I the uppermost regions and so on. But the breath also takes with it the subtle *prana*, the spiritual breath which the Greek initiates called *pneuma*, the breath of God. The whole of a region filled with *pneuma* could thus be seen as a manifestation of the Divine.

Hence it is by no means so irrelevant that the Graeco-Egyptian papyri should speak of the ruler of the gods, the king Adonai, as 'Lord I – A – O – U – E – Ae', or refer to the 'Eye of the World I–E–O–U–E–Y'. And when we investigate the composition of the Jewish name of God, *Jehovah*, we find that it is likewise based on the vowels 'I – E – O – U – A'. While the Hebrew script indicates these 'most secret' letters only by means of dots, they are none the less often to be found in our own Christian mythology, in those codified symbols that serve as vehicles for its wisdom. Christ said : 'I am Alpha and Omega.' This means : the beginning and the end, and thus the whole alphabet, i.e., Lord of heaven and earth.

On the subject of mantric exercises Karl Weinfurter writes : 'As elements of speech the letters are the simplest of concepts, the basis not only of speech but also of thought, and if with the aid of our thoughts and imagination we can suffuse our whole body first with the vowels and then with the consonants we teach its every fibre and cell to speak with the spirit. And here I come to the most important secret of these exercises, namely that one must *begin with the feet*. Man is linked with the higher worlds not via his head but via his feet. We know for a fact that a person dying of natural causes first loses all sense of feeling in his feet and all control over them. The same happens when the astral body leaves the physical body, for then, too, everybody feels the feet stiffen first.'*

From these statements it is quite apparent that the practical use of *mantra* is known even in the West, especially in initiated mystic circles. That is how one of the oldest *mantras* of Egyptian origin has survived, using only the vowels of our (German) language :

A

E E

Ae Ae Ae

I   I   I   I

O O O O

U U U U U U U

Nevertheless only a true initiate would have the key to such a tradition, having himself received every last detail of its pronunciation from a Master who belongs to a school of the greatest antiquity. These schools exist in the East *and* the West. It is merely that, on account of the general materialistic climate of the West, they are even *more* secret here than in the East.

Even the Christian tradition possesses a considerable *mantra* tradition, but unfortunately this is disappearing more and more

* Weinfurter : *Der Brennende Dornbursch*, Lorch-Württemberg, 1962, p. 108 f.

from current religious practice through being mistakenly regarded as a form of 'mumbo-jumbo'. One needs only to consider the Catholic Marian devotions with their long intercessions, the use of the rosary – which helps to induce very powerful meditative states – or the litanies with their continually recurring phrase: 'Good Lord, hear us'. In the case of monastic chanting, too, the psychological effect depends not only on the suprapersonal, contemplative power of the old church modes, but also on the fact that there is no fixed rhythm and therefore the chanting follows the natural rhythm of the Latin spoken word.

The impersonal nature of these chants, which admit of no individual feelings or personal styles of composition, is particularly suited to the Holy Office and the Holy Mass, devoted as it is to proclaiming the word of God, and not that of man. Many Gregorian chants end with an elaborate, several-minute-long AMEN. And there are also medieval chants, especially those of the blessed Hildegard von Bingen (1098–1179), which conclude an antiphon with a kind of Christian *mantra* consisting purely of vowels. There can be no doubt that these groups of vocalic seed-syllables derive from a pre-Christian gnostic school (see Example No. 4). Since the influence of particular sequences of linguistic sounds is a significant means of communication with the soul, the relics of this ancient knowledge can be detected in all religious chants and liturgies. In the West such secrets are clearly passing into oblivion, and are being handed on purely as rules and rituals without any realisation of their deeper content.

In the East the tradition of the inward speaking and simultaneous outward recitation of a *mantra* is still alive, but it is being overshadowed, often being degraded, in its commercial caricatures, into a form of superstition. And where a cult is pursued solely as a form of outward ritual the power of *mantra* is totally lost. On the other hand a person trying to attain higher forms of inner vision purely through the physically audible sound, unwittingly becomes, as Bô Yin Râ has warned, 'merely the most effective of collaborators with all the "hostile" or, as it were, poisonous powers of the invisible physical world, and the imagined flashes of realisation, however lofty they may seem, are nothing but self-produced phantasmagoria with no relation to reality.'*

Bô Yin Râ also warns the Westerner to speak *only* inwardly

* Bô Yin Râ: *Mantrapraxis*, Zürich 1967, p. 37 f.

during the practice of a *mantra*, and to avoid completely even the slightest murmuring or movement of the lips. Where the influence of the inwardly-spoken word is to be used for the moulding and self-experience of the soul, no strain, not even the slightest moral self-coercion should be applied. Lama Govinda, too, makes it clear in the following observations on the subject of the OM, that a *mantra* is more than a mere fashionable piece of merchandise – more, too, than just a mechanical technique: 'The sound of the syllable OM opens a person's innermost being to the vibrations of a higher Reality. OM is a means of tearing down the walls of our ego. OM is the original, deep note of time-less Reality which thrills through us out of a beginningless past, and whose sound comes to meet us when we have developed our sense of inner hearing through stilling of the mind. This transcendental sound is like an opening of the arms to embrace everything that lives, when it is spoken in the heart of one who is truly striving in devout faith. It is an expression not of self-aggrandisement or of self-expansion, but of acceptance and sacrifice ... Giving and taking at the same time: a taking that is free of desire, and a giving that does not attempt to impose its will on others.'*

Since northern Buddhism possesses one of the most vigorous mantric traditions, it is appropriate to mention here the links with some of the other spiritual aids whereby the Mahayana-Buddhist adds realism to his perception. In addition to the *mantras*, his tools are the *mudras* and the geometric *mandalas* (known as *yantra*). The latter, a visual starting-point for meditation, are circular cosmological paintings which are inwardly visualised as archetypal symbols. The physical gestures (*mudras*) accompany ritual performances and reflect the worshipper's inner disposition; arms, posture and finger-positions combine quite specific inner energy-currents and serve as outward signs of the inner contemplation. Now the holy sounds (*mantras*) which are imparted to the pupil by his guru bring his inner being into the correct state of vibration and potentialise the inner experience. Through what the Buddhist calls the *tantric* co-operation of all three – mind, body and speech – the adept can build up his spiritual vision bit by bit. *Tantra* means roughly 'weaving' or 'thread', as well as 'interwoven-ness'.

* Govinda: tr. from *Grundlagen Tibetischer Mystik*, p. 45 f.

As cults of actual physical union, the old Hindu tantric rites have nothing to do with the Buddhist concept of the union of masculine and feminine in the sense of resolving the principle of duality, a form of self-realisation in which there is 'no understanding without feeling, no knowledge without love, no perception without compassion, but the synthesis of heart and head, feeling and understanding, highest love and deepest perception' (Govinda). Enlightenment thus finds its symbol in the most universal and also the most human of activities – the union of lovers.

Finally, let Lama Govinda's words re-express the deep meaning of the most celebrated mantra of Tibetan Buddhism, *om mani padme hum hrih* (pronounced 'om mani peme hung hri'):

> OM is the ascent to the All, HUM the descent of the All into the depths of the heart. HUM is the middle way that loses itself neither in the finite nor in the infinite, commits itself to no extreme ... In the OM we open ourselves, in HUM we surrender ourselves. OM is the gate of knowledge, HUM the gate of living manifestation ... The syllable HUM consists of a breath consonant, a long vowel and the resonating final consonant, which in Sanskrit approximates to a nasal 'ng'. The breath consonant is the sound of breathing, the quintessence of all that lives, the sound of *prana*, the breath of life; the life-force flowing in and out, and bound up with all things (Atman). The vowel-sound U is the sound of those depths that pass over into the inaudible. U is the lower limit of the scale of human voice-sounds, the threshold of silence or, as it is called in Tibetan, 'the gate to the inaudible'.

> OM   mystery of the universal body – the All-experience.
> MANI   the illuminating power of the immortal spirit, awakener of the soul-consciousness, of vision and inspiration.
> PADME   mystery of the all-transforming spirit, unfolding in the lotuses of the centres of consciousness.
> HUM   synthesis, integration, manifestation.
> HRIH   is the inner voice, the intuitive and spontaneous 'knowing better'. It possesses the heat of the sun – is itself a mantric sun-symbol, a light, upward-striving sound made up of the pranic breath-

consonant H, the fiery R (as in RAM, the seed-syllable of fire) and the high I-sound, which expresses upward movement and intensity.

All these associations with light and fire in the universal sphere are linked with *Amitabha*, the Buddha of eternal light, to whom the element fire, the colour red and the direction of the setting sun are dedicated, while the ideal and emotional associations in the human sphere refer to *Avalokitesvara*.*

This *Amitabha Buddha* is revered in Japan as *Amida*, and whoever in faith or knowledge has kept the *mantra* '*namu amida butsu*' on his lips and in his heart his whole life long, and who dies in union with him, is reborn in the *shukavati* heaven, the 'Western Paradise'.†

THE HUMAN ORGANISM AND ITS ACOUSTIC LAWS

In the course of my description of how the basic intervals of the harmonic series (octave, fifth and fourth) can be arrived at with the aid of the monochord, it became clear that our ear can tell exactly when a string is correctly divided according to the simplest mathematical ratios. These proportions are physically rooted in us via our sense of hearing and are thus a natural phenomenon. In fact our ear is so designed that it actually 'corrects' its hearing of inexact intervals. How often I have sat down at out-of-tune pianos, both grand and upright, and winced at the first notes as I pressed the keys; nevertheless, after playing the simplest pentatonic chords for a while, I have found that from the moment when I started to enjoy the music my ear started to correct the inaccuracies. My listeners too, as they adjusted themselves inwardly to these out-of-tune sounds, experienced this odd phenomenon, with all the intervals suddenly seeming to be in tune. Only when the piece came to an end, and I took off my musician's hat, so to speak, did the out-of-tune sounds once again become apparent and unpleasant to hear.

Even a piano that is in tune is of course not 'perfectly tuned', but equally-tempered – i.e., the octave is divided into twelve equal semitones according to the method devised by Andreas

---

* Govinda : tr. from *Grundlagen Tibetischer Mystik*, p. 148 ff., 276 ff.
† Compare D. T. Suzuki : *Amida – der Buddha der Liebe*, Munich 1974.

Werkmeister in the 15th century in order to make it possible to play on keyboard instruments the polyphonic music that was then coming into vogue, with its chords and modulations.

The champions of tempered tuning invoke the 'tolerance' of the ear to support their argument, maintaining that it perceives small variations within a certain pitch-range as 'properly-tuned' notes, and is no longer capable of distinguishing or identifying quarter-tone sequences as intervals at all.* To this it may be objected that a musician engaged in playing unison/melodic or modal/harmonic music, which relates to a *single* keynote, *immediately* perceives any lack of tuning in the piano. The Indian singer Pandit Patekar found he was unable to sing his Raga Bhairavi (corresponding to the Phrygian mode) when accompanied purely in fourths and fifths on a newly-tuned grand piano. 'They are not in tune!' he kept saying. For chromatic or dodecaphonic music, however, tempering is essential, even though it compromises the music's consonance. The criterion for consonance is the degree to which the harmonic overtones accord with the notes of any given chord struck. As a result of the equal-tuning of the intervals under the tempered system there are no longer any pure harmonic relationships. We get by only because our ear is prepared to reconstitute the natural order of things. Indeed, the ancients already knew that the inner man possesses all the proportions as a primal creative force. Octave, fifth and fourth were held by the Byzantines to be 'spiritual sounds', *pneumata*, while the intervals of the third and fourth octaves of the harmonic series, i.e., the seconds and thirds, were called *somata*, bodily sounds. This is also the source of the theory that 'spiritual' music can in fact contain only fourths and fifths, whereas 'worldly' music, for its part, can have thirds and seconds as well. And in the Middle Ages this was indeed the chief difference between church and folk music.

The original musical ratios $\frac{1}{2}$, $\frac{2}{3}$, $\frac{3}{4}$ etc. were discovered throughout nature. And it was one of the most important achievements of the astronomer and astrologer Kepler to show the correspondences between these intervals and the spacings of the planets. Kepler deduced from this that the musical proportions must be inborn in the human soul, a notion reminiscent of C. G. Jung's archetypes of the collective unconscious. Kepler

* Compare M. and W. Keyserling : *Das Rosenkreuz*, Vienna 1956.

takes the view that, thanks to the primal relationships which are native to it, the soul reacts *spontaneously* to external harmonic manifestations.

Present-day study of these correspondences between man, the planetary cycles and note-relationships is a razor-edged path between intuition and exact science. Among other things, Thomas Michael Schmidt, who like Wilfried Krüger is pursuing this path, shows in his book *Musik und Kosmos als Schöpfungswunder* (published privately) the proportional correspondences in man himself. Our body is subdivided in the vertical by various significant points such as leg-sockets, navel, nipples, arm-sockets etc. A subdivision is also apparent in the proportions of the limbs, and specifically in terms of the positions of the joints. If the lengths of these subdivisions of the body or of individual limbs are now compared with each other or with the body's total height, T. M. Schmidt's researches show that the resulting proportions are precisely those with which we became familiar during our work on the monochord.

In a person 172 cm. high, for example, the navel lies at a height of 103 cm. The two measurements stand almost exactly in the ratio 5:3, the Golden Mean, corresponding to the interval of the sixth. The height of the body is related to the height of the nipples as 4:3, i.e., in the proportion of the fourth. The fifth is expressed more or less by the position of the navel, inasmuch as the height of the navel, expressed as a proportion of the distance from the navel to the crown of the head, is as 3:2. A further proportion corresponding to the fourth is expressed by the height of the arm-socket, which is related to that of the navel as 4:3. The inner side of the forearm including the palm likewise expresses the ratio of the fifth, 3:2, when compared with the length of the forearm without the hand.

'Furthermore the listed proportions of the human body correspond to the mathematical relationships between the planetary cycles. If the nipples divide the body roughly in the ratio 4:3, this corresponds not only to the musical fourth, but also to the relationship between the synodic periods of Mars and Venus. For every proportion of the human body that has a musical counterpart, a corresponding relationship between two or three planetary cycles can be demonstrated.

'Thus the two supposedly unconnected worlds of sound and

planetary motion also find in the human body a direct, visible expression. Here the links between man and cosmos are the musical ratios, which thus represent in the truest sense of the term a principle of universal order.'*

Other proportions of the human body concern man's inner organs, the physiological glands and their 'underlying' *chakras.* Here we find the most mysterious correspondences – correspondences which must already have been known, empirically at least, to the Mongolian shamans and Tibetan lamas with their strange chants.

In this connection we should also mention briefly the correspondences between sound and light. It is not merely that an optical term was chosen to designate the whole natural harmonic series – *spectral* harmonics and the overtone-*spectrum* : the colours of the spectrum also stand in a causative relationship to the harmonic spectrum. Already among the alchemists a given colour was assigned to each planet, in early Indian music each interval of the scale has a given colour assigned to it, and the ragas also 'colour' the mind, as we noted earlier. From the cabbalistic point of view Jacob's ladder in the Old Testament is a symbol of the seven-coloured rainbow, or a 'prismatic staircase' whose seven steps are, once again, identical to the seven notes. A memory of this unity of sound and light in antiquity is to be found today in the harmonic research of Hans Kayser, who also refers to 'colour-hearing', a form of synaesthesia, which he calls *audition colorée.*

Analogies between Man and the World of Sounds

The correspondences between man's most important proportions and the world of sound are of prime relevance to the arrangement of the glands controlling the inner secretions and of the *chakras* that lie behind them. This analogy can be seen in terms of the connection between the vowels and the natural harmonic series. If we are in the process of learning to sing the overtones of a bass-note, or listening to this process, we can hear exactly how the jump from note to note, the rise and fall of the overtones, is dependent upon the vowel sung, or rather upon the mouth-position that forms or produces such a vowel.

* Th. M. Schmidt: *Musik und Kosmos als Schöpfungswunder,* Frankfurt 1974 (privately published), p. 230 ff.

What is involved here is the gradual transition from one vowel to another – for example from A, via O to U. If we gradually adjust the position of the mouth-cavity from A to U, and are able, by means of a guttural pressure and mental concentration, to bring the second voice, the 'overtone-voice' into play, we can hear quite clearly how the formant-spectrum descends from the seventh overtone to the second. And if we start to form higher harmonics still, we succeed in doing so only if we adjust the shape of the mouth to another, 'higher' vowel.

From my own researches, from Mongolian gramophone-records, from meetings with Tibetan lamas and also from the experiences of the spiritual vocal group *prima materia* it is clear that the gradual transition from the lower to the higher overtones corresponds to the process of vowel-formation leading from U(OO), via O, A and E to I(EE). If, for example, one intones at length a note of middle pitch and at the same time forms the vowel A with exaggerated clarity, while opening the mouth right back to the pharynx, one is able to emphasise a particular overtone – the seventh, for example. If one now decreases the size of the mouth-cavity by the subtlest of movements until the vowel O is produced, the prominent overtone immediately descends to the sixth and fifth positions. The further one adjusts the mouth position in the direction of U (OO), the sooner the octave and fifth, i.e., the first natural harmonics, will sound alongside the bass-note. If one now alters the position of the mouth to an exaggerated E (EH), stretching the lips wide, the higher overtones will automatically sound at the same time. With this nasal singing technique one can produce, let us say from the bass-note C, at least eight or nine overtones in the 'second voice'. There is thus a correspondence between the overtones, the mathematical ratios $2:1$, $3:1$, $4:1$ and so on, and the vowel-sequence U, O, A, E, I.

A further correspondence between the individual vowels and the parts of the body can be demonstrated experimentally. By imagining the inward speaking of the vowels one opens quite specific inner regions of the body to the breath, i.e., it is with the help of inward vowel-formulations that the breath penetrates the most varied zones of the body for the first time. In the various breathing-schools, above all that of Professor Middendorf in Berlin, mutually confirmatory experiments have been carried out to determine which zones of the body can be 'opened' by which vowels. The 'motion' which a vowel causes to be felt has also been investigated; thus, for example, the sound E (EH) produces an outward 'motion', while O produces an inward one, and so on. Although in breathing work this knowledge is never mentioned initially, in order to make it possible for the pupil or patient to achieve his or her own involuntary self-experience, the different correspondences between the vowels and the breath-cavities are here represented purely schematically:

Head cavity	I
Throat and upper chest (but also the sides)	E
Chest cavity (but also the body as a whole)	A
Abdomen (as far as the navel)	O
Pelvis and lower body	U

At this point the step to an even more comprehensive analogy between harmonic ratios, vowels and the various parts of the body can be undertaken with the help of our knowledge of the inner centres. The *muladhara* chakra has its seat by the sex-organs and corresponds esoterically to the element Earth. The second centre, *svadisthana*, has its seat near the suprarenal glands, which regulate the body's water/mineral levels and correspond to the element Water. The *manipura* lotus has its seat in the solar plexus, near the pancreas, which regulates digestion and combustion and corresponds esoterically to the element Fire. The chest-centre, at the level of the heart, is the *anahata* chakra, sited near the thymus-gland and associated with the element Air. The lotus of the throat region, in the area of the thyroid gland, is called *vishuddha* and is associated with the element Ether. The forehead chakra between the eyebrows, the 'third eye', is the *ajna* chakra, which is connected with the pineal gland. Finally the thousand-petalled lotus, the *sahasrara* chakra at the back of the head, corresponds to the pituitary gland at the base of the mid-brain. Since the vowels which are themselves associated with given parts of the body correspond to the harmonic series, it seems reasonable to assume that the bodily proportions between their associated inner centres also reflect the harmonic series. The relationship between the basic vowels, the breath cavities and the associated psychic centres also has a bearing on the fact that the chakras are 'awakened' by vocalic seed-syllables; and that the spacings of the overtones corresponding to inner body-cavities become smaller and smaller, to the point where countless micro-intervals are contained within the space of a single tone, just like the countless petals of the topmost lotus in the *sahasrara* centre.

In this light one can then also start to understand the secret of the unfathomably deep singing of the Tibetan lamas and their mantric formulae, to which a particular overtone is assigned, just like a given inner centre which its associated deity, or a *mudra*, a gesture which can make contact for inner currents to flow between the centres. Production of the overtones through the mouth-positions consequent upon particular vowels, and con-centration on the body regions corresponding to those vowels, can permit, even for Western adepts, the tangible experience of an inner awakening of the psychic centres.

The visible signs of this primal human power are the simplest numerical fractions: $\frac{1}{2}$, $\frac{1}{3}$, $\frac{1}{4}$, etc., or, expressed as ratios, $2:1$, $3:2$, $4:3$, $5:4$ and so on, each of which has its audible equivalent in the harmonic series. We can listen to our own bass-note, which contains within itself not only all notes but all 'dissonances'. If the primal, archaic music of the belly used only the octave, but at the same time was unconsciously aware of all the notes within it; if mythical music emphasised the fourth and the fifth as the polar intervals for modal melodic-music; and if the nascent dualism of the mental consciousness conferred upon the two intervals of the third that appertain to the centre of feeling the distinction between major and minor, then human consciousness, as it ascended to the next centre, would now be able to make a further discovery – the emancipation of dis-sonance, of whole and half tones, out of which a twelve-tone music could be created.

The next step would now seem to be a musical integration of the long-buried, dormant and forgotten fundamental notes, the 'spiritual' intervals of fifth and fourth, the modal scales, the duality of major and minor and the twelve-tone concept. The vehicle for this integration is *tone-colour*, which is deeply rooted spiritually in the primal nature of music. Let us listen to the tone-colour of our own fundamental note, which bears all notes within it, even the 'dissonances' of the 'mental' head-regions which, for all that, must then resonate in harmony.

TONE-COLOUR AS THE VEHICLE OF THE SPIRITUAL

An Armenian folk legend describes the process of 'listening to one's own note' in humorous form: 'A man had a cello with one string, which he used to bow for hours on end, always holding his finger at the same place on the string. For seven months his wife put up with the noise, in the patient expectation that her husband would either die of boredom or smash the instrument. But since neither happened she gently said one evening (if one is to believe it): "I have noticed that when others play this wonderful instrument it has four strings for bowing, and the players keep moving their fingers up and down."

'The husband stopped playing for a moment, fixed a wise old eye on his wife, shook his head and said: "You are a woman, long of hair and short of understanding. Of course the others move their fingers up and down. They are looking for the right place. I have found it." '*

Anybody who has become aware of the special tone-colour spectrum of a single note, or who has even detected isolated overtones within a note, will keep trying to rediscover this natural phenomenon when listening to music. And in the process it will quickly become clear to him that some forms of music positively set out to make the tone-colours audible, while others encourage no such acoustic procedure. Thus the mythical, melodic music of India, the heterophonic music of Indonesia, the modal music of Arabia and the Middle Ages, as well as the rhythmic drum music of Africa, is all tone-colour music to the extent that it makes the harmonic series audible. And the experience of tone-colour listening always had the purpose, as it still has today in works such as Bartók's, of producing an inner, spiritual, sympathetic resonance. Even today it is held in India, for example, that correct inner listening is a condition of the performer's inspiration. Yet tone-colour as such does not merely refer to a reaction in the listener, but is itself an important aspect of style and form, even in Western music. The history of tone-colour is as yet unwritten. For some years the music and art historian Gerhard Nestler has been looking into this subject, how-

---

* Quoted by Stege in *Musik, Magie, Mystik*.

ever, and it is he whom we have to thank for the following brief
résumé :

> The tone-colour epochs characterised by ancient single-line
> melodic music, by polyphonic music and by the re-discovery
> of tone-colour in our own century, stand in clear contrast
> to each other. Yet each is unthinkable without its predecessor,
> and their succession is irreversible.
>
> But even within the larger epochs themselves we may dis-
> cern subdivisions associated with partial aspects of cultures and
> nations. For example, when Greek music gives up the unity
> of music, dance and speech in favour of a purely virtuoso
> music; or when the unison/melodic music of early Christianity
> acquires an architecture based on tone-colour classification,
> as in the case of the Sequence, the Lauda and Cantica; or
> when in early polyphonic music, by contrast with the acoustic
> clarity of Organum and Conductus, superimposed layers of
> tone-colour result from the use of different texts, or indeed
> of different languages (Motet), in order to permit phonetic
> sound-effects in line with contemporary Irish poetry
> (*Hesperica Famina*) and the Irish miniaturists' 'aesthetics of the
> confused and labyrinthine'.
>
> Of even more significance, naturally, is the change of tone-
> colour at the interstices of the main epochs. When, in early
> polyphony, a new sound arose in the new sphere of archi-
> tectonic acoustics as a result of the enrichment of earlier tone-
> colours, a miracle had occurred.
>
> After the prologue of Romanticism, the re-discovery of tone-
> colour in our own century needs to be seen in the same light.
> The incorporation of 'white noise' makes tone-colour uni-
> versal for the first time. At the same time the spiritual acoustic
> sphere is being opened up to a hitherto unimagined extent.
> Unison/melodic music of indeterminate pitch, with its wide
> range of micro-intervals, has a broader expressive basis than
> polyphonic music organised in terms of pitches and intervals.[*]

Early in this present century, Ferrucio Busoni anticipated
in his *Entwurf einer neuen Aesthetik der Tonkunst* something
of the new tone-colour music. Arnold Schönberg longed for tone-
colour melodies; Maurice Ravel and Claude Debussy wrote a kind

---

[*] Introduction kindly placed at my disposal by G. Nestler.

of music devoted exclusively to making tone-colours audible, rather than to melodic or harmonic procedures. The new music of the 'cluster technique' is orientated primarily towards the tone-colours of particular instrumentations, and our ability to produce sounds electronically in any case means a tone-colour renaissance. The very fact that avant-garde and experimental representatives of contemporary music are delving into the non-European cultural traditions has its origin in the prominent place given to tone-colour in those musical cultures.

The attempts to combine European and Asian music with a view to *musical meditation*, the American *periodic* and *minimal music* of composers such as Terry Riley and Steve Reich, or indeed my own compositions, all of which seek to attain an 'integral' state of listening, are possible only through the re-discovery of tone-colour as the vehicle of the spiritual. In fact tone-colour permits certain specific *effects* on the listener. If used correctly, music can heal, remove anxiety and bring re-laxation through the linking of the inner tone-colour zones, i.e, the relative proportions of the 'upper sounds' of a harmonic series, with the corresponding parts of the body and of the inner man.

Through the use of tone-colour, present-day music is once more achieving capabilities that were always familiar to the non-European cultures – those of precipitating an encounter with the collective unconscious and achieving spiritual effects through prolonged chants, periodic rhythms and primal melodic patterns. The suggestive powers of musical resonances are always due to tone-colour. But any new tone-colour music should beware of relapsing into the magical and mythical modes of consciousness. Rather should the latter be consciously recognised, familiarity be gained with their psychosomatic *modus operandi*, and a musical integration be attained through their assimilation into one's own mental consciousness.

'This new music demands "pure listening", i.e., a form of listening which is free from all the old accustomed intellectual and emotional ingredients. It is in this pure hearing of the sound and of its shape that the strong stimulatory power of this music lies. Tone-colour music is the most musical of music, because it is the music of the elemental nature of sound.'*

To the extent that we make ourselves aware of the shamanis-

* Nestler: *Die Form in der Musik*, Zürich 1954 (conclusion).

tic, magical powers of both monotone and rhythm, and grasp the *modus operandi* of the modal scales and chants, with all their harmonic riches, by analogy with the inner man, we could create a form of music founded on basic tonalities, and yet which respects, even within the twelve-tone concept, the harmonic relationships which arise, for their part, from the resulting vertical groupings.

The modal harmonies of such as Olivier Messiaen already point in this direction, but then so do the intuitive improvisations of such as John Coltrane. His periodic figures with their mythical undertones of modal scales are on this same path – *minimal music* – which owes its inspiration partly to magical Africa. Ever since the end of the sixties there have been widespread efforts to bring back into the limelight music's inner powers, as opposed to its intellectual aspects. The result has been meditative, intuitive, spiritual, concentric, periodic, or integral music.

All these initiatives, which we shall be discussing later, are milestones on the road towards musical integration. But at present they find themselves 'between the worlds' – between East and West, between mystic intimation and intellectual rationalism, between magical fascination and technical construction, between intuition and reason.

4 Music Between the Worlds

For an Indian or Arab Sufi, a Hindu mystic or a Buddhist monk it is a foregone conclusion that music, when directed towards God or the Divine, affords the greatest and deepest power of human expression.*

The successors of Inayat Khan's Sufi school, his son Pir Vilayat Khan and his grandson Fazhal Khan, similarly lay great stress on meditative self-realisation through personal music-making, and especially through singing. Their various groups have taken it upon themselves to have the old, mystic instruments of Persia and India reproduced from old drawings and remains, and to distribute them in the West. The very tuning of the various stringed instruments can serve as a spiritual exercise: it concentrates the human mind on the correct consonance of the overtones and thus on one's own inner harmonic attunement.

In many schools – some secret, some misunderstood – the knowledge of the meditative power of music has always existed, and there are plenty of cabbalistic, gnostic and Rosicrucian schools that possess an unbroken, and for the most part secret, tradition. It is interesting to observe just when meditative music came into the forefront of public musical interest and via what musical forms. The search for the origins of the new, meditative methods of performance leads us back to the fathers of the Jazz of the sixties.

* Compare the extract from Hazrat Inayat Khan's *The Sufi Message* in the Appendix.

Spiritual Jazz

For it was Jazz that first burst through the rhythmic barriers, right up to the point of the totally improvised collages of such as Charlie Mingus or Ornette Coleman. And even the basic harmonic sequences, a primitive form of melody accompaniment, for which Jazz is so often criticised, were elevated as early as 1958/9 into a modal performing technique, a scale improvisation. It was primarily Miles Davis and John Coltrane who created this modal and scale-based music, which was then further developed in *My Favorite Things* (1960) by John Coltrane. Coltrane played his soprano saxophone with the oriental sound of the *shenai* or *sukra*, and Jazz expert Joachim E. Berendt points out that this way of playing first achieved world recognition when the musical element was joined by a philosophical one – Coltrane's increasing interest in Asian religion, which finds clear expression in the titles of his discs: *India, Om, Love Supreme, Meditation, Ascension.* Coltrane made a large part of the American Jazz-scene meditation-conscious, and many of his co-performers themselves began to meditate under Coltrane's influence.

On the subject of *Love Supreme*, the work which familiarised a wider public with his spiritual message, Coltrane wrote: 'Praised be the Name of the Lord. Thought-waves – heat-waves – all vibrations lead to God . . . God breathes through us so completely, so gently, we hardly feel it . . . He is our All . . . Thank you, God.'

Writing of Don Cherry, the other important Jazz-musician who has similarly given expression to the spirit of meditation on the musical scene, Joachim E. Berendt says: 'Cherry, who to start with stood totally in Coleman's shadow . . . developed into a poet of Free Jazz, a meditating poet. He has fused the sounds of the world of the American ghettoes and the Red Indian reservations of the mid-West (from which part of his family stems), together with those from as far apart as Bali and China, India and Africa, into an unmistakably personal music.'* Today Don Cherry is a pupil of the Tibetan lama Kalu Rinpoche and of the Indian *vina*-player Zia Dagar, and is directing in Sweden a children's creativity-centre. One of the movements of Cherry's com-

---

* J. E. Berendt: *Musik durch Meditation* in the periodical *Zeitwende,* March 1975.

position *Humus* is entitled *Siddharta*, after Hermann Hesse's book of the same title, of which in recent years a million copies have been sold in the United States. Cherry explains: 'Hermann Hesse was the first to make us all aware of these things – in his *Siddharta* and his other books. He was forty years ahead of us all. One cannot say often enough how much we all owe to Hermann Hesse.'*

Joachim E. Berendt attempts to sum up what music meant to Hesse: 'Mozart and Jazz and the divine music of the spheres, Romantic song and musical *mantra*, music as the content of meditation and as the vehicle of love, medieval and Classical and Indian ... In music too, Hermann Hesse anticipated the mood of a generation. The music that Hesse is really referring to is only hinted at in his works. It is circumscribed, not described ... A new musical culture had arisen to the extent that the categories according to which music was still being "reckoned", and thus split apart – Romantic and Indian, Jazz and Blues and Rock, Classical, contemporary and medieval music and the world's folk-music – were at last being re-assembled into a new, comprehensive whole. No longer were mere snippets wanted; the call was for *whole* music, for total music, for unity, for Oneness.'†

Such observations concur completely with Hermann Hesse's intuitive or periphrastic pronouncements on music and point the way to a 'music of the great synthesis.'

With the Jazz-scene a whole series of musicians split away to follow their own spiritual path. As early as 1964 the well-known Jazz clarinettist Tony Scott released the disc entitled *Music for Zen-Meditation*, on which for the first time he played with Classical Japanese musicians, who accompanied him on *shakuhachi* and *koto*. For many this record was the first important breakthrough into a Western spiritual music. Playing his clarinet with extreme softness and tenderness, Scott here conforms to the spare but enormously relaxing patterns of the Japanese modes.

From the time of the Beatles' Indian trip of 1966/7 only a few compositions of a meditative nature were then still surviving. Only one of their number, George Harrison, was still developing in this direction. At the end of the sixties another important group, *Third Ear Band*, released two discs in which the

---

* Retranslation of the sleeve-text of the LP *Humus*, Philips.
† Accompanying text to the LP *Hesse Between Music*, Electrola.

Indian ragas and scales were integrated into their music
(*Alchemy* and *4 Elements*). Apart from this English group, which
achieved little fame but became a thoroughly magical 'guiding-
star' wrapped in mystery for certain circles of young people in
England, Holland etc., it was the music of saxophonist and
flautist Paul Horn that best embodied the character of this new
'uncategorisable', meditative music. Paul Horn recorded *Inside*,
his finest disc, in the world-famous Taj Mahal in North India.
There he had the opportunity to hear an Islamic singer demonstrate to visitors the exceptional acoustics of the thirty-metre
high dome, and having started to play he was allowed to make
his recording because he was able to assure the singer that he
too was performing for God. Paul Horn recounts: 'I could
hardly believe my ears. Each note lingered in the air for twenty-
eight seconds. The acoustics are so perfect that you can no
longer hear when the voice stops and the echo begins. I simply
let the notes hang in the giant dome. I could play whole chords,
and they would come back to me like choirs of angels.'

The two most successful and best-known Jazz and Pop musicians currently producing meditative music are the guitarist
John McLaughlin and Carlos Santana, leader of the well-known
American group *Santana*. Both have the same guru, Sri Chinmoy,
whom McLaughlin was to quote on discs of his Mahavishnu
Orchestra: 'In the spiritual world it is music, next to meditation,
that best conveys the breathing of the cosmos. Meditation is
being silent . . . After being silent comes that which most nearly
expresses the inexpressible – music.' On his disc *Caravanserai*,
Carlos Santana cites extracts from the well-known *Meditation
for Self-Realisation* by Paramahansa Yogananda: 'The body
merges itself into the universe. The universe melts away in the
voice of silence. The sound melts in the all-illuminating Light.
And the Light enters the womb of eternal joy.'* On the subject
of *Caravanserai*, the 'caravan-journey into the land of the self',
Berendt writes: 'Such musical journeys into the land of the unconscious and subconscious are so numerous in the contemporary music-scene that nobody, surely, would attribute the fact
to mere chance: from Herbie Hancock to *Pink Floyd*, from
McCoy Tyner, John Coltrane's former pianist, to Wayne Shorter,
contemporary musicians journey over seas and through deserts,

* Translated from: *Meditationen zur Selbstverwirklichung*, 3rd edition,
Weilheim 1971, p. 43.

through the cosmos and through Arcadian landscapes – with sounds which leave no doubt that those seas and deserts and landscapes are all symbols of that inner landscape which reveals itself to the meditator.'* The Black pianist McCoy Tyner is a member of the Ahmadiya sect of Islam and his Muslim name is Sulaimon Saud.

The Meditative Wave

Alongside these musicians who deserve to be taken seriously we should not omit to mention how quickly the meditative wave has often been transformed into a mere superficial fashion. In Germany it was bound up with the 'cosmic wave' that derived from *Pink Floyd*'s creative period. This was where a good many no doubt well-meaning musicians and promoters sensed their opportunity. They came up with the 'messianic trip', induced with the aid of hallucinogenic drugs, and used quotes from Timothy Leary, then living in Switzerland, to publicise the new 'cosmic music' movement.

Right up to the present day many musical journalists confuse the much-vaunted 'cosmic music' with the meditative initiative, but the distinction is vital: 'The groups involved in "Cosmic Rock" represent a kind of musical equivalent of the science-fiction novel, and even if they do it as well as *Pink Floyd* did (though only, alas, for a short part of their career) it is no more than the equivalent of *first-class* science-fiction literature. But meditative music has a quite different aim. It seeks its "cosmos" not in the expanses of the Milky Way but within the individual consciousness, within the "Self".'†

Collective sound productions designed 'to reflect the deeper levels of consciousness' (as the already-mentioned group *prima materia* puts it, for example) permit, above all, a self-realisation within a musical development process. This is the precondition for an acoustic 'journey into the depths'. A person who merely conforms unconsciously to a particular stylistic fashion and takes himself to be – on the purely mechanical grounds of accidental encounters and influences – a Jazz, Pop or Classical musician, following his particular fashion as though it were the 'only' one, will never be able to make deep, truly Self-conscious music.

That is precisely why for several years now the Free Jazz

* J. E. Berendt in *Zeitwende*, March 1975.
† Berendt: in *Zeitwende*, March 1975.

musician has been studying Indian tonalities and the Classical interpreter medieval improvisation-patterns; why the guitarist has been learning to play the *sitar*, the electronic do-it-yourselfer has been incorporating natural sounds, and the experimental sound-researcher acquainting himself with the singing techniques of the Tibetans and Mongolians.

In order to be able to play a 'music between the worlds' capable of linking up these worlds into a single, integral entity, completely new modes of music-making need to be developed alongside the ancient methods still in process of rediscovery. In order to permit a Jazz musician, for example, to fit in with an Asian improviser, both need to familiarise themselves with the typical playing techniques and idiosyncracies of the other. Through confronting the strange and the unknown – often, indeed, initially a subject for mirth – the individual learns to recognise that his own method, hitherto imagined to be the obvious, or even the 'only' method, is in fact only one method *among many*, one possibility *among many*. In this way such an encounter 'between the worlds' could point a way out of the dilemma of categorised and compartmentalised thinking, and towards the possibility of *self-realisation through music*. As examples of such 'between-music' I would cite the performances of my composition *Dharana* for orchestra and improvisatory ensemble, the experiments undertaken in the course of concerts in Joachim E. Berendt's 'Jazz Meets the World' series or, similarly, the musical collaboration of the famous Indian *sarod*-player Ali Akbar Khan with the American alto-saxophonist John Handy. This event, originally put on by Joachim E. Berendt at the 1972 Berlin Jazz-festival, represented not merely a *rapprochement* but a form of truly integrative music-making with a common spiritual background. No wonder that these two musicians declared in 1975 their willingness to play together in Germany again.

Even in the ranks of the so-called avant-garde, composers and interpreters are attempting a 'synthesis of contemporary expression with ancient spiritual practice' (*prima materia*) and studying musical and religious traditions other than the Western ones. The result takes the form of static or flowing sound-states, not unlike the music of Stockhausen (*Trans, Hymnen*) or John Cage's music for prepared piano. For years now, Morton Feldman, an American member of Cage's entourage, has been composing static music consisting solely of sustained close harmonies. In his choral piece *Christian Wolff in Cambridge*, Feldman has one and the same sequence sung even more slowly the second time round. In fact, while demonstrating his music, Feldman once fell asleep in front of the assembled audience during a particularly gentle passage in his piece *I met Heine at the Rue Furstemberg*.

The composer Ernst Albrecht Stiebler, a pupil of Stockhausen living in Frankfurt, composes pieces that he calls 'Intonations', in which he has a choir, disposed in various parts of the hall, take up sounds played on the organ. In this way 'wandering bodies of sound' are set up in which one can aurally immerse oneself. A similar aim, though more proper to the therapeutic sphere, is being pursued by the German percussionist Seigfried Fink and clarinettist and psychologist Ernst Flackus. In their meditation-music they 'interpret' the cycle of the times of day as an introductory aid to relaxation and self-absorption prior to exercises in deep contemplation. Fink uses gongs and bells from Japan and Tibet, whose powerful vibrations have a strong suggestive effect.

Furthermore it is possible to observe the shift towards a 'new tonality' in contemporary music generally, not least among Europe's youngest composers. Increasingly the making of music is coming to be seen as a spiritual exercise (*sadhana*) or regarded by group communities as a form of sensitivity training or group-dynamic process. In this connection Michael Vetter and Georg Deuter should be named alongside the already-mentioned American percussionist Michael Ranta, who is involved in the study of Chinese music and *tai chi* (slowly-performed Chinese exercises in movement).

Vetter, until a few years ago a virtuoso flautist working with Stockhausen's intuitive group, is now studying with his Japanese wife in Zen monasteries, singing the various styles of sepulchrally-deep chant, and via his creative work with children has come across a completely new technique that one could describe as 'self-experience through calligraphic improvisation'. Georg Deuter, known in Germany to 'insiders' for his two self-produced discs of spiritual Pop music, belongs meanwhile, under a Sanskrit name, to the circle of pupils of an Indian Master who has developed a form of so-called dynamic meditation. Deuter is a member of a group of Munich musicians who are all following intensive, if different, spiritual paths and attempting to express them through music. The *sitar*-player and guitarist Al Gromer, the flautist Gerd Kraus (who also conducts exercises in improvisation and meditation with various groups) ought to be mentioned, as well as Klaus Wiese (who brought back with him from India and Persia the various types of *tambura* for Classical meditation, as well as the teachings of the Sufi Hazrat Inayat Khan and his school) and not least the composer Florian Fricke, who with his group *Popol Vuh* is a pioneer of the German 'spiritual-music' scene. Fricke is primarily concerned with the re-expression of the ideas of his own Christian gnosis, while reflecting Martin Buber's Hasidism, quoting Jakob Böhme and producing discs with titles such as *Seligpreisungen, In den Gärten Salomons* and *Hosianna Mantra*. *Popol Vuh* is also representative of the new tendency consciously to eschew electronic megalomania. Their most recent recordings use only acoustic instruments, whereas 'cosmic music' cannot get by at all without a forest of electronic apparatus. None the less their acoustically-recorded discs are produced by a multi-track process (one instrument after the other) which still leaves plenty of room for the 'technical demon'.

Meditation and Electronics

It is interesting how many of the 'cosmic messengers' are suddenly no longer using the whole electronic 'works' – apparatus worth thousands of pounds – because they feel intuitively how dangerous, 'sub-physical' and demonic the effect of artificially produced sounds can be. And indeed a debate is now in progress as to whether electronic music can ever be 'spiritual', or whether it is merely comparable to the delusions induced by chemical drugs.

On the other hand, when I asked the eighty-year-old Indian musical philosopher Jaidev Thakur Singh this question, after he had heard some electronic music, he replied that this technique in the hands of a *conscious* person could quite well have a spiritual effect, and he could easily imagine a synthesizer-*tambura*. In fact it would be much better tuned than the mechanical Indian instrument. None the less, if one listens to the first, electronically-produced 'unconscious' efforts of the avant-garde – cold constructions of musical rationality – one can understand the anthroposophists who invoke Rudolf Steiner in support of their judgement that electronic devices in general (including television) spring from 'the inhuman levels of the sub-physical'.

Already in 1972 Walter Bachauer was pointing to the fact that a revolution in the sphere of technical sound-production had followed the interest in exotic and new meditative and archetypal music :

The example of collective concentration on the suggestions of Asian soloists may prove to be of greater significance for the most recent tendencies in Euro-American music than is dreamed of at present. The writing or improvising of music that conveys to massed groups direct, possibly musically archetypal messages, will no longer be able to be regarded as taboo ... At least the most primitive form of musical magic has managed to escape the ban : the magic of duration.

Music as a state of consciousness, no longer subservient to the simple dramaturgy of tension and relaxation, will in future have to be taken as much into account as the stirrings of a compositorial poeticism that has long had to take refuge in Asia and Africa because the vital traditions of musical suggestion have been as good as wiped out in Europe ...

As against the beginnings of a return to the archetypal aspects of music, a technical revolution is also in progress, which will be carried through in the seventies on two fronts. Synthesizers – compact miniature electronics studios – have made music portable and accessible for the concert situation. More : the enormous numbers of units produced are permitting access to previously unobtainable equipment to an extent that one can already call massive. If an English firm has so far (1972) delivered around 4,000 miniature synthesizers to all parts of the world, it is not difficult to imagine that the private production of electronic music could reach previously undreamed of quantities – and, through careful selection, perhaps also qualities.

Comparable with this personalisation of institutional technology is the revolution that will inevitably affect the whole field of electro-acoustics as a result of computerisation. The possibilities will include :

(i)   the whole tone-quality continuum as a programme, in-
      cluding total computer-storability and manipulation of all
      natural sounds;

(ii) thus, too, the sounds of existing musical instruments in
      any desired combination;

(iii) thus, too, any artificial sound, whether or not derived
      from nature;

(iv) thus, too, the ability to mix any desired sounds across
      any desired number of channels as a straightforward
      function of memory-manipulation;

(v)   absolute mastery of all concrete and electronic sounds in
      the illusory sphere . . .*

These technical developments, only gradually being learnt
about and made use of by musicians, are outstandingly well-
suited to the creation of a music which will derive massive effect
from even the most primitive application of acoustic materials. In
its best album, *Ummagumma* (e.g., in *Set the Control for the
Heart of the Sun*) the group *Pink Floyd* has already managed to get by with the simplest structures and scales, using the
exaggerated 'oriental' intervals of a modal scale and a great deal
of ecstatic 'space-flight music' from electrically-amplified instruments.

Likewise the 'cosmic' presentations of such as Klaus Schulze
or the synthetic 'sound-fields' of Eberhard Schoener, the 'electronic trips' of the group *Tangerine Dream*, the *Sonic Seasons* of
Walter Carlos or the *Magnetic Garden* of Alvin Curran are all
acoustically enormously effective – even though they use only
a few run-of-the-mill chord sequences, even fewer motifs, or
simply a single, sustained chord – precisely through their fascinating application of the new technical apparatus, their sophisticated space-effects and their mixing of never-before-heard tone-
qualities. In the process *Tangerine Dream* hovers 'between
pure tone-colour-presentation, Brucknerian cantilenas and Rock
antics. Curran's *Songs and Views from the Magnetic Garden*
combine *musique concrète* with pseudo-Byzantine solo chanting,
live-electronics, cowbells and synthesizer-mechanics.' (From a
broadcast review by Wolfgang Burde.)

But all this is hardly meditative music. For the most part

* W. Bachauer: introduction to the Avante-Garde Festival, Berlin, 1972.

it is merely electronic images, acoustic fantasies, dream events, a haphazard penetration of the unconscious. Only the rarest forms of electronic music can maintain a flowing continuity, bring about a yielding introversion, extend an acoustic germ-cell like a mantra into infinity. Only a few products of this kind have the shape and the power, not to lead the listener into insensibility, but to evoke a contemplative self-absorption.

At this point we should also mention the atmospheric pieces of Sunil, the Indian who, as a novice of the 'Mother' of Sri Aurobindo's ashram in Pondicherry, was inspired to accompany her words and to institute a music of the new 'supramental' consciousness using the organ and various Indian instruments. The result is not lacking in a certain sweetness and unworldliness such as is typical of the taste of the spiritually-committed Hindu.

With meditation now very much *à la mode*, the concept of 'meditative music' is as yet ill-defined, and if one follows the feature sections of the newspapers and the music critics, it soon becomes obvious that any slow, gentle music is immediately dubbed 'meditative'. The concept has been made fun of, primarily by those who have never meditated in their lives, and who link meditation with all sorts of vague notions: drugs, hashish, cosmos, ecstasy, trance. Electronic horror-noises and Buddhist mantra-settings are, for many, one and the same. No wonder that the confusion has arisen: most musicians are themselves not quite clear as to what 'meditative music' really is. Does it even exist?

If one knows how to meditate, and has the necessary patience to press forward into deep inner levels, one listens inwardly, and exterior sources of sound are scarcely perceived at all. He who meditates hears no music. None the less music can provide a meditative point of departure, and in particular can remove one's inner restlessness in the initial stages, quieten the ceaseless reasoning and cogitating. Music can provide a ritual such as may be needed in the early stages to stop oneself running away and to enable one to become really still. Music can also serve as an aid and a tool for relaxation, concentration and the achievement of inner quietness.

Now most of the music which is today categorised as 'meditative' is merely a form of imagery recounting the musician's own spiritual experiences and visions, describing 'the universal consciousness, the cosmic joy' and eagerly using it as an occasion for subjective music – music which, to the 'uninitiated' outsider, can seem naïve, rhetorical, intoxicated or just rubbish. And with a few exceptions the meditator – he who *really* sits and is still and silent – cannot 'use' this music anyway. The only exception would be an improvisatory or contemplative music which is not *about* meditation and the self and God at all (with various spiritual quotations merely printed on the record-sleeve), but which is itself capable of being a vehicle, energy-form and magic force for spiritual self-absorption, a music which has no predetermined, stylistic function to perform, but which flows endlessly and will not be listened to as one listens to Classical music – indeed, which is not there to be perceived at all, but which *works* by virtue of its own inner laws, as soon as the listener learns how to open himself totally to it. It carries him away – to himself.

Now, everybody has his own favourite music which, for him only, has such powers: Mozart or Indian ragas, exotic music or Anton Bruckner. Here, however, we shall be concerned with a special kind of meditative music which to some extent sees itself as having a particular rôle, not as an autonomous art form, but as a vehicle for those energies which aid self-absorption and contemplation, thus making drugs superfluous: *periodic music* and its predecessor, the *minimal music* of the new American composers.

'PERIODIC MUSIC' AND 'MINIMAL MUSIC'

Music should be the expression of lofty, spiritual objectives: philosophy, knowledge and truth – the noblest properties of man. In order to give expression to these objectives, music must necessarily have tranquillity and poise. (Retranslated from Terry Riley)

The chief characteristic of *minimal music* is the repetition of short motifs which alter almost imperceptibly and are varied only minimally. Music is transposed into a state of constant regeneration, so that a 'continuous, iridescent sound results which gradually alters without changing its substance' (Dieter

Schnebel). Through the successive superimposition of minute figures, or through nothing more than the sustaining of a note and the production of its overtones, the distinction between movement and non-movement is dissolved into a kind of synchronicity. Everything proceeds as though the principle of repetition had no other purpose than to hypnotise the listener. At a first hearing, such music sounds 'primitive' and monotonous; yet as soon as one gets the feel of it a deep self-experience becomes possible.

Not the least significant precursors of these endless repetitions, periodic formulae and prolonged sounds are Indian music, African rhythmic figures and gamelan music. The fathers of this new music in the early sixties were the Americans Terry Riley, La Monte Young and Steve Reich, who are still today the most important representatives of this movement, alongside Phil Glass, Robert Moran and Frederick Rzewski. The best-known and most seminal of them is without doubt Terry Riley, who has influenced musicians of all schools.

Terry Riley

Terry Riley was born in California in 1935 and financed his musical studies by playing ragtime piano at the Gold Street Saloon, San Francisco. In 1960 he met La Monte Young and thereafter committed himself to music for good. From 1962 he spent two years touring in France with his show-troupe, played in Paris at a bar on the Place Pigalle and put on musical 'happenings' and street theatre in Scandinavia. He organised all-night concerts and events in which he appeared as a saxophonist and as a performer on all kinds of keyboard instruments.

Here he must have performed his first well-known composition, *Dorian Reeds*. In it he uses for the first time the principle of time-delay. A motif played on the organ or saxophone is recorded on tape: the tape-recorder immediately replays the recording, though with a slight delay due to the relative positions of the recording and playback heads: a second tape-recorder is set up a few yards away, and the same tape likewise runs through this machine, where it takes some seconds to arrive, so that the motif-passage is heard again with a further delay.

In the first half of the sixties Terry Riley composed other pieces that have likewise become very well-known: *In C*, for a variable ensemble, and the *Keyboard Studies* (see illustration in Appendix), both of which were based on the principle of *ad lib.* repetition of melodic patterns, which later became of great significance for the whole 'minimal music' movement in America. Although this music is difficult to fit into the traditional categories, Terry Riley himself calls it 'modal' and 'cyclic', and lays the principal stress on the repeated melodic patterns and the superimposed structures that, according to Riley, 'permit the listener to perceive a tonal, melodic and harmonic landscape from several standpoints.'* Riley further writes:

> In the last ten years I have given up the traditional rôle of the composer in favour of self-interpretative improvisation. Since my ideas derive neither directly from the Eastern nor from the Western tradition, I have devoted a great deal of energy to the composition of formal elements on which the improvisation can be based.
>
> In a sense my music is closely related to the techniques of Classical Indian music, whose exponents are capable of developing endless sequences out of a single theme, a fixed mode or a rhythmic period (10/12/16 beats, and so on). According to this concept the composed portions remain unaltered, but the musician is quite free to spin them out within the limits of his imagination. The mode used (tone-row) and the accompanying melodic figures establish the mood and atmosphere in which the improvisation is carried out. In the presence of these conditions one is free to meditate on the gradual development of a whole musical universe. I play the organ, because it offers a large number of possibilities. It is polyphonal, permits the simultaneous development of diverse and integrated parts and the alternative development of main and subsidiary part-lines out of the same material. It is a kind of integration which I identify as the source of my musical thought.*

In 1968 Terry Riley started on the gradual improvisatory development of possibly his best-known piece, *A Rainbow in Curved Air*, which consists of repeatable phrases based on a cycle of fourteen beats (3 – 3 – 4 – 4) and is performed on the organ and other keyboard instruments. The periods (musical state-

---

* Riley: from the programme-booklet of the Meta-Music Festival, Berlin 1974.
* Riley: *op. cit.*

ments) for the left hand initially comprise two phrases each (see Example 5).

The first period (3 – 3) is constructed very similarly to the second (4 – 4), in order to avoid producing any feeling of beginning and end.

The two periods can be combined with each other in various ways. Any note can be the beginning; the hand plays this figure continuously and lets any stresses arise spontaneously. But the sequence of notes must remain the same, and the same cycle is maintained throughout. The tempo is altered only by whole-number proportions, i.e., the notes are played twice as quickly or twice as slowly.

From the two germ-cells of the basic periods Riley finally developed the retrograde version of the sequence, which is then combined either contrapuntally or consecutively with the original series. Now this sequential pattern can be varied in a whole range of ways which the hands in part discover for themselves during the course of performance. The two basic scales for *Rainbow* are both based on the keynote A, but at times tending towards the D-tonality: A – B – C sharp – D – E – F sharp – G – A and A – B flat – C – E – F – G – A. Another important piece of Terry Riley's is *The Persian Surgery Dervishes*, which takes the basic period of *Keyboard Studies* as the point of departure for its improvisatory development – A flat – G – B flat – F. Riley first began to play this pattern in 1964 under the title *Autumn Leaves*, and later, too, in *The Untitled Organ*: 'The first performances consisted of endless repetitions of this pattern. Later I added yet other repeated phrases of four, five, six, seven and eight notes. This gives the impression that periods of varying lengths are being repeated cyclically. In this kind of music it is important that both hands should be able to play all the periods, so that combinations can be arrived at spontaneously. These short periods generate so much energy that with their help large improvised pieces can be worked up on top of the constant pattern. At each performance I try to find pleasing combinations and a new development for these statements.'*

The mode of the piece (or rather of the various versions of it) is based on the keynote C: C – D – E flat – F – G – A flat – B flat – C (natural minor). The sequel to these improvisation periods, in

* Riley: programme booklet of the Sound-Centre of the exhibition *Weltkulturen und moderne Kunst*, Munich 1972.

which Terry Riley combines the A-tonality with that of C, is called *Descending Moonshine Dervishes*. Here, with the aid of a tape-recorder, he also uses the time-delay already described, though the played material is in this case repeated after only a fraction of a second as a result of using the machine's fastest speed so that the time from recording-head to playback-head is shortened. The result is a fascinating reiteration, a kind of vibrant sound, for Terry Riley uses 'time-delay' so cunningly that it sometimes sounds as though four hands are playing.

The music of Terry Riley has fertilised and inspired a whole range of American and European musicians of the avant-garde, Pop and Jazz. Even in the early sixties Terry Riley had made friends with David Allen, co-founder of the Rock-group *Soft Machine*; the piece *Moon in June*, on their third record, clearly shows his influence. The English group *Third Ear Band* likewise uses modal patterns on the principle of periodic progression. The Pop-group *Curved Air* took its name directly from Terry Riley's above-mentioned piece. John Cale, of the once famous group *Velvet Underground*, recorded the disc *Church of Anthrax* with Riley, and above all the great Jazz musician Don Cherry continually cited Terry Riley as the guiding-star of this new movement and finally, in 1975, played with him, for the first time, *Descending Moonshine Dervishes* on WDR Cologne.

In the sphere of New Music it must also have been Terry Riley who did most to inspire the other well-known musicians of 'minimal music', namely Steve Reich, Phil Glass, Rzewski and Moran, of whom more will be said in due course. And on the German scene too, people were fascinated by Terry Riley and endeavoured to reproduce his special sound-effects. The Berlin Rock-band *Agitation Free* has performed *In C*, and the former synthesizer player of this group, Michael Hoenig, developed a whole sequence of vital and yet sensitive patterns after the Riley model. Not least, my own pieces *Aura, Dorian Dervishes, Beyond the Wall of Sleep* and others were also inspired by Terry Riley's music.

American 'minimal music'

For some years now an outstanding Indian singer has regularly been visiting America to train Western musicians in Classical Indian singing : Pandit Pran Nath, the last great representative of the Kirana school of northern India. His chief pupils are La Monte Young and Terry Riley, who accompany him on his tours. Both distinguish strictly, however, between their Indian musical studies and their own compositions. Whereas Riley takes as his main material the 'patterns', which were then taken up by Steve Reich and Phil Glass, for La Monte Young the initial material is even simpler, more primitive and more 'minimal' : a single note and its overtone-spectrum. Often La Monte will use merely a few sine-waves, in such a way that their frequencies, as he explains, 'bear an integral relationship to each other and thus produce a periodically-structured mixture of sound-waves.'

La Monte, like Riley born in California in 1935, learnt the saxophone from his father even as a child. Later, alongside his musical studies, he devoted himself to Jazz and also made the acquaintance of Don Cherry. In 1964 he founded the *Theatre of Eternal Music* together with his wife Marian Zazeela, Tony Conrad (the well-known producer of 'minimal' films) and John Cale of *Velvet Underground*. It is important to note in this connection that performances of 'periodic music' took place, during the so-called 'time of flux', as theatrical productions in art galleries – in Cologne, for example, at the Friedrich Gallery and at the painter Mary Baumeister's.

The piece *The Tortoise, His Dreams and Journeys*, with which Young and his group *Theatre of Eternal Music* began in 1964, takes place in the 'Dream House' conceived especially for it. In other pieces La Monte lit an open fire, let butterflies flutter round the auditorium or distributed little notes on which was written nothing but a fifth with a pause-sign over it, or the words : 'Draw a straight line and follow it.'

The first sounds to leave a deep impression on Young were the continual, slightly varying sighing of the wind, the humming of insects, the echo across valleys, lakes and plains. In an introduction he writes : '... and in the life of the "Tortoise" there is the drone of the first sound. The drone continues on and on, without ever having begun, but from time to time it is taken up, until it re-echoes as a continual sound in the "Dream House" where many musicians and students live and carry on their musical work. Such houses will help us to produce a music which after a year, ten years, a hundred years or more of uninterrupted playing would not only be a living organism with its own existence and tradition, but would have the ability to carry on under its own power. This music could continue playing for thousands of years without interruption ...'

La Monte Young's pieces always consist of prolonged intervals and chords. The individual notes are derived from the natural harmonic series and La Monte describes them as the 'integral diversity' of a common fundamental tone. The individual performers and singers decide beforehand which of the chosen overtones will be used and which combinations are possible. 'Through reinforcement of the integral frequency ratios one obtains a rich texture of overtones, bourdon sounds, differentials and other combinations of overtones, which gives the performer the chance to achieve an extremely precise intonation.'*

It was precisely the practice of careful tuning that La Monte Young, who had developed a totally new way of playing the saxophone in the sixties, brought to bear when he took up singing seriously. From that time onwards he gave up playing the saxophone, just as Terry Riley had done, in order to devote himself wholly to the chanting of long-sustained notes. Public performances of these chants, accompanied by the keynote sounded by instruments or electronic tones, usually consist of two parts, each of which lasts some two hours and is held in a dark room lit only with calligraphic slide-projections by his wife Marian Zazeela.

At this point we should once more mention the American percussionist Ranta who presented his magical-meditative Multimedia Theater several times before he left the West. He used slides, photographs from nature (rocks, water and flowers), the hall was fitted out with bast-mats and Japanese blinds, a typical lantern from Kyoto spread a dim light, and one could sit on Zen cushions which invited one to meditate. One subtly conceived arrangement (by contrast with other avant-garde performances!) was not visible at all: Ranta had several tape-recorders with a variety of static and periodic sound-material at his disposal. Some was electronic, some he had personally recorded with vibraphones and friction-gongs etc., and some was spliced and stuck together using the methods of *musique concrète*.

*Quotation from La Monte Young in the programme of the Sound-Centre at the exhibition *Weltkulturen und moderne Kunst*, Munich 1972.

Now Ranta blended the periodic sounds of the one tape slowly and imperceptibly into the next and, through fading-over, the sound-picture kept altering imperceptibly like the flowing of a great river. Sometimes he would play yard-long bamboo flutes, light joss-sticks, and in Josef A. Riedl's avant-garde mammoth-spectacle during the Olympiad he even greeted the excited visitors in the guise of a Japanese monk. In his former Cologne studio Michael Ranta put on psychedelic-intuitive improvisations, above all with the outstanding guitarist Karlheinz Böttner, and there one could also hear for the first time in Germany, and perhaps even in Europe, a tape of the typical 'minimal music' of Steve Reich. Frederik Rzewski had brought it with him from New York a few weeks after the first performance.

These pieces that Rzewski also made known in Germany, alongside his own similar piano music, were called *Four Organs* and *Piano Phase*. At the first hearing one felt as though paralysed, and among one's listening brother-composers stern rejection and fascination were almost evenly balanced. At that juncture the course for New Music was being held in Cologne under the direction of Mauricio Kagel, with Rzewski and also the Frenchman Luc Ferrari among the lecturers. At this time many composers must have made their first contact with 'minimal music'.

Then, a few years later, Steve Reich's most famous piece, *Drumming*, made him the most prominent representative of this movement. This percussion piece has four sections of about equal length. These sections are performed in turn on eight, small, tuned drums with male voices, followed by three marimba-phones with female voices, three glockenspiels accentuated by penny-whistle and piccolo notes, and finally all the instrumental and vocal timbres are combined with one another. In a Berlin lecture series, Professor Wolfgang Burde analysed Steve Reich's *Drumming*:

'It begins with a cycle of twelve drum-beats with eleven pauses. Then additional drum-beats are gradually substituted for the pauses, one at a time, until the pattern is fully built up. And nothing other than this pattern is to be heard during this one-and-a-half hour piece. All Reich alters during the course of the four phases of his compositorial process is the tone-colour. And the attraction of the work resides primarily, on the one hand, in the simplicity, the unconditional acoustic transparency of the musical proceedings, but also, on the other hand, in the fact that the music has an inherent scintillation about it.'*

Reich also draws attention to this in a commentary on his piece: 'I have never held much with the use of hidden structural procedures in music. Even when all the cards are on the table and everyone can hear what is being played from moment to moment during the course of a musical performance, there are still plenty of secrets to be discovered. Such secrets are the impersonal and unintentional psycho-acoustic side-effects of the consciously-conceived process: such as sub-themes that one can detect as the patterns repeat themselves, or particular spatial effects that depend on the listener's position in the auditorium, or minute irregularities of performance, or overtones, differentials etc.'†

The most exciting moments in the piece are without doubt the overlappings of the various groups of instruments. When the periodicities of the bongo drums gradually give way to the marimbaphone section and this is later superseded by the glockenspiels, the result is a fascinating superimposition of tone-colours, which is further underlined by the strange singing technique which is used to some extent instrumentally to emphasise the rhythmic and melodic inflexions. The main prototype for these ostinato inflexions is clearly the music of Central Africa, which Steve Reich studied for one-and-a-half years in Ghana under a Drum Master.

'This piece by the American Steve Reich relies primarily on the tool of the ostinato, the constant repetition of a basic pattern which undergoes inner development. It would be somewhat misleading, however, to put Reich's ostinato patterns on a mental par with Carl Orff's. Reich brings traces of long-lost rituals into our consciousness, slips over us an appreciation of time which goes beyond time-and-motion pressures, and thus ties in with our own secret longings.'‡

Apart from *Drumming*, which, as I have said, lasts one and a half hours, Reich has written shorter pieces, in which he has supplemented the technique of phase-delay with that of exten-

---

* W. Burde, Lessinghochschule Berlin, June 1975.
† Quoted from the above lecture.
‡ W. Burde: *Minimal Music und meditative Musik*, lecture-series at the Lessinghochschule Berlin, June 1975.

sion, the lengthening of the initial note values. It is interesting to observe that shorter pieces are more problematical for the listener, as he has insufficient time to let himself sink into the unfamiliar state of relaxed listening. If one fails to 'get inside' the music, but instead stands as it were at a distance from it, the result can be similar to looking at a painting in a gallery with only a single pattern on it: so-called 'Minimal Art'. Steve Reich himself draws attention to the relationship between his music and the 'Minimal Art' of the painter Sol LeWitt, for example. Both concentrate on the most direct, as near complete working out of a given idea as possible. Even the term 'minimal music' is derived from the similarly-named creative-art term. Steve Reich's maturest composition, *Music for 18 Musicians*, shows none the less that minimal development of basic material can be expanded into fascinating, almost rhetorical sound-layers, while the various harmonic relationships can be made audible via effective instrumentation.

Apart from Steve Reich it is Phil Glass who has done most to further in his own way the development of the technique of constant repetition for keyboard instruments. The complete performance of his cycle *Music in 12 Parts* would normally last three evenings. Individual parts of the cycle always emphasise one or more aspects of an essentially compulsory figure, and yet the development pursues unusual paths: it is carried on, so to speak, under a time-magnifying-glass. A short, melodic, motif-like figure is continually repeated, and through overlappings with similar melodic figures, produces new resultant patterns. Of its first performance in Berlin, Glass writes: 'Once it is established that nothing is "happening" in the normal sense of the term, and that instead the gradual "surveying" of the musical material can hold the listener's attention, perhaps he can discover a new kind of attentiveness, one in which neither memory nor anticipation (the psychological axioms of Baroque, Classical, Romantic and modern music) have anything to do with the quality of musical perception. It is to be hoped that music will then become free of dramatic structures, as a pure sound-medium, as "the now".'*

Another American, who in 1974 put on in Berlin his ninety-minute *Eternal Hour* for six vocal/instrumental groups, is

* Programme-booklet of the Meta-Music Festival, Berlin 1974.

Robert Moran. The piece takes for its material only the C major scale, which builds up a suitable acoustic context with the aid of many-layered static sections. On this subject Wolfgang Burde writes: 'Minimal music has, paradoxically, discovered the adventure of macro-time. And quite concretely at that, as an adventure in perception which becomes calmer, more resigned and more emotional the longer the process lasts.'* Moran, who is also exploring the possibilities of the 'prepared piano' is a true 'minimal art' craftsman. In Berlin, he once lived as a live art-object in the shop window of a big store and invited guests to tea with the one condition that they should behave informally and not look outside.

Finally we should mention once more the significant composer and pianist Frederik Rzewski, who has combined periodic figures and modal patterns on the one hand with texts reflecting his political persuasions (for example in the pieces *Attica is in Front of Me* or *Coming Together*), and on the other hand, in the sphere of new American Jazz, has inspired vibraphone-player Karl Berger and his group to take up 'periodic music'. An important stimulus for group-improvisation is provided by his composition *Les Moutons de Panurge*: the first note of the fully-composed tone-row is first played alone, then repeated and played with the second; then notes 1 and 2 are repeated and put with the third – thus, 1, 1-2, 1-2-3, 1-2-3-4 and so on. Once all the notes have been added, with the row being played all the way through, one note after the other is now discarded, starting with the first one, until only the last notes are left – 1-2-3-4-5, 2-3-4-5, 3-4-5, 4-5, 5. This ostinato process, which can be performed by a solo instrument or by a whole orchestra, is accompanied by simple rhythm instruments, such as maracas or several drums, which signal the basic time, a quaver-beat, in fairly quick tempo throughout the piece (see Example 6).

The 'periodic music' of the American avant-garde is commonly referred to as improvised music: this is erroneous. Although Terry Riley often writes no notes down one can hear clearly that given note sequences keep being repeated exactly, as in Indian music. And when Steve Reich is trying out his music with his musicians, the percussionists on marimbaphones and drums and the singers, one notices how exact his ideas are, how pre-

* W. Burde, radio-script, Radio Free Berlin 1974.

cisely a piece is rehearsed, even where there are only brief indications to go on, and no exact score exists.

The conventional musician of the European orchestral tradition does not have the experience to realise such music via improvisation; he needs precise, written notes. I have therefore developed a 'concentric' form of music which can be performed by the traditional orchestra on the basis of periodic techniques with reference to exactly worked-out scores. Some of these compositions are presented in the next chapter.

Meditative music will never stand much chance in the concert hall or the Pop-event. The conventional attitudes and expectations are too alien to it, concentrating as they do on 'the dramaturgy of tension and relaxation, "high point and low point" thinking, fortissimo upheavals and pianissimo murmurs' (Wolfgang Burde). The 'action' of a Rock group, the 'necessary' excesses of the percussionist and all the familiar rigmarole of a Jazz concert are inimical, in most cases, to real meditative self-absorption. Thus the sort of thing that happened at concerts by the guitarist McLaughlin or the group *Santana* was that the stars, photographed in white with their guru on the record sleeves, along with quotations of holy words about cosmic consciousness and divine grace, produced on the stage an unholy racket, a mindless magic, because the audiences were impatient and created an atmosphere that was far from spiritual.

And yet there have been a few concerts at which suddenly another temporal and aural consciousness emerged. The several-hour long organ meditations of Terry Riley, for example, gave rise 'not to structural appreciation, not to reflections on formal relationships, but to an attitude of self-surrender. One had to entrust oneself to the music's flow: a sympathetic vibration was demanded, a new readiness for musical self-surrender, the sensitising of a new, more extensive feeling of time' (Wolfgang Burde).

Dieter Schnebel, the experimental composer, who, though himself a theologian of spiritual New Music, stands somewhat at a distance from the preceding examples, had already put it as follows in 1972:

> The New Music has enriched itself with much that is exotic, sometimes from as far afield as eastern Asia: sustained sounds for aural contemplation, previously unknown instrumental

colours, quotations from alien music, improvisation techniques, strange performance-rituals, music of a quite different spirit, and a different philosophy of music ... This turning away from the Western outlook may have to do with the increasingly intolerable contradictions of the late capitalism of the industrial countries.

What is nevertheless still lacking amidst this more universalised music is a World Music as such. A prime requisite for this would be a real effort to experience the strangeness and peculiarities of the many kinds of exotic music, and that means thoroughly to get to know them.

Only when one can truly see the Other as such, and thus is in a position to have both feeling and respect for it, can it truly be combined with one's Own. Certainly, as long as there is so little movement in this direction in the sphere of political and social relationships, the prospects for World Music itself are slim. It can proclaim the *harmonia mundi* only when this has been accomplished, and even then not in unison, but only in an as-yet unheard polyphony.*

CONCENTRIC AND INTEGRAL MUSIC
(AUTHOR'S OWN COMPOSITIONS)

DHARANA

Concentric composition for orchestra, solo improvisation and tape-recorder (1972)†

'Dharana' means in Sanskrit the deepest inner self-recollection and highest concentration. The piece is based on the tonal centre of D flat, which sounds on the accompanying tape in deep, continuous synthesizer frequencies. These are modulated and overlaid with natural, almost inaudible sounds of wind and water.

For the orchestra, elemental, archetypal states of being have been set to music: between the densest of earthly noises and the subtlest ethereal space-sounds, a pentatonic bourdon com-

* D. Schnebel: article in the catalogue of the Olympic Exhibition *Weltkulturen und moderne Kunst*, Munich 1972.
† Published by Schott's Söhne, Mainz: so far performed by the RSO orchestra on Radio Free Berlin and by the SWF orchestra at the Donaueschingen Music Festival.

bines modal-mantric motifs, its 'unending' progression creating specific overtone-spectra in the upper octaves. The piece
has a mandala-like circular shape and no fixed length : it can be
begun and ended at various points and after any number of run-
throughs. The 'solo' improvisation can be performed by a singer,
an instrumentalist or a whole group.

'If the mind can be fixed on the centre for twelve seconds
it will be a *Dhâranâ*; twelve such *Dhâranâs* will be a *Dhyâna*;
and twelve such *Dhyânas* will be a *Samâdhi*.'* For a time span
of twelve seconds the thoughts must be focussed calmly and un-
disturbedly on a single object. This short concentration is the
first true step in any mystic development: *dharanasu cha yogyata
manasah* : 'Concentration frees the mind for union.'†

DHYANA

*Concentric music for mixed voices, solo improvisation and
bourdon (1972)‡*

The title of the composition is taken from the Sanskrit and
means roughly 'meditation' (see above). The piece is based on a
pentatonic scale (F – G – B flat – C – E flat), which is combined
with an ancient Hindu *sutra* (*dhyanam nirvishayam manah*: 'In
meditation the mind dwells on the uncreated') and with the
antiphon '*O quam mirabilis*' of Hildegard von Bingen (12th
century).

The piece is composed according to the technique of 'concentric musical form', whose chief characteristic is a middle
ground common to both composed and improvised material
based on their relationship to the keynote, their modal harmony
and their overall sound-effect. *Dhyana* develops from a sound
that is at rest via the gradual introduction and repetition of
intertwined motifs. Indian and early Christian hymns are blended together at around the mid-point of the composition. *Dhyana*
should be so performed that the listeners can sing or hum with
it. *Dhyana* is a constant flow of impressions and perceptions. It
is the state of a continual flowing of the mind towards a single
objective, in a single direction, like the flowing of water in a
river.

* Vivekananda : *Raja Yoga*, Calcutta 1970.
† Old Hindu *sutra*, as translated by Sivananda.
‡ First performed at the Kassel Festival of Spiritual Music, 1975.

SAMMA SAMADHI

Concentric music for orchestra, choir and solo improvisation
*(1972)**

The piece is based on the Chinese scale which is derived
from fifths in the ratio 3:2 (heaven and earth), and which is
almost identical to the scale of the Indian ragas Megh, Sarang
and Durga. The modal harmonics of *Samma Samadhi* are developed out of a static underlying string sound and continual
repetitions by individual wind instruments. The voices sing
vowel sounds derived from Sanskrit and ancient Greek. The piece
lasts about twenty minutes and permits a relaxed, expectation-
less inner listening to the self, an intensive aural awareness that
is at once intuitively meditative, perceptive ('assimilation with
self-recollection') and conscious.

Samma Samadhi is in Sanskrit the state of total stillness
and self-immersion. In this state thinking is at one with what
is thought, the tension between subject and object is, so to
speak, removed by the integrating power of pure experience.
Even if this experience is of only slight intensity, Samadhi
will nevertheless be instrumental in widening our horizon,
strengthening our faith, deepening our insight, weakening our
prejudices and purifying our efforts ...
The state of Samma Samadhi has been compared to a massive body thrown into the water, which sinks into the depths
until it reaches the bottom and continues to lie there until it
is brought up again; whereas the purely intellectual concentration of a consciousness imprisoned by the outer world of the
senses resembles a hollow body that has to be forcibly pushed
under the water because otherwise it would immediately
emerge again on the surface.†

---

* First performed by the RSO orchestra on Radio Free Berlin; soloist
Jeffrey Biddeau, congas and marimbaphone.
† L. Govinda: tr. from *Die psychologische Haltung der buddhistischen
Philosophie*, Zürich 1961, p. 87 ff.

ANANDA

Concentric music for string-orchestra, solo oboe and drone-instruments ad lib. (tambura, synthesizer, voice, 1973)*

Ananda is based on the scale of the Indian ragas Kedar and Durga. The main tune comes from a centuries-old Bengali religious chant (the *bhajan; Jai Shiva Shankara*) which I learnt from the singer Aparna Chakravarti in Calcutta and was probably the first to write down. Aparna sings this *bhajan* in honour of her spiritual teacher, the eighty-year-old Bengali Ananda Mayi Ma, who is revered as a saint in her homeland. '*Ananda*' means 'bliss'. The composition unfolds note by note the scale of the Raga Kedar, and presents the micro-aspects of the individual intervals via periodic repetitions. Apart from oboe and oboe d'amore, the piece was composed solely for string orchestra with bourdon, and should not be played 'tempered' but in perfect intervals according to the Hindu *shruti* tradition, under the terms of which the octave is divided into twenty-four micro-intervals. Thus the fourth step, for example (derived from a pure downward fifth) is some fifth of a tone lower than the piano's tempered fourth; the full-tone interval of the second (as the second pure fifth above the keynote) is about one-sixth of a tone higher than its tempered equivalent, and finally the sixth is a pure fifth from the second or third, according to its stress and importance.

In his teachings on musical perception, Helmholtz has already bemoaned the fact that we are accustomed from our youth onwards to compensating for the inaccuracies of the modern equal temperament. As a result of this the whole former diversity of mode- and scale-tonalities has been reduced to the dualistic distinction between major and minor. Through the pure intonation of the scale in special heterophonic groupings, the harmonic spectra can once more be heard resonating in sympathy – like the resonating strings of the Indian *sitar* or *sarangi* in the unison/melodic field – and a new tone-colour music is thus heard in the polyphonic context.

* First performed by the symphony orchestra of Westdeutscher Rundfunk, Cologne; soloist Robert Eliscu, oboe.

HARI OM TAT SAT

Concentric music for Indian chant, keyboard instrument and electronics (1973/4)

For some years now Anatol Arkus's *Belle Epoque Studio* in Berlin has been producing (with my collaboration) highly structured basic electronic sounds which – mixed with concrete natural sounds or used for its richness of tone-colour as 'air-conditioning music' to aid concentration and relexation – can be replayed almost inaudibly as a background. Some of these tapes have also been used in concerts to accompany composed orchestral or chamber music.

In 1973 one of these basic sound-tracks, the result of a series of separate operations, was played back to the northern Indian singer Pandit Patekar. Several synthesizer frequencies had been tuned to the fundamental tone and its first overtones, while others touched in an undulatory way on various of the upper tones of the natural spectrum, especially the second, third and upper fifth.

Patekar accepted this sound-track accompaniment as 'Western tambura' and began to sing very softly to it a few simple variations on the mantra syllables *hari om tat sat* and *namo shivaya*. We were unanimous in choosing the scale of the Raga Maru Bihag, which is closest to the harmonic spectrum and the natural notes suggested by it (C – D – E – F sharp – G – A – B). It corresponds to the Lydian church mode. I then studied the sophisticated sequences of the Raga Maru Bihag and practised it on the various keyboard instruments – organ, electronic keyboard, piano etc. On his European tour Pandit Patekar sang on several occasions to this synthesized ground and my own accompaniment on the electric organ. My task was to underlay the vocal improvisations with modal-harmonic 'sound carpets' together with flowing musical patterns.

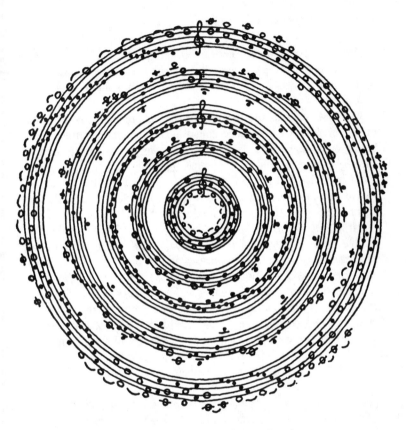

P. M. Hamel: score of *Continuous Creation*

CONTINUOUS CREATION

Concentric music for keyboard-instruments, electronics and rhythm-instruments ad lib. (1974/5)

The term 'continuous creation' was coined by the British astrophysicist Fred Hoyle. He uses it to designate the constant creation of matter out of nowhere, simply appearing and continually unfolding.

The first stage in the realisation of the predetermined modal improvisations of this piece consists, for the one or more keyboard instrumentalists, in the free playing of two patterns for the right or left hand in a relaxed, light-hearted way until the hand is 'doing it by itself' (see Example 7). The figures can be varied relatively within a wide range of modal scales, while the score itself uses the Dorian mode based on D. The individual motif-like seed-phrases are now repeated periodically, while the octave pitch of each cycle can vary. While one hand goes on repeating the periodic seed-phrases indefinitely, the other adds sustained chords and note combinations from the scale in use: thus the Dorian scale is used modal-harmonically, i.e., both in the form of horizontal motifs and vertically in the form of chords. The accompanying tape comprises, for example, deep synthesizer frequencies based on the spectrum of the keynote D.

If one examines the illustrated mandala model, one can see that all the patterns are to be repeated continuously: the third circle is, so to speak, the perpetual motion of the right hand, played by fingers 1 to 3. After a fairly lengthy and intensive period of practice the fourth and fifth fingers are able to add the intervals of the innermost circle. Circles 2 and 4 concern the left hand, and the periodicity of these figures also determines the rhythmic beat. The rhythm should be kept simple to start with, in duple or triple time. The rhythmic impulse is taken over *ad lib.* by several tuned conga drums (G – A – C – D) and intensified. Nevertheless no 'stolid' rhythm should or must develop, but rather the duple and triple periods should flow into each other. Only when both or all the performers are into an involuntary, common rhythmic pulse is this periodicity maintained until the end.

The outermost circle of the composed mandala is to some extent a development of the innermost one: the long-sustained note-sequence can be realised either by a pre-programmed electronic keyboard or by particularly virtuoso 'handling' on the spot. The note combinations which arise out of the improvisation are not to be played schematically, but should be produced in varying forms during the course of the performance. The hands must perform independently of each other, freely and effortlessly. In time the liberated state *between* active and passive will be encountered. Very gradually a moment of dazzling awareness comes into being, and one simply watches one's hands playing away ... an indescribable feeling.

DIAPHAINON

Materials for an integral music for orchestra (1974)

This orchestral composition takes as its basic idea the attitude of consciousness characterised by the spiritual works of the Swiss scholar and cultural philosopher Jean Gebser, who died in 1973. His principal works (*Abendländische Wandlung, Ursprung und Gegenwart, Asien lächelt anders* and *Verfall und Teilhabe*) draw attention to the profound transformation of consciousness which our age has currently to undergo. The aim of the composition is to make audible what Jean Gebser understood by the term 'Diaphainon':

> The undivided, ego-less human being who no longer sees parts but realises the *Self* – the spiritual form of man's being and that of the world – is aware of the Whole, the *Diaphainon* which 'lies before' all origins, which suffuses everything. For him there is neither heaven nor hell, neither Here nor Beyond, neither ego nor world, neither immanence nor transcendence, but through their magical unity, their mythical wholeness, their mental division and synthesis, only the Whole is perceived. We must seek to become aware of this four-dimensional wholeness that is free from space and time, for only from 'within' this spatial and temporal freedom is it possible to perceive the transparency of the spiritual, the *Diaphainon* which cannot be made visibly manifest.*

* J. Gebser: *Ursprung und Gegenwart*, Munich 1973.

Part I

Atomisation (mental): 'cut up, torn apart, divided' (Gebser), highest overtones derived from the note A as sharp, pointed, shrill events: orchestral psychosis.

Part II

Evocation (magical): vital, ecstatic cry, 'the earth is quaking', the deepest notes, shamanistic powers.

Part III

Arché, presentation of the Origin (archaic): the overtone/space-harmony is heard.

Part IV

Soul-dream (mythical): the maternal bosom of Indian raga, modal clearing, ancient Greek pentatonics.

Part V

Alienation (concrete): the modal scale develops into dode-caphonic material; parts I and II combine out of their 'alienation'.

Part VI

Achronon, foundations in the ground of being: a-perspective modal-harmonic scale of the Raga Todi (North India).

Part VII

Taking note – giving note (apperceptive): harmonic/functional abstraction; apotheosis as a stepping-stone.

Part VIII

Manifestation (diaphanous/integral/free of time): the overtones derived from the note A find their fundamental tone on a non-tonal, newly-understood 'atonal' basis, an attempt at acoustic transparency.*

MAITREYA

Experiment in integral music for orchestra (1974)

This composition represents an extension of the musical tech-niques applied in *Diaphainon* to the search for a transparent sound capable of giving audible expression to a new, emerging

---

* First performed at 'musica viva', Munich (Schott's Söhne).

consciousness. By contrast with *Diaphainon*, which is to some extent an 'inventory', in *Maitreya* the individual sections are interlocked or fused together in such a way that its acoustically-presented levels of consciousness arise not one after other but within each other (see page from score in Appendix).

What Gebser describes as the new, integral or diaphanous consciousness, what Sri Aurobindo calls 'supramental' and Teilhard de Chardin 'transparent', is to the Buddhist the living manifestation of the *coming buddha Maitreya*, the great lover who, as a future building force, is infiltrating man's consciousness with ever-growing power:

Maitreya, who was once the symbol for a far-distant future, has now become the living hope of millions of spiritually awakened people throughout the world, and especially all those who, after the dissolution of received traditions and forms of belief, are seeking for new and more living values. For nowadays humanity is becoming aware for the first time of being part of a cosmic unity and a common human heritage that links us in a common destiny ...

This ideal takes on flesh and blood in the figure of Maitreya, for he is, like us, both becoming and being, and all the while we are growing spiritually, we are growing together with him and inwardly merging ourselves with him: he becomes the prototype or embodiment of our own highest consciousness.

The coming Buddha will replace the age of intellectual acquisitiveness with an expanded intuitive awareness, while the feeling and consciousness of an underlying oneness with all life will effect the breakthrough into a deeper feeling of love and an active compassion. This has nothing in common with that sentimental attitude affected by emotional people: rather is it the practical application of the characteristic wisdom of *Amitabha*, in whom warmth of feeling is combined with clarity of inner vision. Maitreya is the embodiment of spontaneous action arising out of selfless love, which does not bind the doer, but frees him and blesses him, because his action is free of egocentric desire.*

* Lama Govinda, extracts from an article in *Maitreya*, Shambala Publications, Berkeley. Translated from the German version in the periodical *Middle Earth*, No. 5.

The integral composition *Maitreya* sets out to bring about these selfless and compassionate states of feeling and consciousness as well as a musical-spiritual integration by means of sounds and notes.*

* Published by Bärenreiter-Verlag, Kassel.

5 Social Practice and Exercise Methods

THE HEALING EFFECT OF MUSIC

Every illness is a musical problem ...
Novalis

The healing of psychic disorders by means of musical sounds
has a centuries-old history stretching back through all cultures.
The task of the medicine-man and shaman was to provide the
patient not with medicines but with healing chants. With rattles
and percussion instruments the evil spirits of disease were driven
out, and a drumbeat accompanied the mesmeric laying-on of
hands. The direct efficacy of these powers is still observable today
in various non-European cultures.

Admittedly this musico-therapeutic potential derives from a
level of consciousness far different from the contemporary
mental one. As soon, in fact, as we start to study the magical
cultures from a therapeutic or medical point of view, we realise
that figures such as the shaman or medicine-man not only see
the world differently, but are able to exercise influences on the
physical world that to us are inconceivable.* We mentally-
orientated Europeans can no longer imagine how it is possible
to heal illnesses by means of sounds. And so it may well strike
us as a form of superstition when we are told that the ancient
Greeks believed it possible to cure sciatica by blowing notes of
the Phrygian mode against the affected parts of the body. And it
is recounted of Pythagoras, too, that he used songs to cure
bodily pains, to soothe the pangs of bereavement, to calm anger
and to still desire.

Later, in the Middle Ages, it was the 'wizards of the massage
of the drumskin' who opened vents through which the 'evil

* Compare G. R. Heyer: *Der Organismus der Seele*, Munich 1958, p. 175.

spirits' could escape. And it was in the last century that observations were at last made of the effects of music on patients.
Thus Dr. Hofgartner of Vienna reported that fast, pleasant music
caused the patient's eyes to sparkle, the pulse to speed up and
the cheeks to redden, while the consequences of slow, mournful
music were a saddening of the eyes, a paling of the face and a
slowing of the heartbeat. In his important book on musical healing, Aleks Pontvik describes the late nineteenth century use of an
orchestra to treat nervous cases, and the foundation of a mental
institution near Naples in which musicians were employed in a
curative capacity.*

From this it has transpired that pieces of music are not medicines that one can simply prescribe. For whether harps are useful
for hysteria, trumpets for persecution-mania, an hour of Handel
for a weak heart, Mozart for rheumatism, or Schubert for in-
somnia (according to the practice at a certain American university) is more than questionable. None the less, during the last
twenty years a music therapy based on the most wide-ranging
of methods has been developed, above all in the U.S.A., though it
is only in the last two or three years that a lively interest in this
area has also started to manifest itself in Germany.

First of all, two principal schools of music therapy need to
be distinguished – that which seeks to work through listening,
and that which would bring help to the patient through his own
involvement in communicative music-making. Behind these two
aspects stand two different ways of looking at the problem. The
representatives of the one place their faith exclusively in the
spiritual powers of music, while the others maintain that the
'anthroposophical mysticism' of countless music therapists is to
blame for the fact that music therapy is seen as vague and sus-
pect by rationally-trained psychotherapists. The latter regard the
'magical use' of music as a heresy, and further maintain that
music is incapable of curing a patient through any purely
musical realisation-experience, whether of spiritual or of mental
illness.

At all events, as the Soviet scientist U. Berdiyev of the
Samarkand Medical High School has established, notes of various
pitches, volumes and tones have a discernible effect on the
cardiovascular system. 'Our organism is subject to biorhythms.

* A. Pontvik : *Heilen durch Musik*, Zürich 1955.

To put it metaphorically, man resonates to music as does a string. The nervous system is such a string *par excellence*. That is why the rhythmic processes of the organism can be strengthened by the use of music as a stimulant.'*

It is a demonstrated fact that fast music also quickens the pulse, and that music can influence both blood pressure and heart-rhythm in terms of an ECG modification. On the other hand Prof. Alfred Schmölz, director of one of the Viennese institutes of music therapy, expects positive results less from 'passive therapy', i.e., listening to music, than from encouraging the patient to participate in spontaneous music-making. The Siegburg behavioural scientist Johannes Kneutgen reports in the collected volume *Neue Wege der Musiktherapie* (Düsseldorf 1974) that debilitated youngsters and even idiots will pass quiet nights under the influence of tape-recorded cradle-songs, while the incidence of bed-wetting decreases by almost two-thirds and the various sleeping-drugs can be dispensed with. The Bonn therapist Georges Hengesch has allowed schizophrenic psychotics (who had often been subjected to electric shock treatment) to play as a group with Orff's school instruments, and achieved a relaxing effect that made it possible to resume speech therapy, when long efforts to this end had hitherto proved fruitless.

The Göttingen psychotherapist Prof. Hanscarl Leuner, who has already been mentioned in connection with psychedelic therapy, has gone on to develop a technique in which it is arranged for the patient to construct mental images that are intensified by listening to music. This so-called 'katathymic image-experience' under the influence of music has already shown itself to be very effective in many therapy groups, as well as in work with 'healthy patients'. These day-dreams under musical influence noticeably lessen the severity of the symptoms, according to Leuner, as, for example, the impulse to stutter in cases of neurotic stammering. The Kassel theologian and psychologist Dr. Ingrid Riedel has further developed this into 'imagination with music' in which several people in a group-circle exchange and analyse psychologically those inner pictures which they have found to be supported or intensified by the music. Leuner, too, proceeds on the assumption that his technique of experiencing day-dreamed pictures under the influence of music can also be

* From: *Medizin, Forschung, Gesundheit*, Rostock, August 1975.

practised in groups, and can help even healthy people 'to achieve a deepened self-discovery and the clarification of personal identity' (Leuner).

Another important application of listening to music is to be found in therapeutic hypnosis. Here music can lead to altered states of awareness – to colour-synaesthesia, for example, which can even occur in allegedly unmusical patients as a result of their making an unconscious association between the experience of the sounds and the corresponding sense impressions of light and colour. It was interesting to observe whether the hypnotic dream-experience altered at the moment when the music started. In fact it was established that, while under hypnosis, patients tended to have negative experiences before the music was faded in, whereas after it had started these gloomy pictures were replaced by happier images. Naturally the choice of music plays an important rôle here.

Another important finding is that subjects or patients could retain in their memories for many years the fragments of music they had heard under hypnosis, and that on hearing them again their former feelings of happiness would often return. The same phenomenon has become well-known in connection with music-listening under the influence of drugs: the music heard in ecstatic moments produces the same intensified feeling when re-heard years later. A further experiment was arranged involving artistically gifted or artistically engaged subjects: in the absence of music, they would draw their pictorial experiences in black and white on 'coming round': but when music was switched on during the hypnosis, their pictorial images changed to full colour. Furthermore, the subjects were able to develop in their sketches or pictures an unconscious aesthetic feeling for the personal style of the composer or the mood of the piece they had been listening to.

Music versus Drug Addiction

The Würzburg clarinettist and psychotherapist Ernst Flackus has brought the therapeutic aspect of listening to music into relationship with methods of autogenous training. Personally familiar with the advanced stages of this relaxation method, he is working on 'deep relaxation through music-listening'. During the course of the 'heaviness exercises' and muscle relaxation starting with suggestions to the patient ('Your arm is quite heavy ... I am completely still ... Breathe deeply'), he plays various records and tapes in the background, as though from far away, all of them of a meditative character. After twenty minutes the beginning of the 'return' is announced by one or more gong-beats, and the patient comes back to full consciousness.

In his paper *Musik gegen Drogen*, Flackus has reported on his relaxation and meditation groups and on his work with drug addicts. After the various exercises each participant completes a personal experience report on the effect of the music and the images evoked by it. On the procedure followed in his courses Flackus reports: 'During the exercise I played Zen meditation music softly over a loudspeaker system, but nevertheless made it clear beforehand that the patient should not listen to the music, but simply concentrate on the weight and warmth of his body ... This introductory exercise was successfully carried out, and encouraged me to introduce specially chosen electronic music from the tenth session onwards. Particularly suitable were tapes on which experiences from nature, such as the pattering of rain with the sun coming out, were represented electronically.'*

In one of his groups one of the participants brought along his favourite Beat discs, reports Prof. Flackus, and the group voted that he be allowed to play them. But after only a short time it became clear that this music, far from promoting the desired relaxation, was actually preventing it. 'This was not only be-cause of the strong beat; for these listeners with experience of drugs, alcohol, ecstatic movement and dances, it was psychic agitation that came to the fore, in natural opposition to the ob-ject of the exercise, namely a personal achievement of deep re-laxation and self-absorption.'†

Flackus goes on to explain why Classical or Western spiritual music did not have too much success in his work, and showed themselves to be hardly suitable. Most subjects found it diffi-cult not to listen to this music and to keep their own bodily pro-cesses at the centre of their attention. For some, these familiar types of music brought back former, ill-digested memories of piano and violin lessons, while for others, on hearing Gregorian hymns, it was the constraints of the convent school that came

* From *Trug der Drogen*, Siebenstern Sammelband 1974, p. 119 f.
† Ibid.

to mind. Many 'enlightened' Europeans find it difficult positively to experience spiritual music and its power, without a disturbing admixture of childhood memories, of the constraints of church and of strict ritual. How many have thrown out the babe of Bethlehem with the bathwater of ecclesiastical and human short-comings and simply cannot bear the sound of the organ!

Apart from his own music and the record *Music for Zen Meditation*, Ernst Flackus finds Classical Zen music and a range of electronic works most useful for his exercises in self-absorption and meditation. They are 'perceived virtually as abstract sounds' and thus make it easy for the subjects 'not to listen to them, but merely to half-perceive them in the background and in this way to allow them, so to speak, to flow into them ... The music hovers in the air as a vibration, as "tone-colour". For the young person this resonance is so soothing, and also removes distortions and excesses, be he never so at home in other familiar "noise scenes" at home, Beat-dive, café or discothèque. Of course the participants first had to learn the other ways in which it is possible, and necessary, to appreciate sounds, if these were to mean any real gain in strength to them. It also dawned on them that one perceives and listens to a concert differently, and more deeply, in a state of relaxation than through any activised or agitated form of participation.'*

The well-known Argentinian avant-gardist Mauricio Kagel even took up the theme of music therapy in one of his annual courses for New Music in Cologne. In the state hospital at Bonn experiments have been undertaken with a view to getting into musical communication with psychically disturbed people. In this case, not only were the traditional, easily-playable instruments used, but other sound sources were specially devised to promote contact with patients. Many socially disturbed patients and schizophrenics, who had in some cases given not the slightest sign of communication for decades, responded to the acoustic opportunity during the several weeks of the study.†

If practical music therapy, carried out by the patient himself, can and must produce all kinds of noise – shrill signs of the distorted psyche, signals of anxiety or helplessness – then any attempt at musical healing, if it is to appeal to the listening patient, should take conscious account of the inner powers of music.

---

* Flackus: article in *Trug der Drogen*, p. 121.
† M. Geck: *Musiktherapie als Problem der Gesellschaft*, Stuttgart 1973.

Anyone who is not himself conscious, from the concrete/intellectual point of view as well as the intuitive/feeling one, cannot heal either. A 'harmonic therapy' reflecting the harmonic laws of musical power would not merely presuppose sensitive doctors and patients for sensitising, but also musical works that give total acoustic expression to *pure* chords and melodies, as a reflection of each individual's own state of 'is-ness'. In his *Lehrbuch der Harmonik* Hans Kayser refers to a healing 'chord-bath' which ought as a matter of course to be brought into a reasonable and coherent shape suited to today's psychotherapeutic methods.

'That, apart from hunger and love, hardly anything affects the life of the soul so much as music is well enough known. And the notion of influencing the human psyche by means of sound, taking this term in the widest sense, is, at the very least, extraordinarily obvious. For any rational psychotherapy there is doubtless here a wide field of unsuspected possibilities. Since, seen from the harmonic point of view, this has to be a matter of resonance-influences on given psychic patterns, the tonal aspect ought initially to be reduced to its simplest expression: to pure, tonal chords above all, plus the simplest of melodic sequences, repeated at regular intervals, from which the "musical doctor" invites the patient to choose. An hour's worth of daily "chord-bath" would indubitably heal many nervous breakdowns more quickly than would some other methods, and a likewise daily immersion in the calming, pleasant sound of a well-loved melody could work wonders for a disturbed nervous system.'*

Music for Relaxation

Using types of music, part-recorded, part-live, that come very near to the idea of a 'chord-bath', I have for two years now been conducting experiments in musical relaxation-therapy in apprentice-halls and leisure centres for Berlin workers. With the encouragement of a political organisation that was not concerned *merely* with the material well-being of the underprivileged, lecture evenings and get-togethers were arranged during the years 1971 and 1972 in Berlin-Moabit.

The evenings took place weekly or fortnightly in a cellar which had no chairs, but was laid out instead with mattresses and blankets. The first evenings generally produced an animated

* H. Kayser: *Lehrbuch der Harmonik*, Stuttgart 1963.

throng of 'customers', but numbers decreased as time went on, which was just as well, for meaningful situations never arose in a group of more than ten people. The available music-making facilities comprised a tape-recorder/amplifer system and a two-manual organ. After a brief explanation a start would be made with a musical improvisation designed to offer either the young apprentice or the older worker a more or less familiar musical sound. Thus, themes from Beatles' songs or other familiar tunes were used. (In addition, half-an-hour's worth of gramophone records – already familiar to the participants – had been played beforehand.) This first improvisation of mine would establish at the outset whether the randomly-constituted audience was ready for concentrated listening. If this was the case, a piece of music announced as 'relaxation-music' would then be played (this was in any case the title of these relaxation evenings). Generally speaking the pieces in question were *A Rainbow in Curved Air* by Terry Riley and the earlier pieces of Steve Reich (*Four Organs, Piano-Phase*). According to a particular audience's acceptance-level, these pieces would be run either for a fairly short time or right to the end, generally for some twenty minutes. Since most of the young workers and apprentices (an age-group ranging from 16 to 24), who in response to the poster announcements were supposed not to have taken any drugs before coming, often brought along cans of beer instead, a discussion would arise as to whether this music went with alcohol. The conversation would then turn to personal conflicts, to problems at work, and to the fact that there was never a proper chance to relax. Soon everybody would start to realise that this was not *merely* the fault of the boss or of exploitation : in fact there *was* time for it, but somehow one was always 'on the go'.

The next stage was generally an improvisation on the organ, beginning with somewhat chaotic and jittery sounds, sometimes frankly shrill and painful, but then leading almost imperceptibly into a periodic sound, a continually-recurring motif or just a static bass-note. The first observable result was that after a time those who had let themselves go into this development-process were suddenly 'far away'. This sudden 'dozing off' was a puzzling phenomenon : it was not that they had become tired, nor, somehow, had they really fallen asleep. Thus everybody was fully aware of when the organ stopped playing. Among the older workers, however, who right from the beginning had been extremely guarded about the whole affair (since this was something that could not be understood on the same sort of level as applied to the discussion of Pop music or other themes) and whose attitude of 'Well, we'll see what happens, but I'm not promising . . .' certainly didn't help to start with, agitated discussions would break out after the various musical performances, to the effect that they knew nothing *about* music, even though they allegedly liked it. Listening – simply the ability to listen – is a process that has to be *learnt* in the earliest years, otherwise there is no possibility of ever using music as a means of relaxation.

None the less it was noticeable during these two years how quickly some people will respond to music as a relaxation aid.

In any case, quite a few workers had come along simply because, just for once, something outside the run of the normal Berlin social amenities was being put on for them. By and large I regard these experiments as a success, even though I received no support, least of all of a material kind, from any quarter. Within the coercive systems of such diverse milieux as factory, office, suburb, block of flats or old people's home, the process of consciousness-expansion and self-realisation still falls within the sphere of social taboo.

This brief report can do no more than serve as a footnote to the very difficult and important task of producing a socially-engaged form of relaxation music. The most important conclusion to be drawn from these experiments in the use of music for inner relaxation has been that music *alone* can do nothing to bring about or maintain in people a truly open state of conscious relaxation. Above all, active participation is of prime importance, particularly for young people. It is here, in the sphere of active improvisation, that music therapy has an important rôle to play for socially and environmentally disturbed and handicapped people, however dilettante the idea may seem. The case of a Berlin working-class youngster speaks for itself. At fourteen almost a medical wreck from 'paint-sniffing' (the inhaling of chemical substances), at sixteen in Borstal for car-stealing, at eighteen unemployed, this youth is nevertheless not so far gone as many of his companions in misfortune, for he has his guitar. He is getting by as an occasional labourer and has become neither a 'fixer' nor an alcoholic, which is something quite rare. After many hours, without any help or encouragement from outside, he has learnt to play a bit of Blues and a few Rolling Stones numbers. He has created his own musical therapy, to which he has to devote some time each day, just to make life bearable. At which point various questions arise. Could efforts not be made for the many others who share a like fate? Or, on the other hand, is this music-making just a form of escape mechanism, a 'music of repression'?

Music critics are quick to make fun of the harmonic music of such as Terry Riley and write it off as 'function-music': 'The more worries there are to forget and repress, the longer and more happily one may lie on one's back and let oneself be lulled by its pleasant sound.'*

A person who cannot surrender himself to sound, who cannot 'let himself go' into a musical state which can only be experienced in this relaxed way, has necessarily to stand outside it and may perhaps be secretly jealous of those who are capable of this form of inner experience. For in fact the healing capabilities of music are intimately bound up with personal experience of the workings of inner relaxation, and with the ability to surrender oneself to one's own breathing which, whether consciously perceived or otherwise, is what supports and makes possible life itself in the first place. To the question of the Berlin worker: 'What am I supposed to do while you're playing, then?' the simplest answer, that he should be aware of his own breathing and observe it, resulted in an immediate initial relaxation.

Music and breathing as a unity stand in the closest of relationships to the healing effects of sound. Meditative music, long-sustained sounds, gentle movements or even a single note can be appreciated and accepted for the first time, even by the most rigidly intellectual or drug-saturated 'nitwit', if only he is given the task of observing his own breathing: when it comes in, when it goes out, whether it is regular or restricted. Body-awareness is certainly a capability, or rather a gift, which is diametrically opposed to our competition-orientated upbringing. We are supposed to have 'no time', we must always be 'on the go', for the first step towards actual thought would bring with it the shock of realising that all haste is in fact pointless and only leads to

* *Süddeutsche Zeitung*, feature-pages, 15/10/74.

further senselessness. How often it has been observed that simple people especially possess without so-called training an astonishing, spontaneous sensibility which nobody has made them conscious of and which has no motivation in any conversation or encouragement on the part of those around them. Moreover, through the drug of television our ability to perceive the subtle processes of our own organism is being stunted, if not killed off entirely. People are concerned less and less with their real selves and tend rather to feel hurt if someone else concerns himself with their inner life.

None the less, ways need to be found to re-discover our inner regions, to become aware of our own breathing, to encourage us to become familiar with our own voices, to enable us to sing, to permit the natural movement of the breath that will allow man once again to find his own vibration, his 'own note'.

THE POWER OF BREATH AND VOICE

From the earliest times the Asian has known the existential meaning of human breathing. If we consider that we can live for weeks without eating, for days without drinking, and yet without breath would die in a few minutes, the significance of breathing is immediately obvious. Man breathes all the time, whether asleep or awake, and the breathing always works in such a way that we generally become aware of it only when we either have problems with it – lack of air during violent exertion, breathing troubles arising from illness, breathlessness as a result of shock – or when we are deep breathing in the fresh air, in the forest.

It is a good test to ask oneself when one is aware of one's breathing. To start with one thinks immediately of inhaling, and consciously breathes in more deeply, while expanding one's chest and thinking: 'Yes, I'm breathing.'

The second stage in the test might be to observe the distinction between how one breathes when one is merely letting the breath flow in and out unconsciously, and how it alters as soon as one starts to think about it. After some time it becomes apparent that as soon as one thinks about the breathing one also simultaneously 'does' it, i.e., one consciously breathes in, and then quite audibly out again. But even if one does not 'will' one's breathing, *it* breathes none the less. How would it be, then, if we were consciously to experience how the breath just goes on breathing ... in other words to watch how the breathing-process goes on even during sleep, without actually 'doing' anything, but merely observing it as it comes and goes? Anyone who tries this test straight away will notice that it is by no means so easy consciously to let *it* breathe. And this is where not only the ancient teaching of *Pranayama* comes in (the Hindus' practice of breath-control), not only, too, the knowledge of the Zen Buddhists on the subject of the 'is-ness' of the breath, but also where the work of a whole variety of Western breathing-institutes begins, whose help is today being increasingly sought after.

The prime rôle of breathing in the Indian yoga schools is demonstrated by the fact that an overwhelming number of yoga exercises are concerned directly or indirectly with the breathing. Within the course of any particular exercise, breath control is combined with various body positions and methods of mind control. In advanced exercises, from the cleansing of the body and mind (*yama* and *niyama*) via the body positions (*asanas*) to *pranayama*, the numerous variations of breathing are very much to the fore. Carefully, via a range of procedures, the breath-organs – nostrils, air-passages and lungs – are 'cleansed'. Various types of breathing rhythm are used. For example in one well-known exercise one nostril is closed while breathing through the other to a given count, the breath is held for a given time (*kumbhaka*), and then the air is allowed to flow out of the formerly closed nostril, once again to a given count.*

The breath is now brought into the various parts of the body by means of a kind of imagined inner pressure, and with the help of the corresponding vowel sounds, for example by constricting the throat or the anus or carrying out various *asanas*. Then follows the regulating of the breathing rhythm, the technique of slowing down the breathing and finally of stopping it. Thus, in the process of uniting or yoking (*yoga*) man with his higher nature, which is at one and the same time the divine, the breath has a prime function. The breath is not only cleansed, but 'it assumes the rôle of our most important ally in the effort

---

* Compare André van Lysebeth on the subject: *Die grosse Kraft des Atems. Die Atemschule des Pranayama*, 2nd edition, Munich 1975.

to transfer outwardly our inner perceptions. Thus the breath is directed to the organs, as they really are and as we imagine them to be, and channelled through them.'*

The very first experiences with yoga and *pranayama* show that the awareness and stimulation of perceptions in the inner centres is promoted by the direction of the breath to particular parts of the body. Here the power of the breath resides primarily in *prana*, the subtle energy which flows through the body via invisible yet tangible channels. *Prana* can be experienced when adrenalin is produced under the influence of a sudden fright and 'shivers run up and down the spine', or when a part of the body 'shudders' on being gently stroked. These fine channels are also known in acupuncture, running just under the surface of the skin as well as within the body, where they run along the spine connecting the various *chakras*. It is through these channels, which are also called *nadis*, that the *prana* passes, and in one particular yoga technique even the sound of the *nadis* becomes audible. Via one of the channels, *susumna*, the *kundalini* serpent-power (already mentioned briefly in connection with the *man-tras*) climbs up through the body from where it slumbers in the lowest centre.

What is of interest to us here, however, is the connection be-tween breathing and consciousness. It is a fact of which the yogis were always well aware that the mind, the centre of think-ing, is unsteady when the breath is disturbed, and vice versa. When the breath is following a free and regular rhythm or even standing still, an achievement learnt by the yogi, the flow of thoughts also quietens down, and the constant thinking comes to a halt. The breathing becomes the sole content of one's con-sciousness. But the goal of the yogi must be to achieve pure consciousness *without* content.

While in the technique of yoga the breathing is consciously manipulated – either rhythmically controlled or slowed down and retained – Zen Buddhism's relationship to breathing is quite different. Since in Zen there exists no duality between controller and controlled, and likewise no duality between mind and body, spiritual and physical, there is in Zen no artificial breathing technique to be followed, but simply a conscious, to some extent psychological observation. None the less great significance is

* W. Haas: *Oestliches and Westliches Denken*, Reinbek 1967, p. 188.

attached to the way in which one breathes. For breathing is not only a vital rhythmic process, but also a procedure in which 'control and spontaneity, voluntary and involuntary action are most clearly identified with one another (Alan Watts).

In his book *The Way of Zen*, Watts explains the significance of the breath in Zen Buddhist teachings and schools:

> Long before the origins of the Zen School, both Indian *yoga* and Chinese Taoism practised 'watching the breath', with a view to *letting*, not forcing, it to become as slow and silent as possible. Physiologically and psychologically, the relationship between breathing and 'insight' is not yet altogether clear. But if we look at man as process rather than entity, rhythm rather than structure, it is obvious that breathing is something which he does – and thus *is* – constantly. Therefore grasping air with the lungs goes hand-in-hand with grasping at life ... The technique therefore begins by encouraging a full release of the breath, easing it out as if the body were being emptied of air by a great leaden ball sinking through the chest and abdomen, and settling down into the ground. The returning in-breath is then allowed to follow as a simple reflex action. The air is not actively inhaled; it is just allowed to come; and then, when the lungs are comfortably filled, it is allowed to go out once more, the image of the leaden ball giving it the sense of 'falling' out as distinct from being pushed out.*

This is precisely where we Westerners are confronted by our main problem. We are accustomed to managing everything, manipulating, acting, using force. And now, of all things, our breathing is supposed to arise 'of itself', involuntarily, and yet be consciously experienced and observed. In order simply to 'let our breath flow' we need composure and self-surrender, as well as attentiveness, if we are to perceive it without disturbing it. The most important thing, according to the teacher of breathing techniques Professor Ilse Middendorf, is 'self-recollection', conscious presence in those parts of the body in which the flowing of the breath is to be experienced. 'Once one has learnt to detect this breath movement and is at the same time "present" throughout one's body, one has a chance to become aware of the primal

* A. Watts: *The Way of Zen*, Pelican 1962, p. 217.

rhythmic movement of the breath without altering it. The un-selfconscious breathing function enters our consciousness ... Through the procedure mentioned we create for ourselves a state of breathing which is under our control and yet whose rhythm is undisturbed by our will ... Out of this comes awareness of hitherto unconsciously followed paths, bodily as well as spiritual, whose energies can now be transformed.'*

This 'practice with the breath' (Graf Dürckheim) is thus no yoga technique, influencing or manipulating the breath, but a return to the natural process of breathing. Here, moreover, no teacher is necessary to 'keep a hand on' the person practising. The hand of the therapist is merely there to lead the patient or exerciser, who is lying down on a flat, firm bed or couch, to the various breath-regions and diagnose where the other's rhythm is disturbed, where and when his breathing is shallow or weak, hard or hasty. The hand's job is to help the exerciser release and 'open' himself, once it has learnt to touch and activate given pressure points and places throughout the body, corresponding to the various breath-regions. These points – lying for the shoulder region in the feet, for example, or for the head in the big toe – are connected with the already-mentioned inner channels and, being directly experienceable and thus demonstrable, can be learnt about at various breathing-institutes.

It is well-known in naturopathy and acupuncture that all the human organs and parts of the body are 'present' or represented in the foot, i.e., that given zones or points in the foot correspond to particular parts of the body. The mantric exercise already mentioned that places the seed-syllables and letters in the feet is based on the same knowledge. The hands, too, have just such a correspondence with the body's breath-regions. As an example of this the following brief exercise deserves to be mentioned. Let the 'patient' sit in a relaxed way and allow the breathing to work by itself. Now place the tips of the two little fingers alongside each other and press them lightly together, while the other fingers are gently spread wide. Next try to detect where the breath is flowing: more upwards or more downwards? Now alter the hand position, press the index-fingers together and keep all the other fingers away: now where is the breath flowing? Anybody can find out the answer for himself. Gradually one senses

* I. Middendorf in the periodical *Atem*, Vol. 3, Bad Homburg 1969.

that each 'circuit' completed by two similar fingers opens a particular region of the body to the breath.

Self-observation demonstrates additionally that the parts of the body into which the breath penetrates more strongly as a result of any given finger-combination are opened even more strongly if the corresponding vowel-sound is also imagined at the same time. As a result of connections and interreactions with the breathing, resonances arise in those parts of the body corresponding to each vowel whenever this is 'thought' or imagined as being sung. This work is very subtle and gentle, yet it always has an effect on body and soul. The breath-suffused body seems to be an instrument which will resonate to every sound, every note, every word in which man can experience and recognise himself, just as he does in his movements (according to Prof. Middendorf).

The assignment of various breath-regions to given vowels can be represented schematically without prejudice to fine distinctions and fluid borderlines. In the following illustration, supplied by the Leser-Lasario school, these correspondences are supplemented by (admittedly subjective) mood and colour associations:

I(EE)	head, mouth	happy	bright yellow
E(Eh)	throat, larynx	cheerful	gold, orange
Ae(Air)	pharynx, apex of lungs		
A(Ah)	upper chest	neutral	blue-green
OA	mid-lungs		
O	heart	serious	purple, crimson
Oe(Er)	diaphragm, liver, stomach		
U(OO)	lower body	deadly serious	dark blue
UI	kidneys, rectum		

If we now recall the close connection between overtones and vowels, we find here a clear link between breath, sound, musical proportion and inner body. Indeed the Indian singers and yogis pursuing *mandra-sadhana* or *nada-yoga* invariably start by singing the purest vowels, followed by a long, hummed 'mmmh'. These are in fact the mantric seed-syllables: *hoooommm, haaaammm, heeeeg, huuuummm, hriiiimmm.*

Voice training, too (a prerequisite for singing and drama instruction, as well as for elocution), has always concentrated on having the basic consonants and vowels sounded and intoned correctly. Physical deportment and so-called 'deep' breathing have also been points of departure for the healing of speech disorders.

An important element in a clear and powerful vocal sound is correct tension. We have already spoken so much of relaxation, but here it is correct *tension* that is necessary. In any case we need to distinguish between strain and tension. Strain overburdens and constricts, and leads to rigidity; but tension balances, yields as a spring does, and is an active power which must never be allowed to lead to strain or forcing. If, on raising the voice, we tension the vocal cords incorrectly, we constrict the throat and compress the airstream, with the result that the sound is distorted and the throat becomes sore. If, on the other hand, we fail to constrict the throat, we lose too much air and cannot sustain the note, given that there is one there at all.

Voice production is closely bound up with tension and with the united concentration of all our inner and outer powers. On meeting a stranger it is immediately possible to detect both personality and level of consciousness by the sound of the voice. Any inhibition, any nervousness, as well as innate goodness and inner peace can be heard quite clearly. So many people are horrified when they hear their voice on tape for the first time : here, not infrequently, they are encountering character-traits and peculiarities that they had never before noticed in themselves.

It is also interesting to observe that the development of correct breathing and suitable voice training tends to make a person much more musically receptive and will even refine a poor ear. I now propose to quote some exercises from the group-work of the Berlin Institute for Breath Therapy and Breathing Instruction (Director : Prof. Ilse Middendorf), which are designed to lead all the way from the conscious experiencing of breathing, via the inner formation of vowels to actual singing.

Exercises in Breathing*

1. Stretch in a spontaneous, natural, animal way, first in the sitting position and then standing up. Yawning is to be encouraged.

* Published by the Institute for Breath Therapy and Instruction, West Berlin 1973. By kind permission of Frau Prof. Middendorf.

2. *Sit properly* on the buttocks (if possible on a wooden surface) in such a way as to feel your full weight on the seat. In this way the lumbar spine is held erect. The back grows upwards, the crown of the head strives heavenward. The shoulders hang square to each side, the hands rest on the thighs near the body. The thighs at the width of the hips, the knees aligned with the feet. The second and third toes are aligned with the knees. Feet spread wide, bearing their full weight.

Lay both palms on the surface of the body and concentrate your awareness at that point. The movement of the breath can be felt under your hands, growing in extent. *Let the breath come*; do not 'inhale'; let it go out, wait until it comes back in again, *by itself*. In this way address the whole torso *with your hands* and encourage the movement of the breath. This promotes sensitivity and composure and increases breath movement.

3. *Stand properly* : the whole body-weight is on the balls of the feet. All joints (in particular the knee joints) are loose and springy. Practise as under 2. (above), apart from differing hand positions. Both hands lie over the surface of the body, hovering in the air during the inbreath, returning to touch the body-surface during the outbreath. This exercise creates numerous individual developmental possibilities and, in particular, improves the quality of breathing.

4. To practise in the morning, or during the day for relaxation after heavy work : *shaking*. Stand with legs slightly apart and transfer the weight from left to right. Constantly alternate so that no tensions arise in the lower leg. Spring up with loose ankles, but *from* the ankles. On coming down again, the heel touches the floor. The springiness must reverberate through all the joints, the spine and all parts of the body. Be aware and composed. Bounce either to a high or a low frequency.

5. Torso-circling: stand with the feet apart at a distance of 20-30 cm. Bending at the waist, lean sideways completely loosely, circle to the front, straighten up. Carry on by leaning slightly backwards and then continue to repeat the circle – twice to the right, twice to the left. Repeat – putting both movements together – so that the shoulders follow a flowing, spiral, twisting movement. The breath comes and goes as it wants to. Only when you are taking a rest and feeling the after-effects do you notice how the breath is going right through you. A good exercise in the

morning. Important for the whole exercise: ensure that the arms and shoulders move *completely freely* . . .

13. Vowel E. Silently sing to yourself or contemplate the sound E (Eh), i.e., feel where the movement of the breath is taking place. E moves the sides in a lateral direction and develops one particular region. Later, the sound can be intoned on the outbreath. But even while breathing in and out silently the breath movement is strong and clear. E signifies movement outwards.

14. Vowel O. As under 13. The sound O has a breath movement which goes backwards and forwards on the same level as E; thus the O-region lies roughly from the middle of the breastbone to around the navel. Likewise for the back. O develops a different breath-region from E. O signifies movement inwards.

15. Vowels U and I. As under 13. U (OO) is sited in the lower, pelvic region. Combined with I (EE) (head and shoulders) it uplifts the spine and the whole torso.

Thus, inwardly singing, speaking, thinking or contemplating a vowel and experiencing one's own breath-regions means *truly letting the breath come*. If the outbreath bears the *sound* of the vowel, the resonance spreads far and wide through the vowel-region and its contours produced during the inbreath . . .

Since the movement of our breath reacts integrally on our whole life-expression, it is not surprising that under such conditions such breath-movement regions are formed. These forms correspond to the vocalic breath-regions. The preconditions are as I have pointed out: the silent sounding of a vowel in full concentration, and feeling the movement of the breath.*

Frau Prof. Middendorf continually emphasises in her lectures, as well as in personal conversation, the distinction between the opening of particular regions by silently thought vowels and the opening of the resonance-regions of sounded vowels. The breath-regions corresponding to inwardly spoken and sung vowels are in fact different. According to Prof. Middendorf the vowel-region pattern of inward speaking experiences the U in the pelvis, the E in both sides up as far as the armpits, the I-region in the upper

* From a lecture by Frau Prof. Middendorf.

shoulders, neck and head. The O-region has a closed and open character, and finally the A takes in all the other vowel and consonant regions, i.e., the whole body.

On the other hand, the bodily regions corresponding to vowels or syllables that are *sung* in the course of vocal improvisation are as already set out in simplified form (on page 180).

Sounded Breathing: Vowel-Improvisation

Various composers, ensembles and music groups have recently been studying the singing techniques of Asia and Arabia, the psycho-physical effects of singing and the dynamic processes of vowel-improvisation. The American composer Pauline Oliveros, who years ago took choral sound, and its modulation by means of electronics, as the point of departure for her work (in her composition *Extended Voices*, for example) has developed *sonic meditations*, meditation patterns in sound, which she has developed partly out of the exercises performed by the 'Living Theatre' of New York and other 'sensitivity' exercises.

The already mentioned group *prima materia* has learnt *multiphonic* singing (the technique of the Mongolians and Tibetans) at least in its initial stages, and practises improvised, sung group-meditations, in which the public are also actively involved. In various places in Germany, in spontaneously assembled groups, a communal form of singing and music making has been developed, using bells, cymbals and gongs.

One such group, whose members vary in number, is called *Singing-Pool*, and is led or rather 'animated' by the sinologist and musician Peter Müller, who has studied instruments and singing techniques in various non-European countries. On the subject of communal singing he says: 'Actually we are all in the same boat. We were told at school and by our parents that we should sing in *one* particular way, that we must not sing "wrong" micro-intervals, and in this way we have been deprived of most of the fun of singing. The voice is a medium that becomes all the more alive and interesting the more we make use of it – and the more we free ourselves from the brutal insistence that we could somehow sing "wrongly".'*

The assembled participants in a *Singing-Pool* self-experience group lie or sit in a relaxed circle and start by letting their voices

* P. Müller: *AUM, Einige Tips für Leute, die gerne singen* (proof copy of *Erdenlogbuch* (Connexions) in *Middle Earth* No. 6.

sound as they breathe out. It is quite possible that no properly-sung note will result from this, but merely a kind of humming. In order to feel how the sound moves through various parts of the body, everyone stops up his ears. By alternately opening and closing each ear, one can also hear how the sound wanders hither and thither in the head. Also during the course of singing, the hands are placed on the heart and the abdomen in order to feel the vibration that is produced in the body by the voice. In smaller groups, a participant may sit chest to chest or back to back with a partner and feel the voice and presence of the other, thus allowing the body to respond to the other's body (according to Peter Müller).

The most important basic exercises in sounded breathing are collected in the famous work by Dr. J. L. Schmitt, *Das Hohe Lied vom Atem*. Two of these exercises are appended here:

Breathe in with a sigh and hold the breath; while holding it, open the mouth wide to the position of the vowel to be sung. To start with: A. Mouth big, wide open, round. The opening should be able to be felt right down past the jaw-socket and into the back of the throat.

With the accumulated breath, the vowel A is now uttered, sounding in the prepared spaces and cavities until all the breath is used up. Wait a little while; breathe in deeply and repeat the vowel seven times in succession. Repeat the whole procedure with E, I, Ue, Oe (roughly 'Er'), O, U (OO) and M.*

A further development of this exercise involves making the vowel louder as one sings it, and perhaps ending it with a final hum. Thus: Maaaaaaaaaaahmmmmmmmm, Heeeeeeeeeehmmm-mmmm, Hiiiiiiiih (no hummed ending necessary here), Vooooooh, Luuuuuuuh and Kuuuuuuuh. At the end of such a series of exercises the individual or group can take up an oriental sitting position, laying the hands on the knees or in the lap. Once the breath is working quietly and involuntarily, the participant takes a particularly deep breath, briefly holds it, contemplates or concentrates on the heart, and sings OM during the slow, gentle outbreath. All of these exercises can be carried out either alone or in a group. The most important prerequisite is a relaxed atti-tude, which may perhaps not be there to start with, but which automatically sets in after a longish period of practice. The myth

* Exercises according to Schmitt: compare *Das Hohe Lied vom Atem*, The Hague, p. 273 ff.

that we cannot sing because we failed to emulate our music teachers at primary school or choir practice is quickly shown to be the falsehood it is. It may well be that we are no good at singing folktunes or arias, but we are quite capable of using our voices in a relaxed, creative way. Perhaps in time we shall also discover our 'own note', that inner sound which is most intimately bound up with our very body and soul.

FINDING YOUR OWN NOTE

Finding your 'own note' is a process that can take some time and demands patience above all else, for although the exercise itself only takes a few minutes, it needs to be carried out regularly over several weeks. Merely trying it out just once will produce no detectable result. For this exercise you need nothing beyond a tuning fork, or some kind of musical instrument, and a carpeted floor or semi-hard couch. The best times to practise it are morning and evening; it is important to be in a calm state and alone in the room.

You lie down, then, on the semi-hard couch, perhaps lighting a candle or a joss-stick to give the whole thing a mildly ritual note, and then begin with conscious breathing. The breathing should be observed, but not controlled. Gradually start to imagine whatever vowel seems nearest to your own inner nature. With time you will come to realise which vowel is truly 'yours'. For people who live more from the middle regions of the body, a 'dark' vowel will in the course of time suggest itself as 'their own'; for people who live more on the mental level (corresponding to throat and head) it could be a 'bright' vowel such as E or I.

With this newly-discovered vowel on your lips, you now concentrate your attention on the corresponding area of the body and, having once reached the point where the breath is coming and going naturally, you form, at first quite tentatively, the vowel you have already spoken inwardly and let it sound freely with each outbreath.

It is quite possible that initially no true singing tone will result, but rather a breathy, sometimes even downright unattractive sound. This should not be consciously modified or 'beautified' into an artificial singing tone, but nevertheless you should endeavour to let the vowel that you breathe out gradually take on the nature of a sung note. It is important not to impose artificial tension on the vocal cords, but to let the vowel gradually form its own note during the outbreath. In this way you will allow the outgoing airstream to give voice, without actually producing any note of your own volition.

To help you in this, you should sing before each chosen vowel an H, or breath-sound ('Haaaaa' or 'Hoooooh' etc.) and, once produced, extend the vowel into a hum – thus, 'Huuuuummm', for example. If during these first runs no truly sung note is produced you should not be put off. After a certain time you will suddenly find yourself singing at a particular pitch, i.e., the breath will automatically discover for itself a natural vibration for the chosen vowel.

The 'own note' that you are seeking can lie at a whole variety of pitches; in other words, you may be singing your 'own note' as an overtone in the next octave up. It is important, however, to find the deepest note within the spectrum of your particular voice. In addition, care should be taken to concentrate equally on the same vowel during the inbreath too. Once you have the feeling that the note *suits you*, once the note audibly gains in resonance, you may go on 'breath-singing' for a while, but should not deliberately alter the pitch. It is of course quite possible that the pitch will alter subsequently, but generally this no longer happens once you have sung the self-same note on a number of occasions.

If you have arrived at a more or less fixed note by the end of the exercise, you must now attempt to establish its *pitch*. For musicians this is no problem, but even for non-specialists it is possible to tune a guitar-string, for example, to the note you are singing, or to establish the exact pitch with the aid of a tuning-fork. It is even easier to keep the last note of the exercise in your mind, switch on a tape-recorder while still humming it and 'fix' it in this way.

The next day you re-start the exercise in the same way as before, without knowing or checking up on last time's note. Once again you finish up with a note. Once again you record it; and perhaps you will find it completely different from the first one. But the very feel of it will tell you which of the various notes has a more pleasant, as it were 'congenial' effect. In time it

may even happen that you will find yourself singing or humming even during your daily work or in quiet moments, thus
resuming, quite unconsciously, work on your 'own note'.

But it is likely that the results of your searching and probing
and humming will vary only within very narrow limits, i.e., you
may find that a variety of notes have been recorded on the tape,
all of very similar or even almost identical pitch. It is also possible that you will discover on it the octave or fifth of one of the
notes you have previously fixed. This will hardly be surprising
when you think of the harmonic series. That is why it is important from now on to go for the lower note whenever your voice
offers you an alternative during the adjustment process.

Meanwhile you will have found a whole series of notes of
various pitches, and it may be necessary to be patient for a while
before you can speak with certainty of *one* note as being your
'own'. It is very important at this point that the encounter
with this 'own note' can be an archetypal experience: you are
immediately aware of it when you are singing your 'own'
note! In many cases, after weeks of sensitising practice, encountering your own note comes as a flash of light, or an inner
quivering and shaking. But it is nothing to be afraid of, but rather
an exalting, blissful and invigorating feeling. Meanwhile, since
people's 'own notes', sung naturally and without forcing, can be
of various pitches, we ought actually to speak of a 'personal
harmonic series'.

Now your own fundamental tone will have a particular name
– B, or D, for example. Incidentally, you should remember at
this point that the name of a note always depends on the tuning
of the particular instrument in use: the note C on an old, out-
of-tune piano will often produce an A lying one and a half tones
lower. On the other hand, a violinist accustomed to today's high
concert pitch will regard an old C as 'too low'. Thus, in finding
your own fundamental tone you should not regard as reliable
the note-names as represented by the family piano.

In any case it is of no great importance what your 'own note'
is called. If Johann Sebastian Bach spoke of the significance of C
major, his comments would need nowadays to be applied to
what to us is B major. And the *B minor Mass* would for Bach's
ear long since have become a *C minor Mass*. You would thus be
well advised to concentrate constantly on the spontaneous production of your 'own note' irrespective of whether it always

bears the same name. It is an interesting fact, but you will never again lose that note, as long as you do not 'lose yourself', i.e., become irritable or aggressive or otherwise 'out-of-tune'.

A sine-wave generator can be of assistance in fixing your 'own note'. In this case you bring the sung note into relationship with the variable pitch of the electronic generator and then relate it to a particular frequency-count, according to which, for example, concert pitch has A equal to 440 Hertz (Hz). Actually, orchestras have for a long time now been using 443 Hz, while today's Indian tuning is still based on the English concert pitch of 1894 – 432 Hz. But the frequency-count (Hz) is a physical characteristic of the note and thus the only objective way of defining its pitch.

Meanwhile your own fundamental tone, the one which feels right for you, will have its overtones – its octave, fifth, super-octave and so on. A hypothesis that has not yet been researched is that the first *nada*-note (mentioned below in an extract referring to *nada-yoga*) is a super-octave or even higher octave of your own personal fundamental tone, and that the second and third *nada*-notes are always in the musical relationship of a fifth or fourth, and are thus contained within your personal harmonic series. Another hypothesis in respect of your 'own note' is to the effect that the *mantra*-note of your inner self is an octave lower than the lowest singable note of your personal harmonic series. This *mantra*-note *is* the acoustic manifestation of the self, *tat tvam asi*. A person who has found his 'own note', whatever its pitch, gradually becomes able to speak uninhibitedly and naturally, without strain, and yet clearly and distinctly and, above all, convincingly. Another point is the fact that, having once found their 'own note', even Westerners are capable of learning the chanting techniques of the Tibetans and Mongolians (multiphonic singing). States of pain and anxiety are soothed by the singing, softly or aloud, of one's 'own note'. But the most important result of these exercises is the fact of having come one step further in one's own self-realisation.

Mandra-Sadhana

Even if the loud notes are still sounding, one should still concentrate on the subtle sound in the heart.

Upanishad

There now follow extracts from the teaching of *mandra-sadhana*, the long-preserved system of Indian voice and singing training, as described by the famous northern Indian singer Omkarnath Thakur. This classical method for cultivating the singing voice is adhered to as much in the realm of the northern Indian *Hindustani*-style as it is in southern Indian *karnatic* music. The aim of Indian musical practice is a release from the body and an attempt to transcend the physiological methodology of singing practice, a process for which knowledge of the inner musculature of the organs, the nervous system and the psychic centres is required.

The best time to practise *mandra-sadhana* – which in translation means roughly 'spiritual practice of the sung note MA (Fah)' – is in the early morning before sunrise. First of all one's individual keynote should be established: the SA (or Doh, the tonic – let us call it C, irrespective of its real pitch) should be sufficiently high for the voice to be able comfortably to descend to the MA a fifth below, which is then the lowest singable note (F, on the basis of the above assumption). Equally, the keynote should permit the voice to rise to the fifth above, PA (Soh, or G), which is generally a simple matter. One should take great care over the establishment of one's individual keynote. An incorrect keynote that lies too high or too low and is unnatural for the voice in question will make *mandra-sadhana* impossible.

Once the Sa (Doh, or C) is established, one tunes one's tambura accordingly (in our case a harmonium, or an electronic source such as an organ or sine-wave generator, or some other tunable instrument will do just as well) and begins slowly to descend to the lowest note – a downward fifth to MA (F). Obviously this bottom note must sound freely, without losing any of its resonant quality or naturalness.

Having arrived at the bottom, one repeats this deepest note, using the longest possible breaths, for at least fifteen to thirty minutes. The note should be sung to all the vowels, which, in this case, will prove almost impossible with I and E, but quite feasible with A, O and U. The articulation of the individual vowels in ever more sustained notes leads to certain physiological changes and phenomena in the stomach, abdomen and breathing etc. Anybody who has only a small voice should practise with 'Ooooo', which strengthens and enlarges the voice and removes any stiffness from it.

Mandra-sadhana is always carried out to the accompaniment of a bass note, whether from a tambura or bowed instrument or as an electronic drone. The many overtones produced by a tambura are important for the singer's concentration and the timbre of his voice. Indeed, these overtones can even be directly sung by the voice in question.

If the singer has tuned his fourth tambura string (which is not tuned to Sa or C) to F (MA), he will hear that the sound of his deepest note MA (F) also bears this Sa within it. Many yogis experience in the singing of MA the maternal power of the centre and repeat this deepest note for hours on end. When the person practising has stayed with the deepest note for no more than thirty minutes, he gradually begins to climb up the scale of the Raga Bhairav (the morning raga dedicated to Lord Shiva) one note at a time. Each note is then repeated for ten minutes, and the higher one climbs up the scale, the shorter the singing time becomes for each individual note (see Example 8).

The regular practice of mandra-sadhana has a positive effect on lungs, abdomen, heart and circulation, lengthens the breath and promotes concentration. Swimming and the techniques of the yoga exercise surya-namaskaram (the greeting of the sun) should follow, if possible, this early-morning exercise.*

Nada-Yoga

He who knows the secret of the sounds knows the mystery of the whole universe.

Hazrat Inayat Khan

For people to whom the world of sound is more immediate than the visible or tangible world, i.e., for musicians, harmonics experts, or the blind, nada-yoga provides an ideal path for self-realisation. The word nada refers to the cosmic sound which is perceived inwardly, a continuous, persistent sound which is ex-

* From Hamel's free translation of Prem Lata Sharma's version in English (published by the Hindu University, Benares).

perienced in the head. It is most readily audible in the stillness of a forest, or in audible proximity to the sound of the sea or, for that matter, after generous indulgence in alcohol. In the latter case the persistent inner sound is an unpleasant warning of imminent unconsciousness, of gradual loss of inner control.

The initial study of the *nada*-note starts with attentive, inwardly-concentrated listening. In *nada-yoga* notes heard inwardly are associated with symbols of states of consciousness or mood: what one hears are vibrations, or acoustic reflections, of one's own being. The brain-waves are reduced (as measured by the electro-encephalograph) to sine-wave type oscillations with a frequency of between 1 and 30 Hz. This frequency is in fact all but inaudible (the human ear can detect a range of 16 to 20,000 Hz at most) yet the properties and effects of these 'undertones' penetrate right into the unconscious.

It is something to be experienced when a sine-wave generator is gradually switched to these lower frequencies while one listens to the process through good loudspeakers or earphones. To start with one hears an almost painful sound that slides even deeper until it changes into a burbling sound. In the end, depending on the quality of the amplifer, one can no longer hear any sound at all, but is sooner or later aware of a rather unpleasant movement of the air which can be physically taxing. The reverse occurs with the highest frequencies. Suddenly the needle-sharp notes at the top are gone, yet are still detectable to the extent that, if the process is persisted with, they will produce a headache.

Ultrasound, beyond the range audibly detectable to human beings, is used as a signal for dogs, in the use of the so-called dog-whistle. Allegedly this high note causes the dog no pain, but on the contrary produces an enjoyable, sexually stimulating excitation. Unfortunately the effects of ultrasound have also been tested by the armaments industry for possible military applications. Sound-cannons have today moved into the realm of real, scientific horror.

In the esoteric lore of the chakras, meanwhile, we have the inaudible sounds of the heart-region. In the centre of the 'voice of silence' the harmony of the suns and planets can be experienced, according to ancient yoga texts. This sound is called by the Sufis *saute surmad*, abstract sound. The prophet Muhammad heard it in the cave of Gare-Hira on taking up his divine mission. Moses heard the same sound on Mount Sinai when he conversed with God, and the same word was revealed to Jesus Christ when he was united with his Heavenly Father in the wilderness. Shiva heard the same *anahad-nada* during his *samadhi* in the Himalayan cave. The flute of Krishna is the symbolic representation, the *nada*-note which, according to the ancient Vedic teachings, was manifested with the help of Brahma, the creator of the world, via the sound of his cymbals. The Divine reveals itself through the *inner word*, through the Christian *logos*, just as much as through *nada Brahman*, the sound that is the Divine itself.

The Technique of Nada-Yoga according to Swami Satyananda

The preparation consists of a two-minute motionless yoga posture, according to whichever way of sitting one prefers. The anal sphincter is then closed as tightly as possible fifty times. Then follows *pranayama*, preferably five complete alternations of the breath (left nostril in – right nostril out – right nostril in – left nostril out, and so on) and seven *brahmaris* (after breathing in deeply, 'hum out' with closed eyes and fingers in the ears) while concentrating on the point between the eyebrows. Then the actual exercise begins : *

Sit in *bhadrasana* (a position in which the legs are crossed in a particular way) on a round cushion, in such a way that you can still stretch out your legs. Then close your ears with the index-fingers, while propping your elbows either on the raised knees or on a small table. With your eyes closed, concentrate on the *bindu* (between the eyebrows) and try to hear something.

The emerging sound can vary – a cloud passing by, a stream, a stormy sea, a bell, twittering birds, the ocean or a clap of thunder, or perhaps the vision of a starry sky. To start with it is very difficult to hear anything because one does not know how it should be heard. If you find it difficult to hear anything while concentrating on *bindu*, feel free to wander around inside your head, into the ear-muscles, the forehead, the mid-brain, or perhaps even into the heart. But for progress in meditation it is

_____

* This account follows the directions of Jyotirmayananda (M. Zaunschirm) in *Medidate the Tantric Yoga Way* (tr. & ed. L. K. Donat), London 1973.

absolutely essential to draw the sound back to the *bindu* even if it is tempting to listen to it in other places.

Once you can hear a sound in *bindu*, let it become clearer and more distinct. Soon, in the background, in the darkness, a second, different sound will emerge, parallel to the first. Leave the first one and try to develop the next one, until this one becomes clear and the first one disappears. Then take a third and carry on as with the second. This procedure can last a very long time and may perhaps succeed only after months of daily practice. Often, too, the first sound will emerge again after the third one, but it does not matter: simply treat it as a new one.

Warning: should you, after a certain amount of practice, start to hear sounds during the day as well, do not continue with this technique. True, it is not a question of hallucinations, but these dubious developments cannot be combined with a normal working life. A *nada-yogi* is certainly capable of hearing voices in the waking state, if he is very advanced. But other preparations, not mentioned here, are necessary for this: one should go no further without a guru.

To hear the 'voice of the unknown' belongs to the *siddhis* (supernatural powers).

Time to practise: to start with, ideally before sunrise and after sunset. For intensive *nada-yoga* the period between midnight and 2 a.m. is the most favourable.

EXPERIMENTAL THEATRE AND COLLECTIVE SELF-EXPERIENCE

During the 1972 Munich Olympiad a significant event was given only a mixed reception and a hardly fitting recognition: the 'play-street'. This multimedia 'big event' brought together more than a dozen internationally recognised theatrical groups and street-theatres, pantomimes and clowns, children's theatres and artistes. Alongside the hundred or more musical ensembles and creative artists, they were the main attraction of the show. Along the 'play-street', on little stages around the Olympic lake, the theatre groups presented scenes from the history of the Olympic Games from ancient times right up to the present and beyond.

The 'City Street Theatre' from New York, the group 'E.T.E.B.A.' from Buenos Aires, the 'Grand Magic Circus' from

Paris, the puppet-theatre from Stockholm were all invited, as were the Italian political group centred on Mario Ricci, the 'Mixed Media Company' from Berlin, and Terayama's 'Tenjo Sajiki' from Tokyo, who put on a pantomime Rock-musical. It is well known that a street-theatre has to rely on methods other than classical drama: it has to work more dynamically, more drastically, than in the theatre where more subtle, linguistic means can be used. Amid all the street-noises a visible dialogue is required, a *body-language*, a form of 'non-verbal communication'.

Since most of the groups who had come from all over the world to the Olympiad were accommodated at a large school, common encounters arose quite spontaneously. Although each group had to perform once or twice a day, they sometimes had a day off in between. Thus a number of the groups would stay in the school all day and carry out their group training on the lawn or in the gymnasium. Within a short time everybody was working and playing together. Out of it all came improvisations in movement accompanied by dance, song and drumming, which must surely have looked to any outsider like a perfectly rehearsed programme. This was possible because, astonishingly, all the groups, whether from Japan, France, the U.S.A. or Germany, were carrying out similar, in fact almost identical, group-exercises, training programmes and communication games. Everywhere one could see practice of the same breathing exercises, the same physical training, the same kinds of rhythmic dance and musical improvisation. It would seem that all these experimental theatre groups are returning to the same teachers and practice methods, and above all, to the drama exercises of the pathfinding Russian director Konstantin Stanislavski, of the beginning of this century, to the movement school of Mary Wigman, and later to Antonin Artaud's 'theatre of horror' and the methods of pantomime acting developed by the Pole Jerzy Grotowski. In his day Grotowski was already incorporating body and yoga exercises into his work and had studied intensively the theatre of India and Indonesia.

It was from these sources that Julian Beck and his wife Judith Malina created the world-famous 'Living Theatre' which they founded in the fifties. This group was itself the inspiration and prototype for most of the committed, experimental theatre groups that were formed subsequently. Mythological materials and themes were employed (in the case of Peter Schumann's 'Bread and Puppet Theatre' giant dolls were brought in) and scenes were played from the Christmas story in the biblical Gospels. These were nevertheless given a socio-political slant.

Over the years the 'Living Theatre' created a large number of exercise patterns which were also taken up by a whole variety of sensitivity-groups. They were then brought to Germany by individual members who set up smaller groups of their own. In addition, the 'Living Theatre' arranged public experiments in Berlin and the Federal Republic of Germany, in which anybody was allowed to participate. It was above all thanks to the director and author Frank Burckner and his Berlin Forum Theatre that these stimulating and exciting guest performances were able to be put on in Germany. A whole range of partly politically, partly esoterically committed groups still have fond memories even today of their encounter with the 'Living Theatre' people.

It was Frank Burckner, too, who from 1970 onwards made an attempt to bring to life a group after the style of the 'Living Theatre'. At his disposal was a vast factory floor in the Kreuzberg district of Berlin, where a mobile multi-media installation was set up with four-channel sound-amplification, slide and film projectors, screens and a music practice room with all kinds of instruments which could even be played by non-musicians.

In various drama schools, in the established children's theatres, in the 'politically committed scene', as well as in the then still extant, but by now almost 'establishment', Underground movement and sub-culture, the news quickly spread that such a group was being formed and that all one had to do was turn up.

Every afternoon a training session was held lasting several hours, with physical and breathing exercises, 'Living Theatre' exercises, talks, discussions on the undertaking's political and social affiliations and its spiritual background. Within a few months a group of some fifteen or twenty young people had become firmly established – actors, students, social workers, musicians, puppeteers and dancers. It was a group-dynamic adventure and, for all those participating, a process of consciousness development which had profound effects in the sphere of personality and ideology.

The group had its own dramatist and playwright, a director,

several good Rock musicians and specialists in all the require-
ments of a fully operative theatrical undertaking. Had the group
not succumbed too early to the exacting demands of a marathon
production for the Olympiad, and had it been given financial
support, it is probable that it would still be surviving today as
one of the most vigorous experimental, committed theatre
groups. The most fruitful period of this Mixed Media Company
was that of the self-experience exercises, a mutual encounter
leading to recognition of oneself in others.

The following description of the course of an exercise session
is not in fact a documentation of the group work in Berlin, nor
does it represent exactly the exercises of the 'Living Theatre'.
Rather is it the practical result of this, as I myself have pursued
it further in a variety of theatre groups and self-experience situations. For each member of our former Mixed Media Company
the procedure must have looked very similar, but it was never
exactly the same process, for it is always the composition of the
group that decides which exercises shall predominate and what
is likely to be most beneficial to the company as actually con-
stituted. As to the question of who originally designed the exercises, this is scarcely answerable. They have been developed in
the course of the group-dynamic process, sensitivity training,
yoga exercises and new communication methods. Today they
are practised in self-experience groups and breathing institutes
both in Western Germany and elsewhere.

Collective Self-Experience

The following exercises can be carried out in the course of a
several-hour long session of group work:

A room should be chosen to suit the size of group. Each participant should have room to lie down and stretch wide his
arms and legs with comfort. The floor should not be cold: a
carpet or large piece of non-slip fabric can serve as an underlay.
Each participant should have a blanket, be lightly clothed and
take off his shoes. A track-suit is ideally suitable for the exercises. At the beginning of the session, as soon as people start to
arrive, silence should be observed. Any greeting of the participants is superfluous. Perhaps individuals will come to realise that
people can actually greet each other more effectively without
words, as well as feeling nearer to each other.

Individual exercises for all to practise together

Relaxation

Lying on the back, try to relax all the muscles by becoming aware of each of them in turn: first the extremities of the limbs, legs, feet, arms, hands; then the head and neck, the shoulders and back, the small of the back as far as the base of the spine, and the bottom. Head and neck are moved loosely to and fro, the shoulders gently rotated.

Once a degree of looseness has been achieved, concentrate on the right foot, tense the muscles of the right leg and foot, stretch and lift the tensed right leg some 20 cm. into the air, and after a few moments let it fall back onto the floor.

Now do the same with the left leg, the arm, the bottom, the back, the shoulders and head (here a cushion would help!).

To start with it helps the group and individual concentration if one particular participant gives each command aloud, together with a commentary to remind everybody of everything to watch out for. He could say, for example: 'Left leg down, stretch the muscles . . . lift . . . and down again . . .'

'Elastic' spine-uncoiling

After a short interval of regular and unrestricted breathing, each lifts his legs from the lying position back over his head. Initially you could turn this into a neck-stand; in which case carry it out correctly, but without straining the muscles in any way. Then let the legs sink further and further over your head, spreading them so that your knees finish up touching the floor near your ears. Now the weight of your body and your centre of gravity are both on the shoulders. Do not forcibly press the legs or knees down, but go back only as far as is necessary to feel the first signs of discomfort.

Gradually you will reach a position where, with quiet, unforced breathing, none of the spine is touching the floor any longer. Hold this position and allow the breath to penetrate all those parts of the body it seldom reaches, which can make your body feel warm. But remember that this position must not involve any tension!

After a time begin very carefully and as slowly as possible to

uncoil the spine. Consciously lower each individual vertebra onto the floor, letting your weight bear on it a little. When, after
quite some time, the back is half-unrolled, take care that the
part of the spine already on the floor does not start to lift off the
floor again, but remains as it were stuck fast, without any gap.
Once each vertebra is down, it should remain firmly on the floor.
Carry out the exercise very slowly. Even the vertebrae of the
lower back should stay stuck to the floor, which for many will
not be possible to start with. No matter! Consciously go on with
the exercise, staying just the bearable side of the pain-barrier
and continuing to breathe easily and naturally, without holding
the breath in any way. Ideally, the breath should be directed to
wherever the pressure is greatest, i.e., to the part of the spine
your weight is on. Through conscious breathing it is possible to
remove any pain there may be at this point.

Eventually you will have to support the seat with the hands
so that you do not lose balance and let it sink to the floor. Once
you reach this point, bring the still-bent legs to the floor, heels
first, and slide the heels slowly away from you until the legs
are stretched, without lifting the back from the floor, and you
are finally lying quite flat and straight. As a test you can feel
underneath your back with your hand to see that there is actually no gap between back and floor.

Relax. Breathe deeply.

Exercises with partner

'Mirror'

Sit in pairs or stand in front of each other and mutually observe each other's breathing. Gently and gradually try to syn-
chronise your own breathing with your partner's, adjusting to
each other's inbreath and outbreath. At the same time watch
your partner's posture and movements very closely and try to
imitate them in every detail. To help this mutual imitation, it is
preferable to carry out each movement in slow motion.

You can sit or stand to do this, as though there were a mirror
between you, with your partner as your own reflection and vice
versa. Gradually you can start carrying out particular hand or
body movements for your partner to reproduce immediately. Or
you can try reacting spontaneously to the initial movements of

your partner. To start with one of you should be the leader, then the other. Be meticulous with your movements! Even facial expressions should be exactly studied and reproduced.

The object of this exercise is to reach a state in which neither is the leader, in which the movements happen spontaneously and simultaneously, in which the active/passive principle is dissolved. This exercise is especially suitable for breaking down aggressive and mutually domineering attitudes. The 'struggle' is pursued more or less soundlessly and, through the mirror-rule of mutual adaptation, leads to an eventual harmony. Any difficult personal conflicts at this point must be very firmly borne on the shoulders of the group as a whole. Encounters of great profundity can also arise.

'Light head'

Your partner lies on his back, while you kneel comfortably by his head (roughly in the Japanese sitting-on-the-heels position) and lean slightly over your prone partner, whose eyes are closed. Reach down and take his head (which could perhaps be resting on a blanket) in both hands, lifting it gently from under the base of the skull, so that your partner can relax his head muscles and 'abandon' his head for a moment. Lift his head slightly and move it in a circular direction with your hands, very gently. Finally, provided you can see his breathing, pull his head a little away from his body as he breathes in, as though you were lifting it off the vertebrae. During the outbreath gently put it back. An exercise in mutual trust.

'Zone-opening'

Your partner's head is once again lying relaxed on the blanket or on a cushion. Go to the other end of him and observe his breath. As you see him breathe in, pull both feet together towards you, grasping them behind the heels, at the bottom of the lower leg. As he breathes out release them again. Then, still in time with his breathing, pull as above on both little toes, two or three times, then the fourth toes, the third and the second, and finally the two big toes – always pulling as he breathes in, releasing as he breathes out. After some time your partner should turn over on to his front, while you stand astride him. Now lift him carefully by the hips to about 30 cm. from the floor as he breathes out, pulling his lower body somewhat towards the feet.

Then slowly replace his body on the floor. Do this two or three times. Then exchange rôles, and repeat the whole exercise in reverse.

The whole group in a circle
'Imitation'

All the members of the group run around in a circle, following one another. As he walks or runs along, the first puts into effect any characteristic gait or particular pattern that occurs to him moment by moment: he limps, stamps rhythmically while making intermittent noises, crawls, makes swaggering arm-circling movements, and so on. Now everybody else in the circle has in turn to imitate *exactly* the person in front. From time to time the first may alter the pattern, which the one behind him then imitates, then the third, the fourth and so on, all copying exactly, with each letting himself be guided solely by the person in front. Everybody concentrates exclusively on his predecessor. As soon as the first person becomes the last, he immediately hands over the leadership to the second, i.e., the circle 'precesses' backwards. So now the second is in command and has to devise his own figures, antics and complicated or original ways of walking.

As soon as the group is out of breath, which can happen very quickly with this exercise, all stand still in a circle and take a short rest, then join hands, form a ring (insofar as this is possible) and close their eyes.

'Quick reactions'

All having joined hands, one person, previously decided on, gives an impulse to his right-hand neighbour by squeezing his hand: the latter then immediately passes this on as quickly as possible. As soon as he detects the impulse from his left he must pass it on to his right-hand neighbour. If everybody really concentrates and nobody causes any interruption the group becomes as it were 'switched on' without any need for electrification.

After a few run-throughs each one lets out a short sharp sound ('Ho', 'Ha' etc.) at the instant of passing the signal on with his hand. These short sounds too should carry on without interruption and follow each other around as quickly as possible. The next stage of the exercise involves singing out a predetermined vowel-sound with each squeeze of the hand, continuing to intone it for the full duration of the outbreath. Thus, with each squeeze of the hand, each participant sings the vowel in question for as long as his breath lasts. When the signal has gone all round the circle and arrived back at the first person, the latter passes on the next agreed vowel-sound along with his hand-signal. If the first vowel was 'Aaaa ...', the next could be 'Eeee ...' and so on.

At this point the enjoyment consists in the fact that some will still be singing the first vowel while on the other side of the circle the second vowel will already be sounding and even, if it is carried out quickly enough, the third too ('Oooo ...' for example). The sound does not have to be kept going right until the next impulse arrives; it is merely a matter of singing each vowel for as long as the breath lasts naturally; and then one concentrates on the arrival of the next impulse so as to be able to pass it on as quickly as possible. Of course in a smaller circle the impulse will sometimes already have arrived while one is still singing. In this case one reacts as quickly as possible and passes on the impulse together with the next vowel. (A similar form of this exercise is also to be found in P. Oliveros's *sonic meditations*.)

'Consonance'

Still standing in a circle, each member of the group now places his arms around his neighbours' shoulders, which means that those of similar height will need to be standing next to each other, so that the shorter ones will not have too much difficulty in reaching the shoulders of the tall ones. Everyone should be able to have his arms relaxed, with sufficient looseness to allow movement.

Twenty seconds' silence; relaxed breathing until the breath is flowing involuntarily, yet still under self-observation. Eyes closed. In time with the natural breathing, all now begin to hum the deepest notes they can, starting gently and in their own time. Not all at once, but in turn so that no silent gaps occur. Now out of these deep humming tones let the syllable 'Uuuum' slowly arise in soft, long-sustained notes, each lasting until the breath runs out. Once the note has been started it is not varied or altered in pitch. During the 'Uuuum' sound concentrate on the lower part of the body.

After some time the sound should become louder, but gradually, not suddenly. Always pay attention to the overall sound. The 'Oooom' (Ohm) sounds come next, while concentrating on the belly region. Gradually the volume increases, and the 'Oooom' sound starts to be sung to somewhat higher notes. With the following 'Aaaam' sound the pitch goes up even further. (During 'Aaaam' concentrate on the chest region).

Everyone sings louder and louder; in fact, the 'Aaaam' can even be shouted. However, no 'solos' should result: instead the crescendo should be carried out in concert. There should be no undulation in the singing, but the chosen note should be sung right to the end without alteration of pitch. Naturally the sound or tone of the note can vary, however. Glissandi and 'siren-wails' are to be avoided.

The climax should be reached together, with the women's voices perhaps going on further to the 'Eeee' (Eh) and 'Iiii' sounds. All take their favourite and easiest vowel (not excluding so-called 'diphthongs' such as 'Aeaeaeae' and so on) and sing it as loudly as they know how. Then, gradually, return slowly via the same route back into the silence. Do not suddenly break off, but come back down again step by step by way of 'Oooo' and 'Uuuu' sounds to the deep humming-sound that you started with. A slow ebbing away. A pause. Eyes open. Slowly disengage the arms from the shoulders.

Group-exercises

'Slow motion'

With eyes closed, a few of the participants stand within a marked-off area of carpet or within the circle of the other members of the group. Moving all their limbs and their bodies as slowly as they possibly can, they now explore each other, get to know each other blindly, by touch alone. 'Slow motion' can be started with a 'heap' of people. All lie on top of one another and disengage themselves in slow motion, form small groups, slowly wander about, spread their arms, find and touch each other and perhaps eventually come nearer and nearer to each other. For many participants this exercise can lead to an awareness of personal conflicts and crises which then have to be taken on by the group as a whole through discussion of them at the end of the exercise.

'Living tableau'

Using a drumbeat or a tape, a clearly audible, simple, slow rhythm is tapped out or played. The exercise should be carried out in a dark room with a projector that can conveniently be switched on and off.

A given rhythmic pattern is agreed on for switching the light on and off; for example, on the first beat the light goes out and it stays out for the next three beats. Exactly on the fifth beat the light is suddenly switched on again, and stays on for beats six, seven and eight. On the next first beat the light is switched off again. Now the idea is that each participant can move only in the dark, and by the time the light comes on again he must have taken up a motionless position which may only be altered when the light has gone out again. No movement when the light is on! The spectators must not see any kind of movement. It is recommended that this exercise first be carried out slowly, while taking special care that no physical movement is visible either in the moment when the light comes on or before it has fully gone out.

Ideally two separate groups should be formed for this, so that each in turn can watch the other and try to improve on the other's performance. In fact this is worth doing with many of the exercises.

Once the principle has been mastered, the tempo or rhythm for switching on and off can be speeded up, and fantastic living photographs can result. The purpose of this exercise is a heightening of bodily discipline, in conjunction with a strengthened sense of rhythm.

'Singing carpet'

For this final exercise, a large room is needed. The first participant lies down in the top right-hand corner in such a way that the second has room to lay his head on the stomach of the first; the third lies with his head on the stomach of the second, the fourth with his head on the third's stomach ... and so on. The whole thing needs to be so organised that the group finishes up lying diagonally across the room from the top right-hand corner to the bottom left-hand corner, like a kind of carpet pattern. The first, third, fifth and so on will be lying parallel to each other, as will the second, fourth, sixth etc. All having taken up their positions, each now adjusts his own breathing to the breathing of the person on whose stomach his head is lying. It is important that the first one should breathe quietly and regularly, so that the others can gradually adjust themselves to it.

After some time the first starts to sing a long note every time he breaths out (an 'Oooom' or 'Aaaam'). The second time he does so, the second begins to sing with him – either the same note, its fifth or its octave. With the third person's note, the first person stops singing, so that it is the third and second notes that are now heard together, and so on. The next stage of the exercise involves each person starting to sing the moment his or her predecessor, on whom he is lying, first begins. A kind of wandering, gliding sound should result. A certain discipline is necessary at this point, as the group's disposition and/or the pattern of its arrangement in the room can often give rise to mirth. If, for example, somebody starts coughing or laughing, the next person is liable to take it up. But then a measure of fun is of course always permissible.

Care should be taken not to spoil the point of these exercises by adopting a stereotyped routine; instead, common discussion should decide which of the various exercises should be concentrated on. This is of course not the place for discussing the vast number of exercises, devised by the 'Living Theatre', which are capable of being carried out only after lengthy practice once an established group has been formed. 'Gastod', 'Soldier', 'Lion' and 'Lee's Piece' are exercises that cannot be put across in words. My purpose here is in any case merely to indicate a few exercises with some kind of acoustic content.

At the end of a practice session, as well as after individual exercises, discussion is very important. How often somebody 'flips out', gets nervous or anxious, or finds some other latent condition coming to the surface. Here the whole group becomes the bearer of the individual's personal conflicts, as well as of many an unspoken, unexpressed crisis of the community as a whole. Harmony and an uninhibited meditative atmosphere only arises when a few crises have occurred and a good few members of the group have felt impelled to leave.

It is a generally valid observation that harmony cannot be

expected to reign right from the word go in any self-experience process. It is precisely the recognition and acceptance of phases of suffering and discord that are necessary to permit the attainment of true inner harmony. In the sphere of personal unfolding, as in that of communication, any artificially assumed aestheticism or pretended spirituality actually hinders any real encounter or true integration.

As a medium, via listening, for relaxation and inner self-surrender, as a symbol of the deepest cosmic relationships, as well as a form of practical improvisation in the context of group work, music particularly can help to achieve this great goal. The final question, then, concerns the actual realisation of all these possibilities, whether ideal or practical.

Prospect

For years now, young people in all countries of Europe have been gathering in spiritual groups and centres, in new religious circles and communes. Masters from Japan and Tibet, yoga and Sufi teachers have been living in our midst and instructing us in a new religious consciousness that is not intolerant, dogmatic or ethnocentric. All the living Masters whom I, like so many others, have been fortunate enough to meet – among them the Dalai Lama, his teacher Lama Ling Rimpoche, Lama Anagarika Govinda, the Indian saint Ananda Mayi Ma and the Japanese meditation-Master Professor T. K. Nagaya – confirm what is also expressed in the works of Suzuki, Sri Aurobindo, Teilhard de Chardin and Jean Gebser: that the time has dawned for a spiritual integration, for a *new consciousness*.

For the last six years, all over the Federal Republic of Germany, conferences have been held that have concerned themselves more and more intensively with this theme. Again and again the point at issue in these seminars, as well as in many conferences and meetings elsewhere, is the polarity between the 'new religion' or spirituality and social practice and progress. In particular, the practice of meditative music, the work of collective-experience groups with musical stimulation and vowel-improvisation, intuitive and spiritual experiences through performing and listening to music – all of these need to be seen in relation to their social context. Thus, musical integration is a social challenge. Inner vaues, spiritual powers and psychic support have today become necessities of life, if we are not to remain sunk in an inward and outward disintegration. And one of the reasons for this very tendency may well be discerned in the dichotomy between the public who listens to music and those who criticise it on the public's behalf. It is not by accident that the catch-phrase 'social-crisis' has come into being. Yet hand in hand with it goes a crisis of critical publicity.

In the great creative eras of the past, a unity reigned between musicians and listeners. They were bound together by a common religion, a morality that was equally valid for all, a single 'world ear' (Akróasis). The artists served, and were part of, a closed society. Now, at a time when a cultural epoch is in decline – whether we call it late-capitalist, early socialist or something else – that unity has been split apart.

Our efforts and first attempts to bring about a musical integration, and on this basis to erect a structure that is 'inhabitable', will only be truly successful when we become prepared to create a world-society. This would be the precondition for a world-culture, which would need to be both willing and able to create and preserve for all the inhabitants of this earth a truly humane existence free of class-distinctions.

Such a world-society will not be built in a day, nor by mere outward revolutions. It is the inner revolution that is most sorely needed. And so it is for each of us to start with himself and, through deepened self-awareness, to take the first step in this direction. Everything that can express man's true humanity can serve as a tool for this much needed self-experience. And of those tools, as I have tried to show, music, thanks to its relationship to the elemental life-processes of the human body, is one of the most effective. Music is part and parcel of man, just as much as his breathing and the rhythm of his daily life. As Franz von Baader, a philosopher inspired by Jakob Böhme, has put it: 'He who makes music does not himself create it, but merely opens the door, to a greater or lesser extent, through which we hear the music of eternity.'

Appendices

TEXTS

Below are reproduced extracts from texts that are obtainable in Germany only with difficulty. The first (*Lü Bu Ve*) is out of print, while the second (*The Sufi Message* by Hazrat Inayat Khan) has not previously been translated into German. Both are eloquent examples of the holistic approach to music typical of Asian cultures.

From : *The Spring and Autumn of Lü Bu Ve**
Notes for the Midsummer Month (Book V, chapter 2)

The origins of music lie far back in time. It arises out of proportion and is rooted in the Great One. The Great One gives rise to the two poles; the two poles give rise to the powers of darkness and light. The powers of darkness and light undergo change; the one ascends into the heights, the other sinks into the depths; heaving and surging they combine to form bodies. If they are divided they unite themselves again; if they are united, they divide themselves again. That is the eternal way of heaven. Heaven and earth are engaged in a cycle. Every ending is followed by a new beginning; every extreme is followed by a return. Everything is co-ordinated with everything else. Sun, moon and stars move in part quickly, in part slowly. Sun and moon do not agree in the time which they need to complete their path. The four seasons succeed each other. They bring heat and cold, shortness and length, softness and hardness. That from which all beings arise and in which they have their origin is the Great One; that whereby they form and perfect themselves is

---

* Edited and translated by Richard Wilhelm, Düsseldorf-Cologne 1971. Reproduced by kind permission of Eugen Diederichs Verlag.

the duality of darkness and light. As soon as the seed-germs start
to stir, they coagulate into a form. The bodily shape belongs to
the world of space, and everything spatial has a sound. The
sound arises out of harmony. Harmony arises out of relatedness.
Harmony and relatedness are the roots from which music, established by the ancient kings, arose.

When the world is at peace, when all things are at rest, when
all obey their superiors through all life's changes, then music
can be brought to perfection. Perfected music has its effects.
When desires and emotions do not follow false paths, then music
can be perfected. Perfected music has its cause. It arises out of
balance. Balance arises from justice. Justice arises from the true
purpose of the world. Therefore one can speak of music only
with one who has recognised the true purpose of the world.

Decadent states and people ripe for decline are admittedly not
lacking in music; but their music is not balanced and cheerful.
The drowning indeed laugh, and those condemned to die indeed
sing, and madmen are ready to fight. Roughly so is it with the
music of an age that finds itself in confusion. Prince and official
do not take their rightful places. Father and son do not find their
right relationship, and the relationships between man and
woman are in disarray. If now the people sigh and complain,
that is held to be music. How perverse is this behaviour!

Music rests on the harmony between heaven and earth, on
accord between darkness and light . . .

Loud music (Book V, chapter 3)

The rulers of this world mostly hold pearls and jewels, spears
and swords, to be their most precious possessions, but the more
they have of them the more the people grumble, the more the
land is endangered, and the more they themselves are dragged
into decline. In fact these conditions lead to the loss of those very
treasures. The music of a perverse generation has the same
effects.

If drums both big and small boom out like thunder, if cymbals
and singing-stones strike like lightning, if flutes and violins, tumul-
tuous dancing and singing sound forth, it is enough to shatter the
nerves, to madden the senses and to cause life to bubble over.
But a music that uses these means does not make one cheerful.
Therefore the louder the music, the more melancholy the people

become, the more the land is endangered, the lower the prince sinks. In this way the true nature of music is lost.

What all holy kings have prized in music has been its cheerfulness. The tyrants Giä of Hia and Chou Sin of Yin made loud music. They thought beautiful the loud noises of big drums and bells, singing-stones, clarinets and flutes, and valued mass-effects. They strove for new and strange sounds, notes that no ear had ever heard before, plays that no eye had ever beheld. They sought to surpass each other and overstepped all rhyme and reason.

The cause of the decline of the Sung state was that it invented a thousand bells; the reason for the fall of the Ch'i state was that it invented large bells. The reason for the fall of the Chou state was that it invented magic music. Such music is noisy enough, but from the point of view of truth, it has strayed from the true nature of music. Because it has strayed from the true nature of music, this music is not uplifting. If music is not uplifting, the people grumble and life is impaired. Under the influence of this music it is with life as with ice in the burning sun, it melts away. All this arises because people do not understand the nature of music, but are only out for noisy sound-effects.

As with the nature of music, so it is with the nature of the bodily organs. Since they each have a particular nature, each needs corresponding care. Cold and heat, over-exertion and indolence, hunger and self-indulgence, these six things do not accord with nature. One who would preserve his life sees to it that what does not accord is replaced by what does accord. Whoever can remain constantly in conditions that accord with nature, he will live long...

On hitting the right note (Book V, chapter 4)

In music there is also the matter of hitting the right note. If it is too loud, one's state of mind is disturbed. If one listens to loud music in a disturbed state of mind, the ear cannot grasp it. If one cannot grasp it, obstructions arise, and, from the obstructions, derangement. If it is too soft, then the state of mind is dissatisfied. If one listens to soft music in a dissatisfied state of mind, the ear is not filled; if the ear is not filled, the stimulation is insufficient, and from insufficient stimulation arises inner emptiness. If the notes are too high the state of mind is too tense; if one hears high notes in a tense state of mind the hearing is distorted. If the hearing is distorted one can no longer distinguish the notes, and, through this inability to distinguish, one becomes exhausted. If the notes are too low, the state of mind is depressed. If one hears low notes in a depressed state of mind, the ear does not comprehend them. If one cannot comprehend them, one becomes distracted and, through distraction, irritable. Therefore: not only music that is too loud or too soft, but also music that is too high or too low, is not hitting the right note.

What is meant by hitting the right note? The mid-point is the right note in music. What is meant by the mid-point? If the size of the instrument does not exceed a Gün and its weight does not go beyond a Shi, that is the mid-point of size and weight. The keynote of the Yellow Bell is the basis of the musical notes. It holds a mid-position between height and depth. If one hears the right note in the right way, a harmonious state of mind arises. That is the state in which cheerfulness is not too great, but a harmonious balance reigns.

Hazrat Inayat Khan: On Music*

Music has been revered by the mystics of all ages. Almost throughout the world music has been the centre of cult and holy office within the innermost circles of the initiates. Among the Sufis, too, music is seen as the source of their meditation, for they feel how the soul is unfolding, how the intuitive faculties can be opened. Their heart opens, as it were, to all the beauties of the inner and outer world, uplifting them and at the same time bringing to them that perfection for which the soul yearns ...

The musicians of India devote twelve hours or more a day to practising various rhythms and their variations. In the end these rhythms produce a psychological effect that is no longer merely musical, but magical. This magic can move a person and touch his heart. On hearing this music one feels as though translated to another world. And yet it is scarcely audible. It is played not before thousands of people, but in gatherings of two or three like-minded people ...

* From: *The Sufi Message of Hazrat Inayat Khan*, Vol. II, 2nd edition, London 1973, by kind permission of Pir Vilayat Khan. Retranslated from Hamel's freely selected German version.

There is no real comparison between the voice and an instrument, for the voice is a living thing. Movement, sight, touch, even the breath flowing from the nostrils, do not have the range that the voice has . . .

In the Middle East it is the custom among orthodox Christians and Armenians not to use the organ in church. They use a chord, a sound that is produced by ten to twelve people with closed lips. Anybody who has heard it will concede that the sound of the organ is extraordinarily artificial in comparison with this sound. It has a wonderfully magical effect. It reaches so deeply into the human heart and creates so religious an atmosphere that one does not miss the organ. This note is itself a natural, God-given organ . . .

The singers of olden times always used to try out the effects of their spiritual exercises on themselves first. They would sing a note for half an hour at a time, observing the effect of this one note on their various body centres: what currents of life-energy it summoned up, how it opened up the intuitive faculties, how far it produced rapture, afforded extra energy, how it soothed and healed. For them it was not a theory but an experience . . .

It is a great pity that in the present-day musical field people are moving further and further away from the natural voice. Commercialisation is to blame. To start with, a hall would be built for a hundred people; then for five hundred; then for five thousand. A person has to shout in order that five thousand people may hear him and in order to be a success (a box-office success, that is). But the magic spell lies in the *natural* voice. Everyone has this gift. God has given him a particular pitch, a natural tone, and if he develops this tone, magic results. He can work wonders. But today he must think of the hall where he is to sing, and of how loudly he will have to shout . . .

It is the nature, the basic principle of sound, that the more it is in tune with nature the more powerful and magical it becomes. Every man and woman has a given vocal pitch, but the voice expert says: 'No, that is contralto', or 'soprano', 'tenor', 'baritone' or 'bass'. He confines what cannot be confined. Are there, then, really so many voices? There are as many voices as souls. They cannot be classified. As soon as a singer is classified, he has to sing at this vocal pitch. If his natural vocal pitch is different, he will not know it.

Because the voice expert has said: 'That is a soprano', this person can no longer be anything else. Moreover, the composer has probably never heard the voice of this particular singer and has written only for a particular vocal pitch. Once a person has been handed over to the composers, and therefore has to sing at a predetermined vocal pitch, he loses the natural voice that he once possessed. But quite apart from singing, one will find, even in speaking, only one person in a hundred who speaks in his natural voice, and ninety-nine who are imitators. They are imitating someone else, even though they perhaps do not know it . . .

In daily life one may sometimes notice annoyance in oneself even before someone has got a single sentence out. This is not because of what he has said but because of his voice. On the other hand one notices, perhaps not every day but none the less from time to time, that one has heard a person speak only once, but has retained in one's mind what he has said. There is something beneficial, soothing and healing about it; one feels inspired and uplifted . . .

There is nothing that can be of greater spiritual help than music. Meditation is a preparation for perfection; but it is music that comes nearest to it. I have seen the psychological power of music work such wonders (only in congenial surroundings), with five or six people, by moonlight, in the twilight or at sunset. It is as though nature itself were conducive to the perfecting of music. Both work together; for they are one . . .

Music is the harmony of the universe in microcosm; for this harmony is life itself, and in man, who is himself a microcosm of the universe, chords and discords are to be found in his pulse, in his heartbeat, his vibration, his rhythm and tone. His health or sickness, his joy or displeasure show whether his life has music or not.

What can music teach us? Music can train us in harmony, and therein lies the secret or the magic of music. If one listens to pleasant music, harmony is brought into one's life. That is why man needs music, yearns for it. Many say that they have no time or room for music, but these people have not yet listened to music. In fact, if they had really listened to music, their soul would have been touched, and they would have been quite incapable of doing anything other than love music . . . In addition, music develops the faculty of appreciating all that is good and beautiful in art and science, for in music and poetic art beauty is revealed to one in every aspect...

The wonderful thing about music is that through it one can achieve concentration and meditation independently of thought. In this sense, it bridges the gulf between conscious and unconscious, between form and formlessness. If there is one thing that can be grasped by the understanding and is effective, yet at the same time has no form, that thing is music.

Poetry suggests form; line and colour suggest form; but not music. Rather does it create a resonance which vibrates through the whole of the inner and outer universe and transcends all notions of the denseness of matter. Music can even transform matter into spirit, into its original state, by touching every atom of a whole, living being, through the law of harmonic vibration.

The beauty of drawing and painting can go a long way; but it has its limits. The joy of scents and perfumes goes even further. But music penetrates our innermost depths and thus creates a new life-force, a breath of air that lends joy to all existence and leads one's whole being to perfection. Therein lies the fulfilment of human life.

Musical Examples

Chant for Mandala Ceremony (Tibetan Gelugpa-sect)

(Start)

① O - - - - - - - - - - - soi hi pò hi dshiu sheng me oi

to - - - tram Schri ra li - g - - - - - shi - - - - Nyi - - -
(Conclusion)

Däe Gyän Pa oi Di Idam Guru Ratna Mandalakam Niryata ya - mi - - -

The Harmonic Series (natural overtones and harmonics of the bottom C-string of a cello)

② Overtones: 1 2 Fifth 3 Fourth Major 4 Minor 5 6 7 8 9 10 11
third third

Whole-tone intervals (seconds)

Harmonics: 1 Octave 2 Fifth 3 Fourth 4 Major 5 Minor 6 7 8 9 10 11 12
third third

Hindu-mantra, as a kirtan-chant

③ Sri Ram Jai Ram Jai Jai Ram

Hildegard von Bingen : ending of an antiphon

④ E - - U - - O - - U - - A E - - -

Musical Examples

Terry Riley: A Rainbow In Curved Air (basic motifs for the left hand)

F. Rzewski: Les Moutons de Panurge (complete modal line)

P.M. Hamel: Continuous Creation (initial pattern)

Mantra-Sadhana (for male voice of medium pitch)   Basic figure

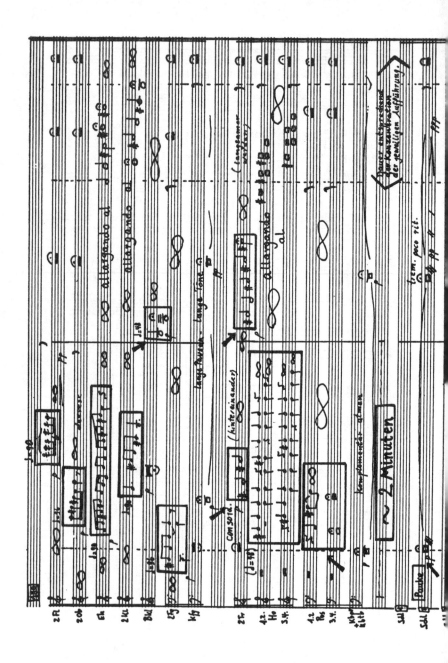

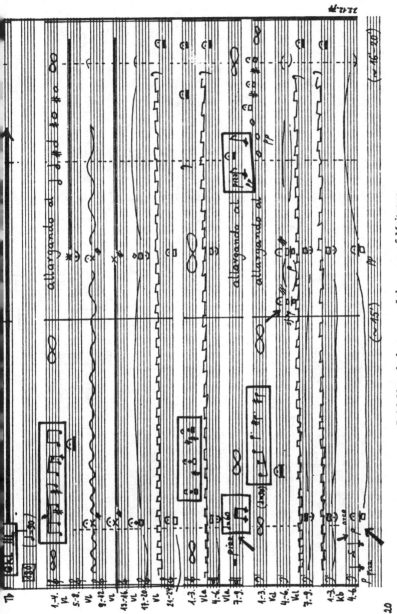

P. M. Hamel: last page of the score of *Maitreya*

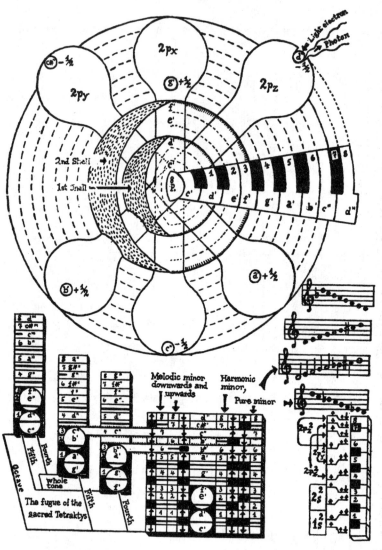

Wilfred Krüger: the oxygen atom complete with ten electrons

Terry Riley: Score from *Keyboard Studies 1967* (No. 7)

Bibliography

Aurobindo Ghose, Sri, *Stufen der Vollendung*, O. W. Barth Verlag, 5th edition, Munich, 1975.

Bergier, Jacques and Louis Pauwels, *Aufbruch ins dritte Jahrtausend*, Scherz Verlag, Bern-Munich-Vienna, 1961.

Bô Yin Râ, *Mantrapraxis*, Kobersche Verlagsbuchhandlung, Zürich, 1967.

Daniélou, Alain, *Einführung in die indische Musik*, Wissenschaftliche Buchgesellschaft, Darmstadt;

—— *Ragas of North Indian Music*, Barrie & Rockliff, London, 1968;

—— *Die Musik Asiens zwischen Missachtung und Wertschätzung*, Heinrichshofen-Verlag, Wilhelmshaven, 1973.

Evans-Wentz, W. P., *The Tibetan Book of the Great Liberation* (with commentary by C. G. Jung), Oxford University Press, London, 1954.

Geck, Martin, *Musiktherapie als Problem der Gesellschaft*, Klett Verlag, Stuttgart, 1973.

Gebser, Jean, *Abendländische Wandlung*, Ullstein Verlag, Frankfurt-Berlin, 1965;

—— *Ursprung und Gegenwart*, dtv-Taschenbuch, Munich, 1973, (3 volumes);

—— *Verfall und Teilhabe*, Otto Müller Verlag, Salzburg, 1974;

—— *Ein Mensch zu sein*, Franke Verlag, Munich-Bern 1974.

Gelpke, Rudolf, *Drogen und Seelenerweiterung*, Kindler Verlag (Taschenbuch-series 'Geist und Psyche', No. 2058), 4th edition, Munich, 1975.

Gespräche mit Komponisten, ed. Willi Reich, Mannesse Verlag, Zürich, 1967.

Govinda, Lama A., *The Psychological Attitude of Early Buddhist Philosophy*, Rider, London, 1969;

—— *Foundations of Tibetan Mysticism*, Rider, London, 1969;

—— *The Way of the White Clouds*, Rider, London, 1966.

Haas, William, *Oestliches und Westliches Denken*, Rowohlt Verlag, Reinbek, 1967.

Helmholtz, Heinrich von, *Ueber die physiologischen Ursachen musikalischer Harmonien*, Kindler Verlag, Munich, 1971.

Hesse, Hermann, *The Glass Bead Game*, tr. R. & C. Winston, Cape, London, 1970.

Heyer, Gustav Richard, *Der Organismus der Seele*, Kindler Verlag, Munich, 1958.

I Ching, The Richard Wilhelm Translation (with a foreword by C. G. Jung), Routledge & Kegan Paul, London, 1951.

Ital, Gerta, *Der Meister, die Mönche und ich*, O. W. Barth Verlag, 3rd edition, Weilheim, 1972.

Jung, Carl Gustav: *Ueber die Psychologie des Unbewussten*, Frankfurt, 1975. (*Symbols of Transformation*, London, 1952.)

Jyotirmayananda (M. Zaunschirm), *Meditate the Tantric Yoga Way* (ed. L. K. Donat), Allen & Unwin, London, 1973.

Kayser, Hans, *Lehrbuch der Harmonik*, Julius Schwabe Verlag, Basel-Stuttgart, 1963;

—— *Akroasis*, Julius Schwabe Verlag, Basel-Stuttgart, 1964;

—— *Orphikon*, Julius Schwabe Verlag, Basel-Stuttgart, 1974.

Keyserling, Graf Hermann, *Das Reisetagebuch eines Philosophen*, 2 volumes, Otto Reichl Verlag, 5th edition, Darmstadt, 1921.

Keyserling, M. & W., *Das Rosenkreuz*, Verlag der Palme, Vienna, 1956.

Khan, Hazrat Inayat, *The Sufi Message*, vol. 2 (The Mysticism of Sound, Music, The Power of the Word, Cosmic Language), Barrie & Rockcliff, 2nd edition, London 1972;

—— *Aus einem Rosengarten Indiens*, Drei Eichen, Munich, 1954.

Krüger, Wilfried, *Das Universum singt*, privately published (55 Trier-Zewen, Auf Blehn 15, W. Germany).

Laing, Ronald, *The Politics of Experience*, Penguin, Harmondsworth, 1967.

Lange, Anny von, *Mensch, Musik, Kosmos*, Novalis Verlag, Freiburg, 1956, (vol. 2 1960).

Lysebeth André van, *Die grosse Kraft des Atems – die Atemschule des Pranayama*, O. W. Barth Verlag, 2nd edition, Munich, 1975.

Nestler, Gerhard, *Die Form in der Musik*, Atlantis Verlag, Freiburg-Zürich, 1954;

—— *Die Geschichte der Musik*, Bertelsmann, Gütersloh, 1961;

—— *Der Stil in der Neuen Musik*, Atlantis Verlag, Freiburg-Zürich, 1958.

Neue Wege der Musiktherapie, Econ Verlag, Düsseldorf, 1974.

Neumann, Erich, *Ursprungsgeschichte des Bewusstseins*, Rascher Verlag, Zürich 1949, republished by Kindler Verlag (Taschenbuch-series 'Geist und Psyche') Munich, 2nd edition, 1974.

Olvedi, Ulli, *Buddhismus – Religion der Zukunft?*, Heyne Verlag, Munich, 1973.

Ouspensky, Peter, *In Search of the Miraculous: Fragments of an Unknown Teaching*, Routledge, London 1950.

Pfrogner, Hermann, *Lebendige Tonwelt*, Langen Müller, Munich, 1976.

Pontvik, Aleks, *Heilen durch Musik*, Zürich, 1955.

Prem, Sat, *Sri Aurobindo, or the Adventure of Consciousness*, Aurobindo Ashram, 1972.

Religion und die Droge, ed. H.-C. Leuner & M. Josuttis, Kohlhammer Verlag, Stuttgart, 1972.

Scheidt, Jürgen vom, *Innenweltverschmutzung*, Knaur Taschenbuch, Munich-Zürich, 1975.

Schmidt, Thomas Michael, *Musik und Kosmos als Schöpfungswunder*, privately published, Frankfurt, 1974.

Schmitt, J. L., *Das Hohe Lied vom Atem*, J. Couvreur Verlag, The Hague, 2nd edition.

Schneider, Marius, *Singende Steine*, Bärenreiter, Kassel, 1955.

Schumann, Robert, *Gespräche und Briefe*, ed. Willi Reich, Manesse Verlag, Zürich, 1967.

Shankar, Ravi, *My Music, My Life*, Jonathan Cape, London 1969.

Steckel Ronald, *Herz der Wirklichkeit*, Jugenddienst Verlag, Wuppertal, 1973.

Stege, Fritz, *Musik, Magie, Mystik*, Otto Reichl Verlag, Remagen, 1961;
———— *Das Okkulte in der Musik*, Bisping Verlag, Münster, 1925.
Suzuki, D. T., *Amida – der Buddha der Liebe*, O. W. Barth Verlag, Munich, 1974.
Tibetan Book of the Dead, The, compiled and edited by W. Y. Evans-Wentz (with psychological commentary by C. G. Jung, introductory foreword by Lama Anagarika Govinda, foreword by Sir John Woodroffe), Oxford University Press, London, 1960.
Trug der Drogen, ed. J. Buck, Siebenstern Taschenbuch, Hamburg, 1974.
Vivekananda, *Raja-Yoga: the Yoga of Conquering Internal Nature*, Advaita Ashrama, Calcutta, 1970.
Walter, Bruno, *Vom Mozart der Zauberflöte*, S. Fischer Verlag, Frankfurt, 1955.
Watts, Alan, *The Way of Zen*, Penguin, Harmondsworth, 1970.
Weinfurter, Karl, *Der Brennende Dornbusch*, K. Rohm Verlag, Lorch/Württemberg, 1962.
Wilhelm, Richard, *Frühling und Herbst des Lü Bu We*, Eugen Diederichs Verlag, Düsseldorf-Cologne, 1971.
Woodroffe, Sir John, *Serpent Power: a brief study of Kundalini Yoga*, Ganesh, 1972.
Yogananda, Paramahansa, *Meditationen zur Selbstverwirklichung*, O. W. Barth Verlag, 3rd edition, Weilheim, 1971;
———— *Cosmic Chants*, Self Realization Fellowship, Los Angeles, new edition, 1974.

Selection of Recorded Music

Items known to be currently unavailable outside Germany, or available only as imports, are marked (G).

MODERN CLASSICS
Maurice Ravel: orchestral works and piano pieces.
Alexander Scriabin: 'Piano Pieces'.
Bela Bartók: Violin Concerto 1938; Music for Strings, Percussion and Celesta; Second and Third Piano Concertos.
Charles Ives: 'Five Symphonies'.
Olivier Messiaen: 'Les Corps Glorieux' for organ; 'Et exspecto ...' and 'Colours of the Celestial City', two orchestral works.
Carl Orff: 'De Temporum Fine Comoedia' (G).
Karlheinz Stockhausen: 'Hymnen' for orchestra and electronics (G); 'Stimmung' for 6 vocalists (G); 'Mantra' for two pianos (G).

INTUITIVE IMPROVISATION
Karlheinz Stockhausen: 'Aus den Sieben Tagen' (G); 'Goldstaub' (G).

PSYCHEDELIC AVANT-GARDE
'wired' – Rant, Lewis, Böttner (in boxset 'Free Improvisation') (G).

PSYCHEDELIC POP MUSIC
'Ummagumma'. Double LP by the group *Pink Floyd*.

PSYCHEDELIC JAZZ
'Karma', by Pharao Sanders (G).

NON-EUROPEAN MUSIC
The *Musicaphon Bärenreiter* UNESCO collection has brought out innumerable and excellent recordings: from Africa, Asia and the whole world. Additionally the following specialities are available:

Tibet: 'Tantric Ritual'. Gyoto Monastery.
'Chants Mongols'. Mongolian chanting and folk music.
'ZEN. Sound and Silence.' Recordings from a Japanese Zen monastery.
Gamelan-music: Boxsets of music from Bali and Java.
Indian music: 'Imrat Khan – Nordindische Ragas live' (G).
'Nikhil Banerjee – Nordindische Ragas auf Sitar' (G).
'South Indian Vocal and Instrumental Music'.

Music from the Morning of the World (Balinese Gamelan).
Buddhist Chant (Japanese temple ritual).
Islamic Liturgy.
A Night at the Taj (Vilayat and Imrat Khan).
A Persian Heritage (Classical music of Iran).
The Ten Graces on the Vina (Music of south India).
Master of the Sarangi (Ram Narayan).

EAST-WEST SYNTHESIS
'Music for Zen-Meditation' with Tony Scott, clarinet, and Japanese
    musicians.
'Tibetan Bells'.
'Buddhist Meditation East-West'. Chants by Tibetan Lamas and elec-
    tronic mantra-music by P. M. Hamel (G).
'Karuna Supreme'. Ali Akbar Khan, sarod, and John Handy, alto-
    saxophone (G).

SPIRITUAL JAZZ
'Love Supreme' and 'Om' by John Coltrane.
'Humus' by Don Cherry.

SPIRITUAL POP MUSIC
Third Ear Band: 'Alchemy' and '4 Elements'.
Paul Horn, flute: 'Inside'.
'Hesse Between Music'. A 'poetry-and-music-production' with texts by
    Hermann Hesse and music by the group *Between* (G).
Santana: 'Caravanserai'.
Soft Machine: 'III – Moon in June'.

ELECTRONIC POP MUSIC
Tangerine Dream: 'Phaedra' and 'Rubycon'.
Klaus Schulze: 'Timewind' and 'Irrlicht' (G).
Michael Hoenig: 'Hanging Garden Transfer' (G).

SACRED POP MUSIC
Popol Vuh: 'Seligpreisungen' and 'Hosianna-Mantra' (G).

MINIMAL MUSIC – PERIODIC MUSIC *from the U.S.A.*
Terry Riley: 'A Rainbow in Curved Air'; 'Happy Ending'; 'The Persian
    Surgery Dervishes'.
Steve Reich: 'Drumming'.

AUTHOR'S OWN COMPOSITIONS (all G)
'HAMEL', 'The Voice of Silence'.
'Einstieg', 'And The Waters Opened', 'Dharana', 'Contemplation', 'Nada',
    all with the group *Between*.